高级商务英语阅读教程
—— 剑桥商务英语证书考试阅读训练

Advanced Business English Reading
—— A Training Course for BEC Reading Test

主　编　徐李洁
副主编　段传铬
编　者　谢　潇　唐智芳　李俏俏　官　科
　　　　傅婵妮　朱曼莉　陈　元

东南大学出版社
·南京·

图书在版编目(CIP)数据

高级商务英语阅读教程:剑桥商务英语证书考试阅读训练/徐李洁主编. —南京:东南大学出版社,2012.3 (2018.8重印)
ISBN 978-7-5641-3333-7

Ⅰ.①高… Ⅱ.①徐… Ⅲ.①商务-英语-阅读教学-教材 Ⅳ.①H319.4

中国版本图书馆 CIP 数据核字(2012)第 022995 号

东南大学出版社出版发行
(南京四牌楼2号 邮编210096)
出版人:江建中
江苏省新华书店经销   江苏凤凰扬州鑫华印刷有限公司印刷
开本:787 mm×1 092 mm 1/16 印张:15.75 字数:393千字
2012年3月第1版 2018年8月第3次印刷
ISBN 978-7-5641-3333-7
印数:4001-5000册   定价:32.00元

(凡因印装质量问题,可直接与读者服务部联系调换。电话:025-83792328)

前　言

随着全球经济一体化的不断深化,中国社会经济的高速发展,社会对商务英语复合型专门人才的需求逐渐加大,对人才的要求也逐步提高。面对这一形势,培养和造就一大批既懂英语又有较扎实商务知识的综合人才是我们的当务之急。

《高级商务英语阅读教程》一书的编写正是为了顺应这一具有鲜明时代特征的人才培养要求。本书宗旨是:通过阅读增强学生对商务知识的理解,扩大学生的视野;通过对商务知识的习得,强化学生的英语阅读能力,实现语言与知识的良性双向互动,不断激发学生对英语语言和商务知识的学习兴趣。

全书共分为16个单元,每个单元由课文(Text A)、课文注释、阅读理解练习、BEC阅读练习(Text B)等部分组成。注释主要提供课文所涉及的背景知识,扩大读者的知识面;阅读理解练习分为问答与正误判断题,以检查和提高读者的阅读能力。书后还附录了所有练习的答案。

本书的编写有以下四个特点:

第一,内容丰富,覆盖面广。全书16个单元基本覆盖了商学的各个分支,如:经济全球化、市场机制、国际贸易、营销策略、物流、电子商务、人力资源管理、知识产权、商业道德、商务礼仪等。有利于学生全面了解商务知识并掌握商务英语的阅读技巧。

第二,选文经典,语言地道。文章大部分选自原版刊物以及经典的外文经贸类教科书。语言地道,内容经典。

第三,编排合理,阅读方便。为了让学生能流畅地阅读,减少因查字典而产生的停顿,连贯把握文章的主要内容,我们将生词以脚注的形式编于页尾,使阅读更加方便。

第四,本书最大的特色在于"Text B"的设置。为方便学生备战剑桥商务英语证书考试,我们按照考试的题型、要求和难度,在每章后编制了一套完整的证书阅读考试模拟练习,阅读选材紧密围绕各章内容,一则可以通过不同题型的强化训练,巩固对本章知识的理解,增强阅读能力;二则可以通过大量练习,熟悉并掌握剑桥商务英语证书考试中阅读部分的做题方法。

此外,在本书附录中,我们还增加了三套剑桥商务英语证书考试阅读真题,作为学生考试前的热身训练。

本书主要供高等院校商务英语专业、经贸商务类专业、相关专业的双学位学生,也可供致力于提高商务英语阅读能力的社会人士自学之用。教师可以根据学生的英语程度,在二年级或三年级开设。本书可供1个学期使用,每学期18个教学周,每周2课时。

编者

2011年12月15日

Contents

前言	(1)
第 1 单元　经济全球化　Economic Globalization	
Text A	(1)
Text B　BEC Reading Texts	(6)
第 2 单元　市场机制　Market Mechanism	
Text A	(14)
Text B　BEC Reading Texts	(19)
第 3 单元　国际贸易　International Trade	
Text A	(26)
Text B　BEC Reading Texts	(31)
第 4 单元　营销策略　Marketing Strategy	
Text A	(38)
Text B　BEC Reading Texts	(43)
第 5 单元　广告和促销　Advertising and Promotion	
Text A	(50)
Text B　BEC Reading Texts	(56)
第 6 单元　商业合同　Business Contract	
Text A	(64)
Text B　BEC Reading Texts	(69)
第 7 单元　企业管理　Corporate Management	
Text A	(77)
Text B　BEC Reading Texts	(82)
第 8 单元　物流　Logistics	
Text A	(89)
Text B　BEC Reading Texts	(94)

第9单元　商业道德和社会责任　Business Ethics and Social Responsibility
　　Text A ……………………………………………………………………………… (102)
　　Text B　BEC Reading Texts ……………………………………………………… (106)

第10单元　电子商务　Electronic Business
　　Text A ……………………………………………………………………………… (114)
　　Text B　BEC Reading Texts ……………………………………………………… (120)

第11单元　信息时代的会计　Accounting in the Information Age
　　Text A ……………………………………………………………………………… (128)
　　Text B　BEC Reading Texts ……………………………………………………… (134)

第12单元　知识产权　Intellectual Property
　　Text A ……………………………………………………………………………… (141)
　　Text B　BEC Reading Texts ……………………………………………………… (147)

第13单元　人力资源管理　Staffing and Human Resource Management
　　Text A ……………………………………………………………………………… (154)
　　Text B　BEC Reading Texts ……………………………………………………… (160)

第14单元　货币和银行　Money and Banking
　　Text A ……………………………………………………………………………… (167)
　　Text B　BEC Reading Texts ……………………………………………………… (172)

第15单元　商务礼仪　Business Etiquette
　　Text A ……………………………………………………………………………… (180)
　　Text B　BEC Reading Texts ……………………………………………………… (185)

第16单元　股票市场　Stock Market
　　Text A ……………………………………………………………………………… (192)
　　Text B　BEC Reading Texts ……………………………………………………… (197)

附录一　剑桥商务英语证书考试真题（一） ……………………………………………… (205)
附录二　剑桥商务英语证书考试真题（二） ……………………………………………… (215)
附录三　剑桥商务英语证书考试真题（三） ……………………………………………… (225)

参考答案 ……………………………………………………………………………………… (235)

第 1 单元 经济全球化
Unit 1 Economic Globalization

Text A

Ⅰ. 课文导读

经济全球化,有利于资源和生产要素在全球的合理配置,有利于资本和产品在全球流动,有利于科技在全球性的扩张,有利于促进不发达地区经济的发展,是人类发展进步的表现,是世界经济发展的必然结果。但它对每个国家来说,都是一柄双刃剑,既是机遇,也是挑战。特别是对经济实力薄弱和科学技术比较落后的发展中国家,所遇到的风险、挑战将更加严峻。进入21世纪以来,经济全球化与跨国公司的深入发展,既给世界贸易带来了重大的推动力,同时也给各国经贸带来了诸多不确定因素,使其出现许多新的特点和新的矛盾。

Ⅱ. Text

Although globalization is discussed everywhere—television shows, Internet chat rooms, political demonstrations, parliaments, management boardrooms①, and labor union meetings—so far there is no widely accepted definition. In fact, its definition continues to broaden. Now, for example, social scientists discuss the political, social, environmental, historical, geographical, and even cultural implications② of globalization. Some also speak of technological globalization, political globalization, and the like.

However, the most common definition and the one used in international business is that of economic globalization—the international integration of goods, technology, labor, and capital; that is, firms implement③ global strategies which link and coordinate their international activities on a worldwide basis.

There are five major kinds of drivers④, all based on change, that are leading international firms to the globalization, namely (1) political, (2) technological, (3) market, (4) cost, (5) competitive drivers:

(1) Political driver. There is a trend toward the unification and socialization of the global

---

① boardroom: 董事会会议室
② implications: 内涵
③ implement: 实施;执行
④ driver: 驱动器

community. Preferential ①trading arrangements, such as the North American Free Trade Agreement and the European Union, that group several nations into a single market have presented firms with significant marketing opportunities. Many have moved swiftly to enter either through exporting or by producing in the area.

Two other aspects of this trend are contributing to the globalization of business operations: (a) the progressive reduction of barriers to trade and foreign investment by most governments, which is hastening the opening of new markets by international firms that are both exporting to them and building production facilities in them, and (b) the privatization② of much of the industry in formerly communist nations and the opening of their economies to global competition.

(2) Technological driver. Advances in computers and communications technology are permitting an increased flow of ideas and information across borders, enabling customers to learn about foreign goods. Cable TV systems in Europe and Asia, for example, allow an advertiser to reach numerous countries simultaneously, thus creating regional and sometimes global demand. Global communications networks enable manufacturing personnel to coordinate production and design functions worldwide so that plants in many parts of the world may be working on the same product.

(3) Market driver. As companies globalize, they also become global customers. For years, advertising agencies established offices in foreign markets when their major clients entered those markets to avoid having a competitor steal the accounts. Likewise③, when an automaker, about to set up a foreign plant where there was no tire factory, asked a tire company if it was interested in setting up a plant in this new market, the response was, "When do you want us there?" It is also quite common for a global supplier to make global supply contracts with a global customer.

(4) Cost driver. Economies of scale to reduce unit costs are always a management goal. One means of achieving them is to globalize product lines to reduce development, production, and inventory④ costs. The company can also locate production in countries where the costs of the factors of production are lower.

(5) Competitive driver. Competition continues to increase in intensity. New firms, many from newly industrialized and developing countries, have entered world markets in automobiles and electronics, for example. As you saw in the opening incident, import penetration⑤ has increased markedly for five of the six major trading nations over the past 29 years. Another competitive driving force for globalization is the fact that many companies are defending their home markets from competitors by entering the competitors' home markets to distract them.

The result of this rush to globalization has been an explosive growth in international busi-

---

① preferential: 优惠的；优先的
② privatization: 私有化
③ likewise: 也；同样的
④ inventory: 库存
⑤ penetration: 渗透；打入（某一地区或国家市场）

ness.

The primary evidence for globalization is the rapid growth in the volume① of cross-border trade and investment that we have witnessed over the last three decades. The most recent data from the World Trade Organization and the United Nations indicate that in recent years the growth in cross-border trade and investment has accelerated②, suggesting that the world is moving ever more rapidly toward a global growth.

Is the shift toward a more integrated and interdependent global economy a good thing? Many influential economists, politicians, and business leaders seem to think so. They argue that falling barriers to international trade and investment are the twin engines that are driving the global economy toward ever-greater prosperity. They maintain that increased international trade and cross-border investment will result in lower prices across the border for goods and services. They believe that globalization stimulates economic growth, raises the incomes of consumers, and helps to create jobs in all countries that choose to participate in the global trading system.

The arguments of those who support globalization have considerable foundation. Nevertheless, despite the existence of a compelling body of theory and evidence③, over the last few years globalization has been the target of a growing number of critics.

One frequently voiced concern④ is that falling barriers to international trade destroy manufacturing jobs in wealthy advanced economies such as the United States. The basic thrust⑤ of the critics' argument is that falling trade barriers allow firms to move their manufacturing activities offshore⑥ to countries where wage rates are much lower.

Supporters of globalization reply that critics such as Barlett and Steele miss the essential point about free trade—the benefits outweigh the costs. They argue that free trade results in countries specializing in the production of those goods and services that they can produce more efficiently, while importing goods that they cannot produce as efficiently from other countries. When a country embraces⑦ free trade there is always some dislocation⑧—lost textile jobs at Harwood Industries, for example—but the whole economy is better off as a result. In this manner, supporters of globalization argue that free trade benefits all countries that adhere to a free trade regime.

A second source of concern is that free trade encourages firms from advanced nations to move manufacturing facilities offshore to less developed countries that lack adequate regulations

---

① volume: 份量；容量
② accelerate: (使)加快
③ a compelling body of theory and evidence: 一系列令人信服的理论和事实根据
④ concern: 忧虑；担心
⑤ basic thrust: 要旨
⑥ offshore: 境外的
⑦ embrace: (欣然)接受；(乐意)采取
⑧ dislocation: 混乱；紊乱

to protect labor and the environment from abuse by the unscrupulous①. One point often made by critics is that adhering to labor and environmental regulations significantly increases the costs of manufacturing enterprises and puts them at a competitive disadvantage in the global marketplace vis-à-vis② firms based in developing nations that do not have to comply with such regulations. If this is the case, one might expect free trade to lead to an increase in pollution and result in firms from advanced nations exploiting the labor of less developed nations.

Supporters of free trade and greater globalization express serious doubts about this scenario. For a start, they point out that tougher environmental regulations and stricter labor standards go hand in hand with economic progress. Furthermore, supporters of free trade point out that it is possible to tie free trade agreements to the implementation of tougher environmental and labor laws in less developed countries. Moreover, business firms are not the amoral③ organizations that critics suggest. The vast majority of business enterprises are staffed by managers who are committed to behave in an ethical④ manner.

A final concern voiced by critics of globalization is that in today's increasingly interdependent global economy, economic power is shifting away from national governments and toward supranational organizations such as the WTO, the European Union, and the United Nations. In this manner, claim critics, the ability of the national state to control its own destiny is being limited. Many economists and politicians argue that bodies such as the United Nations and the WTO exist to serve the collective interests of member-states, not to subvert⑤ those interests. Moreover, supporters of supranational organizations point out that in reality, the power of these bodies rests largely on their ability to persuade member-states to take a certain action. If these bodies fail, those states will withdraw their support. In this view, real power still resides with⑥ individual nation states, not supranational organizations.

Ⅲ. Notes

1. North American Free Trade Agreement（北美自由贸易协议）. NAFTA is an agreement signed by the governments of Canada, Mexico and the United States, creating a trilateral trade bloc in North America. The agreement came into force on January 1, 1994. It superseded the Canada-United States Free Trade Agreement between the U. S. and Canada. In terms of combined GDP of its members, as of 2010 the trade bloc is the largest in the world. The North American Free Trade Agreement has two supplements, the North American Agreement on Environment Cooperation (NCAAEC) and the North American Agreement on Labor Cooperation

---

① unscrupulous: 肆无忌惮的；无道德原则的
② vis-à-vis: 面对面地
③ amoral: 不属于道德范畴的
④ ethical: 道德的
⑤ subvert: 破坏；搅乱
⑥ reside with: （权利、权力等）归于；属于

(NAALC).

2. European Union（欧洲联盟）. EU is a unique economic and political body between 27 European countries. It has delivered a century of peace, stability and prosperity, helped raise living standards, launched a single European currency, and is progressively building a single Europe-wide market in which people, goods, services and capital move among Member States as freely as within one country.

3. Barlett and Steele. Donald L. Barlett and James B. Steele are one of the most widely acclaimed investigative reporting teams in American journalism. They have worked together for more than three decades, first at The Philadelphia Inquirer, (1971—1997) where they won two Pulitzer Prizes and scores of other national journalism awards, then at Time magazine, (1997—2006) where they earned two National Magazine Awards, becoming the first journalists in history to win both the Pulitzer Prize for newspaper work and its magazine equivalent for magazine reporting, and now at Vanity Fair as contributing editors. They also have written seven books.

4. Harwood industries（哈伍德工业公司）. Based in Tyler, Texas, Harwood Industries Inc. manufactures products, components and accessories for the racing and street performance industry. Operating for over 35 years, the company's products range includes hoods, body panels, scoops, carbon fiber, lexan windows and accessories such as scoop plugs, hood springs and cowl panel. Its operation includes product design, construction, packaging and shipment and it also offers servicing and maintenance support. Harwood Industries Inc. has also received various awards for its products, including National Hot Rod Association (NHRA) Best Engineering Awards and Composite Industry Awards.

IV. Useful Expressions

1. contribute to: 有助于, 促成; 是……的部分原因
2. increase in intensity: 增加强度
3. participate in: 参加
4. one frequently voiced concern: 一个常常被提到的忧虑
5. The benefits outweigh the costs: 利润超过成本
6. be better off: 境况好起来
7. advanced nations: 先进国家; 发达国家
8. for a start: 首先
9. member-states: 成员国
10. rest largely on: 主要依赖于……
11. reside with: 归于; 属于……

V. Reading Comprehension

Questions

1. What is the definition of economic globalization?
2. What are the five drivers that promote globalization of international firms?

3. What is the primary evidence for globalization?

4. What are the voiced concerns about globalization by the critics?

5. What are the advantages of globalization according to the supporters?

Decide whether each of the following statements is true or false.

1. Globalization is a relatively new phenomenon. ( )

2. The definition of globalization denotes an integration of goods, technology, labor and capital among different countries. ( )

3. Advanced technology makes it possible that many companies over the world may be working on same product, so it puts them at a competitive disadvantage in the global market. ( )

4. The Internet and network computing enable small companies to compete globally because they make possible the rapid flow of information regardless of the physical location of the buyer and seller. ( )

5. Trade barrier is not a threat to the company's business. ( )

6. Multinational company can take their capital and leave to invest in lower-wage countries. ( )

7. Globalization is the automatic and unstoppable consequence of the emergence of new technologies. ( )

8 Globalization concedes that the wage rate enjoyed by unskilled workers in many advanced economies has declined in recent years. ( )

9. The writer of this article is in favor of globalization rather than against it. ( )

10. Globalization is a double-edged sword. It is predicted that its promise will exceed. ( )

VI. Discussion

What measures can be taken to gain the best interests for a country out of globalization?

Text B
BEC Reading Texts

PART ONE
Questions 1—8

- Look at the statements below and the five extracts about globalization from an article.
- Which extract (A, B, C, D or E) does each statement (1—8) refer to?
- For each statement (1—8), make one letter (A, B, C, D or E) on your Answer Sheet.
- You will need to use some of these letters more than once.

1. The Linder theory deduces that international trade in manufactured goods will be greater between nations with similar levels of per capita income than between those with dissimilar levels of per capita income.

2. It is about absolute advantage.

3. Some management theorists argue that firms that enter the market first (first movers) will not soon dominate it.

4. It can be concluded that a nation having absolute disadvantages in the production of two goods with respect to another nation has a comparative advantage in the production of the good in which its absolute advantage is less.

5. The First Mover Theory were flawed because they were based on surveys of surviving firms and didn't include a large number of the true pioneers.

6. The goods that will be traded are those for which there is an overlapping demand.

7. We infer that Japan had a comparative advantage in producing automobiles.

8. No single country can do everything well.

A. Adam Smith claimed that market forces, not government controls, should determine the direction, volume, and composition of international trade. He argued that under free, unregulated trade, each nation should specialize in producing those goods it could produce most efficiently. Some of these goods would be exported to pay for imports of goods that could be produced more efficiently elsewhere.

B. Ricardo demonstrated that even though a nation held an absolute advantage in the production of two goods, the two countries could still trade with advantages for each as long as the less efficient nation was not equally less efficient in the production of both goods. Note that the United States has an absolute advantage in producing rice and automobiles. Compared with the United States, Japan is less inefficient in automaking than in producing rice.

C. Swedish economist, Stefan Linder's demand-oriented theory stated that customers' tastes are strongly affected by income levels, and therefore a nation's income per capita level determines the kinds of goods they will demand. Because industry will produce goods to meet this demand, the kinds of products manufactured reflect the country's level of income per capita. Goods produced for domestic consumption will eventually be exported.

D. Some countries have special strengths that make them the best place in the world for certain industries. This gives them an absolute advantage relative to competitors in other nations. Some countries can produce products more efficiently than others, giving them a comparative advantage. However, these advantages may change over time.

E. It was an American firm, Ampex, that made the first VCRs, but because it charged so much ($50,000), it sold only a few. Sony and Matsushita saw the market potential and worked for 20 years to make one to sell for $500. They reached that goal and cornered the market. The authors argue that the early success has gone to the companies that entered the market on average 13 years after the "first movers".

PART TWO
Questions 9—14

- Read the text about body language in cross-cultural situations
- Choose the best sentence to fill each of the gaps.
- For each gap (9—14), mark one letter (A-H) on your Answer Sheet.
- Do not use any letter more than once.

Beware of Body Language in Cross-Cultural Situations

As the trade barriers come down in Europe and contact is increased, cross-cultural misunderstandings are bound to rise. As often as not, many of the misunderstandings in communications will arise not from what is said, (9)...

Attaining fluency in a foreign language is often only half the battle when it comes to mastering effective cross-cultural communications. (10)... This "silent language", or the actions that accompany our words, includes such dimensions as touching, distance between speakers, facial expressions, speech inflection or volume, pauses, as well as hand and arm gestures. (11)...

Very seldom do we speak without an accompanying action in which hands invariably play a crucial role.

(12)... The Italians and the French are renowned for relying heavily on hand gestures to replicate or mimic ideas that they are simultaneously communicating in words. Germans often raise their eyebrows in recognition of a clever idea. (13)...

The French have some of the most expressive hand gestures. To symbolize exquisiteness, a Frenchman pinches his fingertips, raises them to his lips, and softly tosses a kiss into the air with his chin held high. (14)..., he's warning "*something smells bad,*" "*be cautious,*" "*we can't trust these people.*"

Very similar is the Italian gesture of tapping the side of the nose with the forefinger. Its meaning: *Take care. There is danger ahead. They are getting crafty*. In the Netherlands, this gesture means *I'm drunk* or *you're drunk*. In England, a forefinger tap on the side of the nose means conspiracy or secrecy.

A. The same expression in Britain is a sign of skepticism

B. but from a lack of awareness of the various interpretations different cultures ascribe to nonverbal forms of behavior

C. Culture has a powerful impact on people's behavior

D. Of equal, and at times, greater importance is the knowledge of nonverbal communication, or body language

E. On the other hand, if a Frenchman rubs the base of his nose with his forefinger

F. A good way to become more aware of cross-cultural differences is to look at oneself through the eyes of people from other cultures

G. Even clothing and colors are symbolic and have different meanings depending on the part of the world

H. The use of gesticulations varies according to culture

PART THREE
Questions 15—20

· Read the following article on the reason why U. S. wants to import more shoppers to boost flagging economy,

· For each question (15—20) mark one letter (A, B, C or D) on your Answer Sheet for the answer you choose.

The United States has long imported its food and fuel, its cars and clothes. Now the faltering economy has sparked a push for another type of import: shoppers.

For the first time, lawmakers, businesses and even White House officials are courting consumers from cash-rich countries such as China, India and Brazil to fill the nation's shopping malls and pick up the slack for penny-pinching Americans. They are wooing travelers with enticements such as coupons, beauty pageants and promises of visa reform. The payoff, they say, could be significant: 1.3 million new jobs and an \$859 billion shot in the arm for the economy over the next decade.

"They're their own little stimulus program," said David French, senior vice president for government relations at the National Retail Federation, a trade group. The trend underscores the depth of the United States' reliance on countries once considered to be at the bottom of the global totem pole. The nation already counts on China and other countries to manufacture its goods, creating a \$45 billion trade imbalance that is paid for with money borrowed from their coffers. Now officials are encouraging foreign travelers to buy some of those products back — and a growing number are happy to oblige.

Guo Hui, 37, who lives in Beijing, recently returned home from a two-week tour of Yellowstone National Park, Houston and Los Angeles. He estimated he spent \$2,000 to rent a car and pay for gas and lodging for himself and his wife. Then there was the Ed Hardy T-shirt, the Apple laptop, the HP laptop, even baby food and formula for his child, totaling an additional \$6,000.

Still, Guo said prices are significantly cheaper than in China — a pair of Adidas sneakers costs only \$25 at a U. S. outlet mall. "For that price in China, you can't even buy counterfeits," he said.

In contrast, spending by American shoppers — long considered the engine of the nation's economy — has slowed to a crawl as families struggle under high unemployment rates and depressed home prices. The U. S. gross domestic product last year grew an anemic 3 percent, while China's and India's shot up 10 percent. Brazil's clocked in at about 7.5 percent.

Those shifting dynamics have spawned a movement to encourage foreigners to spend their newfound wealth in the United States, placing the country in the unfamiliar role of supplicant. Over the summer, President Obama's jobs council deemed international travel among the "low-hanging fruit" for stimulating the economy. The Corporation for Travel Promotion, a public-private partnership created by Congress last year, will announce next month the first U. S. advertising campaign to promote the nation as a tourist destination. Rebecca Blank, the acting commerce secretary, called tourism a key component of "America's exports success story."

15. What does America want to import from other countries recently?

A. food and clothes

B. raw materials

C. travelers

D. labor forces

16. Why did America prefer consumers from China, India and Brazil?

A. Because the consumers from those countries often pay for goods in cash.

B. Because they have strong purchasing power.

C. Because they find the quality of goods in America is better than that in their native countries.

D. Because they hope that they can get preferential terms for visa.

17. What can we learn from paragraph 4&5?

A. Chinese travelers are often purchasing when traveling in America.

B. Chinese travelers are very fond of American brands.

C. There are various goods for travelers to choose when shopping.

D. Chinese travelers are sensitive to price.

18. Which statement is not true about American buyers?

A. American buyers can't afford goods because of depressed home price.

B. American buyers prefer goods of foreign countries.

C. Many Americans are facing a serious problem of unemployment.

D. American buyers made great contribution to American economy in the past.

19. Why is tourism called a key component of "America's exports success story" in the last paragraph, according to Rebecca Blank?

A. The purchases of foreign shoppers are counted as exports on the country's balance sheet.

B. American exports a large number of goods to China, India and Brazil.

C. American economy has been recovered by foreign shoppers.

D. American economy largely relies on China and other countries to manufacture goods and export to America.

20. What benefits can America get from importing shoppers according to the passage?

A. There are more new jobs.

B. American people have greater confidence in boosting their economy.

C. Tourism promotes the national consumption.

D. Both A and B.

PART FOUR
Questions 21—30

· Read the article below about hiring.

· Choose the correct word to fill each gap from A, B, C or D.

· For each question (21—30), mark one letter (A, B, C or D) on your Answer Sheet.

What Can You Ask When You're Hiring

Once upon a time, if a job applicant was sitting on the other side of your desk, you (21)... ask her about her disabilities and what it might take to accommodate her in your company. This was true even if the applicant's disability was obvious because she was in a wheelchair or using a seeing-eye dog. (22)... the applicant herself made reference to her disability, the employer was (23)... in what he could ask.

(24)... things changed in October 1995. Ten Equal Employment Opportunity Commission revised its guidelines for the American with Disabilities Act (ADA). With the new guidelines in place, it is (25)... for employers to make inquiries about obvious disabilities or ask questions if the applicant (26)... she is disabled or will require reasonable accommodation.

The idea behind the new guidelines, called "ADA Enforcement Guidance: Pre-employment Disability-Related Questions and Medical Examinations," is to allow employers to address the accommodation issue at the (27)... interview stage. However, the guidelines do not allow an employer to go on archeological digs through their applicants' pasts. For example, an applicant's workers-compensation history can be (28)... territory. And some questions about drug and alcohol use are off-limits, (29)... others are not. An employer may ask about current illegal use of drugs, because it's not protected under the ADA. On the other hand, the employer needs to be very careful asking about drinking habits-information on how much the applicant drinks could indicate alcoholism, and (30)... is protected.

The guidelines are available in a question-and-answer format from the EEOC. Asking the right questions at an early stage of the job-application process could save you, and your applicant, a lot of bother later on.

21. A. mustn't   B. mightn't   C. couldn't   D. needn't
22. A. However   B. Even if   C. If   D. If only
23. A. restricted   B. limited   C. confined   D. bound
24. A. But   B. As   C. Although   D. Since
25. A. probable   B. imaginable   C. feasible   D. possible
26. A. reveals   B. opens   C. demonstrates   D. discloses
27. A. initial   B. primary   C. first   D. beginning
28. A. awkward   B. sensitive   C. tricky   D. confidential
29. A. as   B. while   C. when   D. even though
30. A. this   B. so   C. which   D. that

PART FIVE
Questions 31—40

· Read the article below about expert systems in the workplace.

· For each question 31—40, write one word in CAPITAL LETTERS on your Answer Sheet.

Expert Systems in the Workplace

Science fiction writers have long imagined computers with humanlike intelligence, machines that actually think (31)... themselves. Well, they're here, and they're called expert systems. If you've (32)... for a loan or a credit card recently or even had a can of Campbell's soup, you may already have benefited (33)... them.

Like many computer programs, expert systems function primarily by going through hundreds of "if... then" (34)..., doing the kinds of simple "thinking" that we use to run our lives. But expert systems tackle questions more sophisticated than "Should I get up now?" They help American Express decide whether to issue someone a credit card and they enable Hewlett-Packard to find flaws in faulty disk drivers in 30 seconds (35)... than in days. They also help make scores of decisions at Digital Equipment Corp., ranging from how shifts in demand will affect production and inventory, to which accessories a customer will need with a mainframe order.

Computer can do all this (36)... they are programmed with facts about their subject and with rules that human experts use to make decisions based on those facts. These facts and rules make up the system's "knowledge base," (37)... is, ideally, similar to the heedful of experiences and information that a human expert carries around. In fact, that's (38)... knowledge bases come from. A "knowledge engineer" endlessly questions human experts, trying to determine the facts and rules that the human uses to make a decision. The engineer then programs the computer's knowledge base to mimic the human's. If all goes well, the computer becomes the novice (39)... best friend, helping the employee make difficult decisions (40)... calling in the boss or waiting until the technician is free.

PART SIX
Questions 41—52

· Read the text below from a report about competition.

· In most lines (41—52), there is one extra word. It either is grammatically incorrect or does not fit in with the sense of the text. Some lines, however, are correct.

· If a line is correct, write CORRECT on your Answer Sheet.

· If there is an extra word in the line, write the extra word in CAPITAL LETTERS on your Answer Sheet.

Here Comes The Competition

41. The Wadson Company is a management research firm which headquartered in New

Jersey. The company was recently hired by a large conglomerate with a wide range of products, ranging from

42. toys to electronics and financial services. This conglomerate wants Wadson to help them identify

43. an acquisition target. The conglomerate is not willing to spend up to \$2.5 billion to buy a major

44. company at anywhere in the world. One of the things the research firm did was to identify the amount of foreign direct investment in the United States by overseas companies. The research group also compiled a list of major acquisitions by non-U.S. firms. It gathered these data to show

45. the conglomerate in the types of industries and companies that are currently attractive to the international buyers. "If we know what outside firms are buying," the head of the research firm

46. noted, "this can help us identifying out similar overseas businesses that may also have strong

47. growth potential. In this way, although we will not confine our list of recommendations to U.S

48. firms only." In terms of direct foreign investment by industry, the researchers had found that the

49. greatest investment was being made in manufacturing. Then, in descending order, they came wholesale trade, petroleum, real estate, and insurance. On the basis of this information, the

50. conglomerate has had decided to purchase a European firm. "The best acquisitions in the United States have already been picked," the president told the board of directors. "However, I'm

51. convinced that there are highly profitable enterprises in Europe that are ripe for the taking over.

52. I'd particularly like to focus my attention on France and Germany." The board gave to the president its full support, and the research firm will begin focusing on potential European targets within the next 30 years.

第 2 单元　市场机制
Unit 2　Market Mechanism

Text A

Ⅰ. 课文导读

市场经济是一种经济体系,在这种体系下,产品和服务的生产及销售完全由自由市场的自由价格机制所引导,而不是像计划经济一般由国家所引导。在市场经济里并没有一个中央协调的体制来指引其运作,但是在理论上,市场将会透过产品和服务的供给和需求产生复杂的相互作用,进而达成自我组织的效果。市场经济的支持者通常主张,人们所追求的私利其实是一个社会最好的利益,即市场实际是受到亚当·斯密所谓"看不见的手"所支配。

Ⅱ. Text

We actually take for granted the smooth running of the economy. When you go to the supermarket, the items you want—bread, cereal, and bananas—are usually on the shelf. You pay your bill, pop the food in your mouth, and have a juicy meal. What could be simpler?

If you pause for a moment and look more closely, you may begin to appreciate the complexity of the economic system that provides your daily bread. The food may have passed through five or ten links before getting to you, traveling for days or months from every state and every corner of the globe as it moved along the chain of farmers, food processors, packagers, truckers, wholesalers, and retailers①. It seems almost a miracle that food is produced in suitable amount, gets transported to the right place, and arrives in a palatable② form at the dinner table.

But the true miracle is that this entire system works without coercion③ or centralized direction by anybody. Literally millions of businesses and consumers engage in voluntary④ trade, and their actions and purposes are invisibly coordinated by a system of prices and markets. Nobody decides how many chickens will be produced, where the trucks will drive, and when the supermarkets will open. Still, in the end, the food is in the store when you want it.

Markets perform similar miracles around us all the time, as can easily be seen if only we

---

① wholesalers and retailers: 批发商和零售商
② palatable: 好吃的
③ coercion: 强制
④ voluntary: 自发的

observe our economy carefully. Thousands of commodities are produced by millions of people, willingly, without central direction or master plan①. Indeed, with a few important exceptions (like the military, police, and schools) most of our economic life proceeds without government intervention, and that's the true wonder of the social world.

A market economy is an elaborate mechanism for coordinating people, activities, and business through a system of process and markets. It is a communication device for pooling② the knowledge and actions of billions of diverse individuals. Without central intelligence or computation, it solves problems of production and distribution involving billions of unknown variables and relations, problems that are far beyond the reach of even today's fastest supercomputer. Nobody designed the market, yet it functions remarkably well. In a market economy, no single individual or organization is responsible for production, consumption, distribution, and pricing.

How do markets determine the price, wages, and output? Originally, a market was an actual place where buyers and sellers could engage in face-to-face bargaining. The marketplace—filled with slabs of butter, pyramids of cheese, layers of wet fish, and heaps of vegetables—used to be a familiar sight in many villages and towns, where farmers brought their goods to sell. In the United States today there are still important markets where many traders gather together to do business. For example, wheat and corn are traded at the Chicago Board of Trade, oil and platinum③ are traded at the New York Mercantile Exchange, and gems are traded at the Diamond District in New York City.

More generally, a market should be thought of as a mechanism by which buyers and sellers can determine prices and exchange goods and services. There are markets for almost everything, from art to pollution. A market should be centralized, as in the case of houses or labor. Or it may exist only electronically, as in the case of many financial assets④ and services, which are traded by computer. The crucial characteristic of a market is that it brings buyers and sellers to set prices and quantities.

A market is a mechanism by which buyers and sellers interact to determine the price and quantities of goods or services.

In a market system, everything has a price, which is the value of the goods in terms of money. Prices represent the terms on which people and firms voluntarily exchange different commodities. When I agree to buy a used Ford from a dealer for $4050, this agreement indicates that the Ford is worth more than $4050 to me and that the price of $4050 is worth more than the Ford to the dealer. The used car market has determined the price of a used Ford and, through voluntary trading, has allocated⑤ this goods to the person for whom it has the highest

---

① waster plan: 总体计划
② pool: 将……集中起来
③ platinum: 铂金
④ assets: 资产
⑤ allocate: 分配

value.

In addition, prices serve as signals to producers and consumers. If consumers want more of any goods, the price will rise, sending a signal to producers that more supply is needed. For example, every summer, as families set out on their vacations, the demand for gasoline rises, and so does the price. The higher price encourages oil companies to increase gasoline production and, at the same time, discourages travelers from lengthening their trips.

On the other hand, if a commodity such as cars becomes overstocked, dealers and automobile companies will lower their prices in order to reduce their inventory. At the lower price, more consumers will want cars, and producers will want to make fewer cars. As a result, a balance, or equilibrium, between buyers and sellers will be restored.

What is true of markets for consumer goods is also true of markets for factors of production, such as land or labor. If computer programmers rather than textile workers are needed, job opportunities will be more favorable in the computing field. The price of computer programmers (their hourly wage) will tend to rise, and that of textile workers will tend to fall, as they did during 1980s. The shift in relative wages will attract workers into the growing occupation.

The nursing crisis of the 1980s shows the labor market at work. During that decade the growth in the health-care sector led to an enormous expansion of nursing jobs with far too few trained nurses to fill them. Hospitals offered all sorts of fringe benefits[1] to attract nurses, including subsidized[2] apartments, low cost of on-site child care[3], and signing bonuses as high as $10,000. One hospital even ran a lottery[4] for nurses, with the prize being a gift certificate at a nearby department store. But what really attracted people into the nursing profession was rising wages. Between 1983 and 1992, the pay for registered nurse rose almost 70 percent, so they were making about as much money as the average accountant or architect. The rising pay drew so many people into nursing that by 1992 the nursing shortage had disappeared in most parts of the country.

Prices coordinate the decisions of producers and consumers in a market. Higher prices tend to reduce consumer purchases and encourage production. Lower prices encourage consumption and discourage production. Prices are the balance wheel of the market mechanism.

The orderliness of the market system was first recognized by Adam Smith, whose classic work *The Wealth of Nations* (1776) is still read today. Smith proclaimed the principle of the "invisible hand." This principle holds that, in selfishly pursuing only his or her personal goods, every individual is led, as if by an invisible hand, to achieve the best goods for all. Smith held that in this best of all possible worlds, government interference with market competition is almost certain to be injurious.

---

① fringe benefits: 附加利益
② subsidize: 补贴
③ on-site child care: 在工作场所儿童照管处
④ lottery: 彩票

Smith's insight about the functioning of the market mechanism has inspired modern economists—both the admirers and the critics of capitalism. Economic theorists have proved that under restrictive conditions a perfectly competitive economy is efficient (remember that an economy is producing efficiently when it cannot increase the economic welfare of anyone without making someone else worse off).

After two centuries of experience and thought, however, we recognize the scope and realistic limitations of this doctrine①. We know that there are "market failures" and that markets do not always lead to the most efficient outcome. One set of market failures concerns monopolies② and other forms of imperfect competition. A second failure of the invisible hand comes when there are spillovers③ or externalities outside the marketplace—positive externalities such as scientific discoveries and negative spillovers such as pollution. A final reservation comes when the income distribution is politically or ethically unacceptable. When any of these elements occur, Adam Smith's invisible-hand doctrine breaks down and government may want to step in to mend the flawed invisible hand.

Ⅲ. Notes

1. Chicago Board of Trade (芝加哥商品交易). Established in 1848, it is the world's oldest futures and options exchange. On 12 July 2007, the CBOT merged with the Chicago Mercantile Exchange (CME) to form the CME Group, a CME/Chicago Board of Trade Company. CBOT and three other exchanges (CME, NYMEX, and COMEX) now operate as designated contract markets (DCM) of the CME Group.

2. New York Mercantile Exchange (纽约商品交易所). NYMEX is the world's largest physical commodity futures exchange. It is located at One North End Avenue in the World Financial Center in the Battery Park City section of Manhattan, New York City. Additional offices are located in Boston, Washington, D. C., Atlanta, San Francisco, Dubai, London, and Tokyo.

3. Diamond District (钻石区). The Diamond District is the world's largest shopping district for all sizes and shapes of diamonds and fine jewelry at tremendous prices and value. When you shop for diamonds and fine jewelry, this is the first and only place to shop-New York's Diamond District. The Diamond District is located on West 47 the Street between Fifth and the Avenue of the Americas (Sixth Avenue) in midtown Manhattan.

4. Adam Smith(亚当·斯密). Adam Smith (1723—1790) is a Scottish social philosopher and a pioneer of political economy. One of the key figures of the Scottish Enlightenment, Smith is the author of The *Theory of Moral Sentiments* and *An Inquiry into the Nature and Causes of the Wealth of Nations*. The latter, usually abbreviated as *The Wealth of Nations* 《国富论》, is considered his magnum opus and the first modern work of economics. It is a reflection

---

① doctrine: 教条;信条
② monopoly: 垄断
③ spillovers: 伴随的发展;影响

on economics at the beginning of the Industrial Revolution and argues that free market economies are more productive and beneficial to their societies. The book is a seminal work in classical economics.

5. The Invisible Hand (看不见的手). In economics, the invisible hand, also known as invisible hand of the market, is the term economists use to describe the self-regulating nature of the marketplace. This is a metaphor first coined by the economist Adam Smith in *The Theory of Moral Sentiments*, and used a total of three times in his writings. For Smith, the invisible hand was created by the conjunction of the forces of self-interest, competition, and supply and demand, which he noted as being capable of allocating resources in society. This is the founding justification for the Austrian laissez-faire economic philosophy, but is also frequently seen in neoclassical and Keynesian economics.

6. Imperfect Competition(不完全竞争). In economic theory, imperfect competition is the competitive situation in any market where the conditions necessary for perfect competition are not satisfied. It is a market structure that does not meet the conditions of perfect competition. Forms of imperfect competition include: monopoly, in which there is only one seller of a good oligopoly, in which there are few sellers of a good and monopolistic competition, in which there are many sellers producing highly differentiated goods.

IV. Useful Expressions

1. take ... for granted: 把……看作理所当然
2. engage in: 从事
3. far beyond the reach of...: 远远超出……的范围
4. consumer goods: 消费商品
5. be true of...: 适用于
6. at work: 起作用
7. worse off: 更贫困;更糟糕
8. break down: 失效;出问题

V. Reading Comprehension
Questions

1. What is the nature of prices?
2. How do prices work in a market mechanism?
3. How does the "invisible hand" work?
4. What are the "market failures"?
5. How does the nursing crisis prove about market mechanism?

Decide whether each of the following statements is true or false.

1. Before the food arrives at the dinner table, it has passed through different links. (   )
2. The economic system is working under force.   (   )

3. Prices and markets decide the businesses and the engagement of consumers.　(　)

4. There is a master plan controlling the production of commodities.　(　)

5. Economy is an elaborate mechanism for coordinating people, activities, and business through a system of process and markets.　(　)

6. In the economic market, buyers and sellers determine prices and exchange goods and services.　(　)

7. Economy can increase the economic welfare of anyone.　(　)

8. The author used the nurse crisis to explain the importance of rising wages.　(　)

9. Prices are more important than wages in the market mechanism.　(　)

10. Adam Smith's invisible-hand doctrine will break down when any of the three "market failures" occurs.　(　)

Ⅵ. Discussion

Smith held the view that 'government interference with market competition is almost certain to be injurious'. Do you agree with him? Illustrate your point.

Text B
BEC Reading Texts

PART ONE

Questions 1—8

· Look at the statements below and the five extracts about free market from an article.

· Which extract (A, B, C, D or E) does each statement (1—8) refer to?

· For each statement (1—8), make one letter (A, B, C, D or E) on your Answer Sheet.

· You will need to use some of these letters more than once.

1. This is the contemporary use of the term "free market" by economists and in popular culture; the term has had other uses historically.

2. The theory holds that within an ideal free market, property rights are voluntarily exchanged at a price arranged solely by the mutual consent of sellers and buyers.

3. By owning economic interests or offering subsidies to businesses.

4. Free markets contrast sharply with controlled markets or regulated markets, in which governments more actively regulate prices and/or supplies.

5. A free market is a competitive market where prices are determined by supply and demand.

6. Advocates of a free market traditionally consider the term to imply that the means of

production is under private, and not state control or co-operative ownership.

7. In a free market, the system of prices is the emergent result of a vast number of voluntary transactions, rather than of political decrees.

8. A free market is not to be confused with a perfect market where individuals have perfect information and there is perfect competition.

A. However, the term is also commonly used for markets in which economic intervention and regulation by the state is limited to tax collection, and enforcement of private ownership and contracts. Free markets differ from situations encountered in controlled markets or a monopoly, which can introduce price deviations without any changes to supply and demand.

B. A free-market economy is one within which all markets are unregulated by any parties other than market participants. In its purest form, the government plays a neutral role in its administration and legislation of economic activity, neither limiting it nor actively promoting it.

C. By definition, buyers and sellers do not coerce each other, in the sense that they obtain each other's property rights without the use of physical force, threat of physical force, or fraud, nor are they coerced by a third party.

D. Where substantial state intervention exists, the market is a mixed economy. Where the state or co-operative association of producers directly manages the economy to achieve stated goals, economic planning is said to be in effect; when economic planning entirely substitutes market activity, the economy is a Command economy.

E. The freer the market, the more truly the prices will reflect consumer habits and demands, and the more valuable the information in these prices is to all players in the economy. Through free competition between vendors for the provision of products and services, prices tend to decrease, and quality tends to increase.

PART TWO
Questions 9—14

- Read the text about the need of government intervention in the market.
- Choose the best sentence to fill each of the gaps.
- For each gap (9—14), mark one letter (A-H) on your Answer Sheet.
- Do not use any letter more than once.

Market Failure

The market does not work equally well in all situations. In fact, in some circumstances, the market mechanism might actually fail to produce the goods and services society desires.

(9)... Most people want to feel that their nation's borders are secure and that law and order will prevail in their communities. But few people can afford to buy an army or maintain a legal system. (10)..., he or she might decline to do so. After all, a military force and a legal system would benefit everyone in the community, not just those individuals who paid for it.

Recognizing this, few people would willingly pay for national security or a system of criminal justice. They would rather spend their income on ice cream and DVD players, hoping someone else would pay for law and order. (11)..., no money would be spent on national defense or a legal system. Society would end up with neither output, even though both services were widely desired.

In other situations, (12)... If there were no government regulation, then anyone who had enough money could purchase and drive a car. Little kids from wealthy families could hit the highways, and so could adults with a history of drunken driving. Moreover, no one would have to spend money on emissions-control systems, lead free gasoline, or mufflers. We could drive as fast as we wanted.

(13)... Others, however, would be concerned about safety and pollution. They would realize that the market's decisions about who could drive and what kinds of cars were produced might not be so perfect. (14)... To assure safer and cleaner driving, people might agree to let the government regulate speed, auto emissions, and even drivers.

A. Even if someone were rich enough to pay for such security
B. If everyone waited for a free ride
C. The government makes no attempt to intervene.
D. Some people would welcome unregulated roadways as a new utopia
E. the use of the market mechanism does not imply a free market.
F. They would want the government to intervene
G. National defense is an example
H. the market might produce too much of a good or service

PART THREE
Questions 15—20

· Read the following article on the great depression.

· For each question (15—20) mark one letter (A, B, C or D) on your Answer Sheet for the answer you choose.

In 1929 it looked as though the sun would never set on the American economy. For eight years in a row, the U.S. economy had been expanding rapidly. During the Roaring Twenties the typical American family drove its first car, bought its first radio, and went to the movies for the first time. With factories running at capacity, virtually anyone who wanted to work readily found a job.

Under these circumstances everyone was optimistic. In his acceptance address of November 1928, President-elect Herbert Hoover echoed this optimism by declaring: "We in America today are nearer to the final triumph over poverty than ever before in the history of any land... We shall soon with the help of God be in sight of the day when poverty will be banished from this nation."

The booming stock market seemed to confirm this optimistic outlook. Between 1921 and 1927, the stock market's value more than doubled, adding billions of dollars to the wealth of American households and businesses.

The party ended abruptly on October 24, 1929. On what came to be known as Black Thursday, the stock market crashed. In a few hours, the market value of U. S. corporations fell abruptly, in the most frenzied selling ever seen. The next day President Hoover tried to assure America's stockholders that the economy was "on a sound and prosperous basis." But despite his assurances and the efforts of leading bankers to stem the decline, the stock market continued to plummet. The following Tuesday (October 29) the pace of selling quickened. By the end of the year, over $40 billion of wealth had vanished in the Great Crash. Rich men became paupers overnight; ordinary families lost their savings, their homes, and even their lives.

The devastation was not confined to Wall Street. The financial flames engulfed the farms, the banks, and industry. Between 1930 and 1935, millions of rural families lost their farms. Automobile production fell from 4.5 million cars in 1929 to only 1.1 million in 1932. So many banks were forced to close that newly elected President Roosevelt had to declare a "bank holiday" in March 1933 to stem the outflow of cash to anxious depositors.

Throughout these years, the ranks of the unemployed continued to swell. In October 1929, only 3 percent of the workforce was unemployed. A year later over 9 percent of the workforce was unemployed. Still, things got worse. By 1933 over one-fourth of the labor force was unable to find work. People slept in the streets, scavenged for food, and sold apples on Wall Street. The Great Depression seemed to last forever. In 1933 President Roosevelt lamented that one-third of the nation was ill-clothed, ill-housed, and ill-fed. Thousands of unemployed workers marched to the Capitol to demand jobs and aid.

15. Which of the following is not the description of "Roaring Twenties"?

A. Economy had been expanding rapidly.

B. Stock markets boomed.

C. People could travel by driving their cars.

D. There were noises everywhere.

16. What is the meaning of Herbert Hoover's declaring?

A. Poverty will be banished from U. S.

B. America at that time was nearer to the final triumph over poverty than ever before in the history.

C. America has been successful with the help of God.

D. He showed his optimism towards the development of the country.

17. Which of the following is not the description of "The Great Depression"?

A. Families lost their savings.

B. Banks were forced to close.

C. The stock market crashed.

D. The industry of the country was prosperous.

18. Which of the following was not affected by the Great Depression?

A. Employment

B. Farm

C. Banks

D. Pessimism

19. Why does president Hoover assure America's stockholders that the economy was "on a sound and prosperous basis"?

A. To cheat America's stockholders.

B. To encourage America's stockholders to buy stock.

C. To tell America's stockholders the economy is really prosperous.

D. To avoid stock's plummeting.

20. What might be the most appropriate title of the passage?

A. Stock Market

B. The Outcome of Roaring Twenties

C. The Great Depression in 1929

D. People's life during the Great Depression

PART FOUR

Questions 21—30

· Read the article below about the dilemma between income and leisure.

· Choose the correct word to fill each gap from A, B, C or D.

· For each question (21—30), mark one letter (A, B, C or D) on your Answer Sheet.

Income vs. Leisure

Because both leisure and income are (21)..., we confront a tradeoff when deciding whether to go to work. Going to work implies more income but less leisure. Staying home has the opposite consequences.

The (22)... tradeoff between labor and leisure explains the shape of individual labor-supply (23)... As we work more hours, our leisure time becomes scarcer—and thus more valuable. We become increasingly (24)... to give up any remaining leisure time as it gets ever scarcer. People who work all week long are reluctant to go to work on Saturday. It's not that they are physically exhausted. It's just that they want some time to enjoy the (25)... of their labor. In other words, as the opportunity cost of job time increases, we require (26)... higher rates of pay. We will supply additional labor—work more hours—only if higher wage rates are offered: this is the message conveyed by the upward-sloping labor-supply curve.

The upward slope of the labor-supply curve is (27)... with the changing value of income. Our (28)... motive for working is the income a job provides. Those first few dollars are really precious, especially if you have bills to pay and no other source of support. As you work and earn more, however, you discover that your most (29)... needs have been satisfied. You may still want more things, but your consumption desires aren't so urgent. In other words, the marginal (30)... of income declines as you earn more. You may not be willing to work more hours unless offered a higher wage rate.

21. A. necessary   B. indispensable   C. dispensable   D. valued
22. A. intractable   B. awkward   C. inevitable   D. cruel
23. A. graph   B. diagram   C. chart   D. curves
24. A. impatient   B. reluctant   C. repugnant   D. hate
25. A. fruits   B. happy   C. comfort   D. gains
26. A. respectively   B. correspondingly C. fairly   D. equally
27. A. stimulated   B. reinforced   C. provoked   D. aroused
28. A. ultimate   B. essential   C. primary   D. potential
29. A. expected   B. important   C. urgent   D. internal
30. A. utility   B. effect   C. function   D. avail

PART FIVE
Questions 31—40

· Read the article below about the side effect of market mechanism.

· For each question 31—40, write one word in CAPITAL LETTERS on your Answer Sheet.

The Side Effect of Market Mechanism

The market mechanism might also select the wrong choice about HOW to produce. Consider the message that unregulated markets communicate to producers. In an unregulated market, (31)... price would be charged for using air or waterways, since (32)... is owned by any individual. Producers, (33)..., would regard the use of air and waterways as a "free" good. Under such circumstances it would be a lot cheaper for a factory to dump its waste into nearby waterways than to dispose of it more carefully. It would also be (34)... for power plants to let waste gases and soot go up in smoke than to install environmental safeguards. The resulting pollutants are an externality—a cost imposed (35)... innocent third parties. Consumers would be worse off as the quality of the air and water deteriorated.

Profit-driven producers would seldom worry about externalities in a completely unregulated marketplace. (36)... profit-and-loss considerations the only determinant of HOW goods were produced, we might end up destroying the environment. To prevent such a calamity, we look (37)... the government to regulate HOW goods are produced, thereby rectifying market failures.

The market might also (38)... to distribute goods and services in the best possible way. A market system rewards people (39)... to their value in the marketplace. Sports stars, entertainers, and corporate executives end up with huge paychecks while others toil for meager wages. Big paychecks provide access to more output; people with little paychecks get much less of (40)... is produced.

PART SIX
Questions 41—52

- Read the text below about central planning mechanism.
- In most lines (41—52), there is one extra word. It either is grammatically incorrect or does not fit in with the sense of the text. Some lines, however, are correct.
- If a line is correct, write CORRECT on your Answer Sheet.
- If there is an extra word in the line, write the extra word in CAPITAL LETTERS on your Answer Sheet.

Central Planning

41. Karl Marx saw things differently. In his view, a freewheeling marketplace would cater to the whims

42. of the rich and neglect to the needs of the poor. Workers would be exploited by industrial barons

43. and great landowners. To "leave it off to the market," as Smith had proposed, would encourage

44. exploitation. In the mid-nineteenth century, Karl Marx who proposed a radical alternative:

45. over-turn the power of the poor elite and create a communist state in which everyone's needs

46. would be fulfilled. Marx's writings (Das Kapital, 1867) encouraged communist revolutions and the

47. development of central planning systems. The (people's) government, not from the market,

48. assumed responsibility for deciding what goods were produced, at what prices they were sold,

49. and even who got them. Central planning is still not the principal mechanism of choice in some

50. countries. In North Korea and Cuba, for an example, the central planners decide how many cars

51. to produce and how much bread. They then assign workers and other resources according to

52. those industries to implement their decisions. They also decide who will get the bread and where the cars that are produced. Individuals cannot own factors of production nor even employ other workers for wages. The WHAT, HOW, and FOR WHOM outcomes are all directed by the central government.

第 3 单元　国际贸易
Unit 3　International Trade

Text A

I. 课文导读

21世纪初期,国际贸易发生了巨大的改变。国际贸易区域化使国际经济变得错综复杂。除带来了贸易快速发展外,还促进了贸易自由化,从而带动了贸易组织的发展。国际贸易组织促成了区域经济体内对外贸易以及经济的蓬勃发展,但是对于区域国家和地区影响力有限。只能由非成员国与成员国进行合作来减轻区域化带来的负面影响。经济全球化带来了全球经济的腾飞,但区域化却与全球化不相符合。新旧国际贸易体系存在矛盾,但同时也都在快速改变中。

II. Text

As we approach the 21st century, the international trade arena① is a mixture of successes and failures of the recent past which have created a composite of unknowns, uncertainties, and apprehensions. Unquestionably, the global trading arena has undergone some profound changes during the last decade. These changes have, on the one hand, brought about a greater degree of trade liberalization than ever before. Tariffs are at the lowest levels they have ever been, non-tariff barriers② have been reduced to unprecedented levels, and trade liberalization has become the dominant philosophy of trade ministers, international trade organizations, corporate executives, and certainly the academicians.

One of the greatest economic dichotomies③ of our time is the parallel development of greater regional economic or trading blocs④ such as the European Union and the North American Free Trade Agreement, and serious attempts to liberalize trade at the global level. During the last few years of the 20th century, the number of countries belonging to regional blocs mushroomed. While this trend may be beneficial to the member states of such trading blocs, its total effect on the global trade picture, particularly its impact on non-members, is at best questionable. Probably

---

① arena:(古罗马圆形剧场中央的)角斗场,表演场;喻指竞争场所
② non-tariff barrier: 无关税堡垒
③ dichotomy: 二分法
④ regional economic or trading blocs: 区域经济或贸易集团

the most important argument centers on the question of trade creation versus trade diversion.

Those who favor a regional approach to trade liberalization①, argue with some justification, that regional trading blocs create specialization and thus greater productivity. They further argue that the increase in income resulting from improved productivity will generate greater demand for all products, including imports. Thus, the conclusion is that regional trading blocs create more international trade.

Those who oppose regionalism counter that even if regional trading blocs do increase international trade, most, if not all, of the increase is in intra-bloc trade and non-members do not benefit; in reality they lose part of their export market. They further argue that the increase in the intra-bloc trade is in fact larger than the total increase in global trade, and the difference is the reduction in trade between members and non-members. They particularly point to the significance of non-tariff barriers in creating this situation. In short, they argue that tariff rates in major trading countries have already been reduced to a point that they have little or no effect on imports. For example, the average tariff rate in the United States is about 3 percent. Thus a product imported from Mexico under NAFTA will have a 3 percent price advantage over an identical product imported from Brazil or Malaysia. This is simply not enough to convince a buyer to purchase one product over another. The non-tariff barriers, on the other hand, do play a significant role.

By definition, regional trading blocs are discriminatory. They may be innocuous② in their discrimination, and they may even be legal under the prevailing international commercial law, but they are nevertheless discriminatory. They favor trade with (more accurately imports from) certain countries than with others. This bias is not because some countries produce better quality or less expensive products, but rather because of their geographical location or strong political connections. It would be naive to advocate that political realities, including long-term relations between neighboring countries, could be or even should be ignored. It would be as naive to disregard the reason why countries join regional trading blocs, namely the fact that such agreements are created for the benefit of their member states, and not to enhance the global economic well-being.

Given the contemporary economic and political realities, those unfortunate countries which do not happen to be in the right geographical location or have the right political connections have few options. They can join a few of their neighboring countries and form their own free trade area. In fact, more than ten such attempts were made during the last ten years; however, none experienced much success. In part they failed because they were not genuine policy initiatives; rather they were reactions against other more successful attempts at creating regional trading blocs. More significantly, they failed because they did not have some of the major ingredients that are needed to make a free trade agreement a success, namely sufficient economic

---

① trade liberalization: 贸易自由化
② innocuous: 无伤大雅的

power and adequate trade infrastructure①. An economic integration agreement needs an 'anchor'② to maintain it, otherwise it will drift away. The European Union has been successful because it includes France, Germany, and Italy to serve as an anchor. Despite many problems, NAFTA will succeed because it includes the United States, which has been willing to play the same role. On the other hand, numerous other attempts have failed because they lacked the 'anchor'. ASEAN (the Association of South East Asian Nations) is a good illustration of this point. It included some of the fastest growing economies of the world, and logically its creation should have contributed significantly to the economic development of its member states. In reality, however, almost three decades after its formation, ASEAN is still in its developmental stage, precisely because it does not have an economic power base—the anchor—that a successful alliance requires.

A second alternative available to the countries which are not members or potential members of existing economic groupings is to seek concessionary③ agreements from these blocs. While this may not be the most elegant approach, political realities may make them less unacceptable; after all, they may serve the purpose of giving non-members some reprieve④. The European Union has provided several examples of how this approach might work. The EU has eliminated all trade barriers among its member states, thus putting non-members at a distinct disadvantage in trading with its member states. To alleviate the burden this has placed on some of its previously major trading partners, the European Union has negotiated a number of concessionary agreements giving preferential treatment to certain countries. While these agreements do not give anything close to full membership to these countries, they do provide some benefits for these nations. Most signatories⑤ to these preferential agreements had special trade relations with one or more members of the European Union before it was formed. For example, many are former French colonies in Africa or former British colonies and members of the Commonwealth.

While there seems to be a general consensus⑥ that globalization of trade will have a positive effect on the world economy as a whole; this unity does not exist when the aggregate⑦ picture is broken down into different national or regional units or groups. Also, the question of who the major beneficiaries of global trade liberalization are is left largely unanswered. Some argue that for two reasons, most of the gains generated by an expansion of international trade are directed at the industrialized countries. First, according to this hypothesis, any policy which expands international trade would more probably benefit those who are heavily engaged in it. The proponents of this theory point to the volume of trade and the fact that industrialized countries

---

① trade infrastructure: 贸易基础
② anchor: 锚;常喻指精神支柱,靠山
③ concessionary: 特许
④ reprieve: 暂时宽限
⑤ signatory: 签署国
⑥ consensus: 共识
⑦ aggregate: 全面的

make up more than 70 percent of global exports. Second, in a convoluted① way, they argue that industrial countries' tariff rates are already low, and multilateral trade negotiations are merely a ploy by them to force the developing countries to lower their protective trade barriers and expose their fragile industries. Others, on the other hand, maintain that because most developing countries are in the early stages of establishing their export markets, any liberalization will open up vast markets of the industrial world to them, and therefore will benefit them the most. For example, numerous studies substantiate② the advantages of mass production and the economies of scale. Accordingly, industrial production requires a minimum level before the production of manufacturing products becomes economically viable③. Different products have different points at which the benefits of mass production are realized. Nevertheless, most products do have a minimum, economically feasible, level of production. Furthermore, many developing countries are too small to reach this level with their indigenous④ demand. Consequently, the only way that the production of such manufacturing products can be globally competitive would be through exports. In other words, without exports smaller countries would not be able to industrialize their economies, regardless of the cost involved.

Ⅲ. Notes

1. European Union(欧盟). EU is an economic and political union of 27 independent member states which are located primarily in Europe. The EU traces its origins from the European Coal and Steel Community (ECSC) and the European Economic Community (EEC), formed by six countries in 1958. Important institutions of the EU include the European Commission, the Council of the European Union, the European Council, the Court of Justice of the European Union, and the European Central Bank.

2. North American Free Trade Agreement(北美自由贸易协定). NAFTA is an agreement signed by the governments of Canada, Mexico, and the United States, creating a trilateral trade bloc in North America. The agreement came into force on January 1, 1994. It superseded the Canada-United States Free Trade Agreement between the U.S. and Canada.

3. Association of South East Asian Nations(东盟). ASEAN is a geo-political and economic organization of ten countries located in Southeast Asia, which was formed on 8 August 1967 by Indonesia, Malaysia, the Philippines, Singapore and Thailand. Since then, membership has expanded to include Brunei, Burma (Myanmar), Cambodia, Laos, and Vietnam. Its aims include the acceleration of economic growth, social progress, cultural development among its members, the protection of regional peace and stability, and to provide opportunities for member countries to discuss differences peacefully.

---

① convoluted: 错综复杂的
② substantiate: 证实
③ viable: 可行的
④ indigenous: 当地的,本土的;固有的

4. The Commonwealth（英联邦）. The Commonwealth of Nations, normally referred to as the Commonwealth and formerly known as the British Commonwealth, is an intergovernmental organization of fifty-four independent member states. The member states cooperate within a framework of common values and goals as outlined in the Singapore Declaration. Activities of the Commonwealth are carried out through the permanent Commonwealth Secretariat, headed by the Secretary-General, and biennial meetings between Commonwealth Heads of Government.

Ⅳ. Useful Expressions

1. bring about: 导致
2. trade liberalization: 贸易自由化
3. be beneficial to: 对……有利
4. intra-bloc trade: 集团内部之间的贸易
5. In short: 总之
6. tariff rates: 关税率
7. average tariff rate: 平均关税率
8. play a significant role: 起到巨大的作用
9. make up more than 70 percent of global exports: 占有百分之七十以上的国际出口率
10. multilateral trade negotiations: 多边贸易谈判
11. in other words: 换句话说

Ⅴ. Reading Comprehension

Questions

1. What great changes have taken place in the global trading arena?
2. What does the economic dichotomy refer to?
3. How do people argue for and against regionalism?
4. In what way do regional trade blocs impede global economic well-being?
5. Who are the major beneficiaries of global trade liberalization?

Decide whether each of the following statements is true or false.

1. Regional economic or trading blocs lead to trade diversion of the world.   (   )
2. Regional trading blocs increase the trade among blocs, so international trade increases.   (   )
3. Regional trading blocs increase the trade among blocs but reduce the trade between members and non-members.   (   )
4. Trading blocs intend to liberalize trade at the global level.   (   )
5. Geographical location is an important factor for countries to form trading blocs. (   )
6. Preferential agreements are only offered to member countries.   (   )
7. As more countries are industrialized, international trade will expand.   (   )
8. Liberalization will create vast markets of the industrial world, and therefore will benefit

developing countries the most.

9. Members of NAFTA get most benefit in global trade liberalization. ( )

10. Industrial production requires a medieval level before the production of manufacturing products becomes economically viable. ( )

VI. Discussion

What is your opinion of regional trade blocs?

Text B
BEC Reading Texts

PART ONE
Questions 1—8

- Look at the statements below and the five extracts about diminishing returns from an article.
- Which extract (A, B, C, D or E) does each statement (1—8) refer to?
- For each statement (1—8), make one letter (A, B, C, D or E) on your Answer Sheet.
- You will need to use some of these letters more than once.

1. The effect is that the efficiency with which the cocoa industry uses labor will decline, and returns will diminish.

2. Diminishing returns show that it is not feasible for a country to specialize to the degree suggested by the simple Ricardian model outlined earlier.

3. It is more realistic to assume diminishing returns for two reasons. First, not all resources are of the same quality.

4. Diminishing returns to specialization occurs when more units of resources are required to produce each additional unit.

5. A second reason for diminishing returns is that different goods use resources in different proportions.

6. However, it is more realistic to assume diminishing returns to specialization.

7. Thus, the basic conclusion that unrestricted free trade is beneficial still holds, although because of diminishing returns, the gains may not be as great as suggested in the constant returns case.

8. The simple comparative advantage model developed above assumes constant returns to specialization.

A. By constant returns to specialization we mean the units of resources required to produce a good (cocoa or rice) are assumed to remain constant no matter where one is on a country's production possibility frontier (PPF). Thus, we assumed that it always took Ghana 10 units of resources to produce one ton of cocoa.

B. While 10 units of resources may be sufficient to increase Ghana's output of cocoa from 12 tons to 13 tons, 11 units of resources may be needed to increase output from 13 to 14 tons, 12 units of resources to increase output from 14 tons to 15 tons, and so on.

C. For example, imagine that growing cocoa uses more land and less labor than growing rice, and that Ghana tries to transfer resources from rice production to cocoa production. The rice industry will release proportionately too much labor and too little land for efficient cocoa production. To absorb the additional resources of labor and land, the cocoa industry will have to shift toward more labor-intensive methods of production.

D. As a country tries to increase its output of a certain good, it is increasingly likely to draw on more marginal resources whose productivity is not as great as those initially employed. The result is that it requires ever more resources to produce an equal increase in output.

E. Diminishing returns to specialization suggest that the gains from specialization are likely to be exhausted before specialization is complete. In reality, most countries do not specialize out, instead, produce a range of goods. However, the theory predicts that it is worthwhile to specialize until that point where the resulting gains from trade are outweighed by diminishing returns.

PART TWO
Questions 9—14

- Read the text about the international trade.
- Choose the best sentence to fill each of the gaps.
- For each gap (9—14), mark one letter (A-H) on your Answer Sheet.
- Do not use any letter more than once.

What International Trade is about?

International trade is the exchange of capital, goods, and services across international borders or territories. In most countries, such trade represents a significant share of gross domestic product (GDP). While international trade has been present throughout much of history, (9)...

Industrialization, advanced transportation, globalization, multinational corporations, and outsourcing are all having a major impact on the international trade system. (10)... Without international trade, nations would be limited to the goods and services produced within their own borders.

International trade is, in principle, not different from domestic trade as the motivation and the behavior of parties involved in a trade do not change fundamentally regardless of whether trade is across a border or not. (11)... The reason is that a border typically imposes additional costs such as tariffs, time costs due to border delays and costs associated with country differences such as language, the legal system or culture.

Another difference between domestic and international trade is that factors of production such as capital and labor are typically more mobile within a country than across countries. (12)..., and only to a lesser extent to trade in capital, labor or other factors of production. Trade in goods and services can serve as a substitute for trade in factors of production.

Instead of importing a factor of production, (13)... An example is the import of labor-intensive goods by the United States from China. Instead of importing Chinese labor, the United States imports goods that were produced with Chinese labor. One report in 2010 suggested that international trade was increased when a country hosted a network of immigrants, but the trade effect was weakened when the immigrants became assimilated into their new country.

International trade is also a branch of economics, which, (14)...

A. The main difference is that international trade is typically more costly than domestic trade

B. International trade allows us to expand our markets for both goods and services

C. its economic, social, and political importance has been on the rise in recent centuries

D. Increasing international trade is crucial to the continuance of globalization

E. a country can import goods that make intensive use of that factor of production and thus embody it

F. in which prices, or supply and demand, affect and are affected by global events

G. together with international finance, forms the larger branch of international economics

H. Thus international trade is mostly restricted to trade in goods and services

PART THREE
Questions 15—20

· Read the following article on the international trade.

· For each question (15—20) mark one letter (A, B, C or D) on your Answer Sheet for the answer you choose.

The great strength of the theories of Smith, Ricardo, and Heckscher-Ohlin is that they identify with precision the specific benefits of international trade. Common sense suggests that some international trade is beneficial. For example, nobody would suggest that Iceland should grow its own oranges. Iceland can benefit from trade by exchanging some of the products that it can produce at a low cost (fish) for some products that it cannot produce at all (oranges). Thus, by engaging in international trade, Icelanders are able to add oranges to their diet of fish. The theories of Smith, Ricardo, and Heckscher-Ohlin go beyond this commonsense notion, however, to show why it is beneficial for a country to engage in international trade even for products it is able to coproduce for itself. This is a difficult concept for people to grasp. For example, many people in the United States believe that American consumers should buy products produced in the United States by American companies whenever possible to help save American jobs from foreign competition. Such thinking apparently underlay a 2002 decision by President George W. Bush to protect American steel producers from competition from lower cost foreign producers.

The same kind of nationalistic sentiments can be observed in many other countries. However, the theories of Smith, Ricardo, and Heckscher-Ohlin tell us that a country's economy may gain if its citizens buy certain products from other nations that could be produced at home. The gains arise because international trade allows a country to specialize in the manufacture and export of products that can be produced most efficiently in that country, while importing products that can be produced more efficiently in other countries. So it may make sense for the United States to specialize in the production and export of commercial jet aircraft, since the efficient production of commercial jet aircraft requires resources that are abundant in the United States, such as a highly skilled labor force and cutting-edge technological know-how. On the other hand, it may make sense for the United States to import textiles from China since the efficient production of textiles requires a relatively cheap labor force and cheap labor is not abundant in the United States.

Of course, this economic argument is often difficult for segments of a country's population to accept. With their future threatened by imports, U. S. textile companies and their employees have tried hard to persuade the government to limit the importation of textiles by demanding quotas and tariffs. Although such import controls may benefit particular groups, such as textile businesses and their employees or unprofitable steel mills and their employees, the theories of Smith, Ricardo, and Heckscher-Ohlin suggest that such action hurts the economy as a whole. Limits on imports are often in the interests of domestic producers, but not domestic consumers.

15. Why does the author offer an example of Iceland?

A. To emphasize the great strength of the theories of Smith, Ricardo, and Heckscher-Ohlin.

B. To explain the connotation of international trade.

C. To prove the benefit of some international trade.

D. To show the exchange of orange and fish in international trade.

16. By the word "underlay"(line 12, paragraph1), the author means _____.

A. influenced

B. determined

C. supported

D. accounted for

17. What does "nationalistic sentiments" mean in the passage?

A. Sentiments are held by the whole nation.

B. People are patriotic towards their homeland.

C. Consumers should buy products produced in their own country.

D. Countries should not import products.

18. What does "this"(line1, paragraph 3) refer to?

A. United States should specialize in the production and export of commercial jet aircraft.

B. United States should import textiles from China for its cheap labor force.

C. Consumers should buy products produced in their homeland to help save jobs.

D. A country's economy may gain if its citizens buy certain products from other nations that could be produced at home.

19. What does theories of Smith, Ricardo, and Heckscher-Ohlin suggest when a country limits its importation?

A. It hurts the economy as a whole.

B. It helps increase job opportunities.

C. The international trade is not beneficial to the country.

D. Domestic consumers are beneficial from limiting importation.

20. Which is the main idea of the last paragraph?

A. Persuasion of U. S. textile companies

B. The difficulty to accept theories of Smith, Ricardo, and Heckscher-Ohlin.

C. Limits on imports.

D. The influence of limits on imports.

PART FOUR

Questions 21—30

· Read the article below about the specialization and international trade.

· Choose the correct word to fill each gap from A, B, C or D.

· For each question (21—30), mark one letter (A, B, C or D) on your Answer Sheet.

Specialization and International Trade

The high (21)... of specialization in our society increases the standard of living of all by making more goods and services available. But specialization necessarily implies trade and cannot occur without it. This (22)... from the fact that people usually want to have a "(23)... diet." The specialized producer uses only a small part-maybe none-of his own product for his personal (24)..., and he exchanges his surplus for the goods and services of other specialized producers.

The exchange of goods and services among residents of the same country is usually called (25)... trade. Countries cannot live alone any more effectively than individuals can. Thus, each country tends to specialize in the production of those commodities which it can produce relatively more (26)... than other countries, exchanging its surplus for the (27)... of other countries, of goods and services which they produce relatively more cheaply, or which the first country cannot produce at all. This process brings (28)... an international division of labor which makes it possible to make more goods and services available to all countries. (29)..., the international division of labor and specialization increases the standard of living in all countries in the same way that the division of labor and specialization within a single, (30)... economy increases the standard of living of all of its residents.

21.	A. grade	B. level	C. degree	D. extent
22.	A. arises	B. follows	C. differs	D. gains
23.	A. healthy	B. natural	C. balanced	D. proper
24.	A. consumption	B. opinion	C. habit	D. need
25.	A. international	B. border	C. domestic	D. free
26.	A. attractively	B. preciously	C. rarely	D. cheaply
27.	A. commodities	B. deficit	C. currency	D. surplus
28.	A. about	B. forth	C. out	D. into
29.	A. Therefore	B. However	C. Moreover	D. Besides
30.	A. open	B. closed	C. prospect	D. world

PART FIVE
Questions 31—40

- Read the article below about the comparative advantage in international trade.
- For each question 31—40, write one word in CAPITAL LETTERS on your Answer Sheet.

The Comparative Advantage

In economics, the law of comparative advantage says that two (31)... will both gain from trade if, in the absence of trade, they have different relative costs for producing the same goods. Even if one country is more efficient in the production of all goods (32)... the other, both countries will still gain by trading with each other, as (33)... as they have different relative efficiencies.

For example, (34)..., using machinery, a worker in one country can produce both shoes and shirts (35)... 6 per hour, and a worker in a country with less machinery can produce (36)... 2 shoes or 4 shirts in an hour, each country can gain from trade because their internal trade-offs between shoes and shirts are (37)... The less-efficient country has a comparative advantage in shirts, so it (38)... it more efficient to produce shirts and trade them to the more-efficient country for shoes. Without trade, its (39)... per shoe was 2 shirts; by trading, its cost per shoe can reduce to as low as 1 shirt depending on how much trade occurs. The more-(40)... country has a comparative advantage in shoes, so it can gain in efficiency by moving some workers from shirt-production to shoe-production and trading some shoes for shirts. Without trade, its cost to make a shirt was 1 shoe; by trading, its cost per shirt can go as low as 1/2 shoe depending on how much trade occurs.

The net benefits to each country are called the gains from trade.

PART SIX
Questions 41—52

- Read the text below from a report about sale contact.
- In most lines (41—52), there is one extra word. It either is grammatically incorrect or

does not fit in with the sense of the text. Some lines, however, are correct.

· If a line is correct, write CORRECT on your Answer Sheet.

· If there is an extra word in the line, write the extra word in CAPITAL LETTERS on your Answer Sheet.

Sale Contact

41. Should the Sellers fail to load the goods within the time as notified as by the Buyers, on board the

42. vessel booked by the Buyers after its arrival at the shipping port of shipment, all expenses such

43. as dead freight, demurrage, and consequences thereof shall be borne by the Sellers. Should if

44. the vessel be withdrawn or replaced or delayed eventually or the cargo should be shut out etc. ,

45. and the Sellers are not informed in goodtime to stop delivery of the calculation of loss for storage

46. expenses and insurance premium thus be sustained at the loading port should be based on the

47. loading date notified by the agent to the Sellers (or based on the date of the arrival of the cargo at

48. the loading port in case the cargo should arrive there not later than the notified loading date). The

49. above mentioned loss is to be calculated from the 16th day after expiry of the free storage time at

50. port should be borne by Buyers with the exception of Force Majeure. However, and the Sellers

51. still undertake to load the cargo immediately upon the carrying vessel's arrival at the loading port

52. at their own risks and expenses. The above payment of aforesaid expenses shall be effected against presentation of the original vouchers after being checked.

第4单元 营销策略
Unit 4 Marketing Strategy

Text A

I. 课文导读

当代的公司,国内的或是国际的,不论规模大小,营利或是非营利,都非常重视市场营销。过去,人们将市场营销看作是销售和广告。然而,市场营销应该包含诸多活动于其中,而这些活动是被设计来满足消费者需求的。现代市场营销策略,是以顾客的需要为出发点,根据获得的顾客需求量以及购买力等信息、商业界的期望值,有计划地组织各项经营活动,通过相互协调一致的产品策略、价格策略、渠道策略和促销策略,来获取更大利益。

II. Text

Marketing, more than any other business function, deals with customers. Understanding, creating, communicating, and delivering customer value and satisfaction are at the very heart of modern marketing thinking and practice. Marketing is the delivery of customer satisfaction at a profit. It can also be defined as managing markets to bring about exchanges and relationships for the purpose of creating value and satisfying needs and wants of consumers. The twofold goal of marketing is to attract new customer by promising superior value and to keep current customers by delivering satisfaction.

Wal-Mart[①] has become the world's largest retailer by delivering on its promise, "Always low prices—always." FedEx[②] dominates the U. S. small-package freight industry by consistently making good on its promise of fast, reliable small-package delivery. Ritz-Carlton[③] promises and delivers truly "memorable experiences" for its hotel guests. Coca-Cola, the world's leading soft drink, delivers on the simple but enduring promise, "Always Coca-Cola"—always thirst-quenching, always good with food, always cool, always a part of your life. These and other highly successful companies know that if they take care of their customers, market share and profits will follow.

Sound marketing is critical to the success of every organization-large or small, for-profit or

---

① Wal-mart: 沃尔玛公司
② FedEx: Federal Express, 联邦快递
③ Ritz-Carlton: 利兹-卡尔顿酒店

not-for-profit, domestic or global. Large for-profit firms such as Microsoft, Sony, FedEx, Wal-Mart, IBM, and Marriott① use marketing. But so do not-for-profit organizations such as colleges, hospitals, museums, symphony orchestras, and even churches. Moreover, marketing is practiced not only in the United States but also in the rest of the world. Most countries in North and South America, Western Europe, and Asia have well-developed marketing systems. Even in Eastern Europe and other parts of the world where marketing has long had a bad name, dramatic political and social changes have created new opportunities for marketing. Business and government leaders in most of these nations are eager to learn everything they can about modern marketing practices.

You already know a lot about marketing—it's all around you. You see the results of marketing in the abundance of products in your nearby shopping mall. You see marketing in the advertisements that fill your TV, spice up② your magazines, stuff your mailbox, or enliven your Internet pages. At home, at school, where you work, and where you play, you are exposed to marketing in almost everything you do. Yet, there is much more to marketing than meets the consumer's casual eye. Behind it all is a massive network of people and activities competing for your attention and purchasing dollars.

Today, marketing must be understood not in the old sense of making a sale—"telling and selling"—but in the new sense of satisfying customer needs. Selling occurs only after a product is produced. By contrast, marketing starts long before a company has a product. Marketing is the homework that managers undertake to assess③ needs, measure their extent and intensity, and determine whether a profitable opportunity exists. Marketing continues throughout the product's life, trying to find new customers and keep current customers by improving product appeal④ and performance, learning from product sales results. If the marketer does a good job of understanding customer needs, develops products that provide superior value and prices, distributes, and promotes⑤ them effectively, these products will sell very easily. Thus, selling and advertising are only part of a larger "marketing mix"—a set of marketing tools that work together to affect the marketplace.

We define marketing mix as the set of controllable, tactical marketing tools that the firm blends to produce the response it wants in the target market. The marketing mix consists of everything the firm can do to influence the demand for its product. The many possibilities can be collected into four groups of variables known as the "Four 'P's": product, price, place, and promotion. Product means the goods-and-service combination the company offers to the target market. Price is the amount of money customers have to pay to obtain the product. Place includes

---

① Marriott: 万豪国际集团
② spice up: 增加趣味
③ assess: 评估
④ appeal: 吸引力
⑤ promote: 促销

company activities that make the product available to target consumers. Promotion covers activities that communicate the merits of the product and persuade target customers to buy it.

Some critics feel that the Four 'P's may omit and underemphasize certain important activities. For example, they ask, "Where are services?" That they don't start with a 'P' doesn't justify omitting them. There is another concern, however, that is valid. It holds that the Four 'P' concept takes the seller's view of the market, not the buyer's view. From the buyers' viewpoint, in the age of connectedness, the four 'P' might be better described as the Four 'C's: customer solution, customer cost, convenience, communication.

Thus while marketers see themselves as selling a product, customers see themselves as buying value or a solution to their problem. Customers are interested in more than the price; they are interested in the total costs of obtaining, using, and disposing① of a product. Customers want the product and services to be as conveniently available as possible. Finally, they want two-way communication. Marketers would do well to first think through the four 'C' and then build the four 'P' on the platform.

The most basic concept underlying marketing is that of human needs. Human needs are states of felt deprivation②. They include basic physical needs for food, clothing, warmth, and safety; social needs for belonging and affection; and individual needs for knowledge and self-expression. These needs are not invented by marketers; they are a basic part of human makeup.

Wants are the form human needs take as they are shaped by culture and individual personality. An American needs food but wants hamburgers, French fries, and soft drink. A person in Mauritius③ needs food but wants a mango, rice, lentils, and beans. Wants are shaped by one's society and are described in terms of objects that will satisfy needs.

People have almost unlimited wants but limited resources. Thus, they want to choose products that provide the most value and satisfaction for their money. When backed by buying power, wants become demands. Consumers view products as bundles of benefits and choose products that give them the best bundle for their money. A Honda Civic④ means basic transportation, affordable price, and fuel economy; a Lexus⑤ means comfort, luxury, and status. Given their wants and resources, people demand products with the benefits that add up to the most satisfaction.

Outstanding marketing companies go to great lengths to learn about and understand their customers' needs, wants and demands. They conduct consumer research about consumer likes and dislikes. They analyze customer inquiry, warranty⑥, and service data. They observe customers using their own and competing products and train salespeople to be on the lookout for unful-

---

① dispose: 清除
② felt deprivation: 感到匮乏的(状态)
③ Mauritius: 毛里求斯共和国
④ Honda Civic: 本田思域汽车
⑤ Lexus: 雷克萨斯，日本丰田汽车旗下的豪华车品牌
⑥ warranty: 保修卡

filled customer needs.

In these outstanding companies, people at all levels—including top management—stay close to customers. For example, top executives from Wal-Mart spend two days each week visiting stores and mingling with customers. At Disney world, managers spend a week each year on the front line—taking tickets, selling popcorn, or loading and unloading rides. At AT & T①, CEO C. Michael Armstrong often visits one of the company's customer service centers to get a better sense of the problems and frustration that customers may face. At Marriot, to stay in touch with customers, Chairman of the Board and President Bill Marriot personally reads some 10 percent of the 8,000 letters and 2 percent of the 750,000 guest comment cards submitted by customers each year. Understanding customer needs, wants and demands in detail provides important input② for designing marketing strategies.

Ⅲ. Notes

1. Wal-Mart Stores, Inc.(沃尔玛公司). Branded as Walmart since 2008 and Wal-Mart before then, it is an American public multinational corporation that chains of large discount department stores and warehouse stores. The company is the world's 18th largest public corporation, according to the Forbes Global 2000 list, and the largest public corporation when ranked by revenue. It is also the biggest private employer in the world with over 2 million employees, and is the largest retailer in the world.

2. The Ritz-Carlton(利兹卡尔顿酒店). It is a brand of luxury hotels and resorts with 75 properties located in major cities and resorts in 24 countries worldwide. It also has major service training operations in its Ritz-Carlton Learning Institute and Ritz-Carlton Leadership Center, created by Ritz-Carlton executive *(emeritus)* Leonardo Inghilleri, where nearly 50,000 executives from other companies worldwide have been trained in the Ritz-Carlton principles of service. The Ritz-Carlton Hotel Company LLC is now a wholly owned subsidiary of Marriott International. The Ritz-Carlton Hotel Company currently has 32,000 employees. The Ritz-Carlton headquarters are found in Chevy Chase, Maryland, a community along the border of Washington, D. C. .

3. Marriott International, Inc.(万豪国际)(NYSE: MAR). It is a worldwide operator and franchisor of a broad portfolio of hotels and related lodging facilities. Founded by J. Willard Marriott, the company is now led by son J. W. (Bill) Marriott, Jr. Today, Marriott International has about 3,150 lodging properties located in the United States and 68 other countries and territories.

4. AT & T Inc.(美国电信公司)(sometimes stylized as at & t; NYSE: T, for "telephone"). it is an American multinational telecommunications corporation headquartered in Whitacre Tower, Dallas, Texas, United States. It is the largest provider of mobile telephony and

---

① At & T: 原为 American Telephone & Telegraph 的缩写,是一家美国电信公司

② input: 投入

fixed telephony and in the United States, and is also a provider of broadband and subscription television services. As of 2010, AT & T is the 7th largest company in the United States by total revenue, as well as the 4th largest non-oil company in the US (behind Walmart, General Electric and Bank of America) In 2011, Forbes listed AT & T as the 14th largest company in the world by market value and the 9th largest non-oil company in the world by market value. It is the 20th largest mobile telecom operator in the world with over 100.7 million mobile customers.

5. Marketing mix（市场营销组合）. The term "marketing mix" was coined in 1953 by Neil Borden in his American Marketing Association presidential address. However, this was actually a reformulation of an earlier idea by his associate, James Culliton, who in 1948 described the role of the marketing manager as a "mixer of ingredients". The marketing mix (price, product, distribution, promotion) forms the entire promotional campaign.

6. Four 'P's. Elements of the marketing mix are often referred to as the "Four 'P's", a phrase used since the 1960's. A prominent marketer, E. Jerome McCarthy, proposed a Four 'P' classification in 1960, which has seen wide use.

7. Four 'C's. Robert F. Lauterborn proposed a four C classification in 1993. The Four 'C's model is more consumer-oriented and attempts to better fit the movement from mass marketing to niche marketing.

IV. Useful Expressions

1. at the very heart of: 在实质上；其核心
2. freight industry: 货运业
3. spice up: 增加趣味
4. go to great lengths: 不顾一切；竭尽全力
5. on the lookout for: 当心，提防
6. thirst-quenching: 止渴的
7. stay in touch with: 与……保持联系
8. mingle with: 与……在一起

V. Reading Comprehension

Questions

1. What is the definition of marketing?
2. What consists of the marketing mix?
3. What is the major difference between the Four 'P's and the Four 'C's?
4. What are the basic human needs?
5. What's the difference between customer's needs, wants and demands?

Decide whether each of the following statements is true or false.

1. Creating value and satisfying needs and wants of consumers are vital in marketing.

(   )

2. Customers create superior value for marketing. ( )
3. Wal-Mart is to attract customers by promising "Always low prices—always." ( )
4. Sound marketing is critical to the success of every organization around the world. ( )
5. Countries in Eastern Europe despise marketing. ( )
6. Only the process of selling products needs marketing. ( )
7. "Marketing mix" refers to a set of marketing tools working together to affect the marketplace. ( )
8. Four 'P' concept means the same as the Four 'C's. ( )
9. Understanding customer needs, wants and demands in detail provides important input for designing marketing strategies. ( )
10. All human needs are invented by marketers. ( )

Ⅵ. Discussion

Discuss and illustrate that human needs are shaped by culture.

Text B
BEC Reading Texts

PART ONE
Questions 1—8

· Look at the statements below and the five extracts about marketing from an article.
· Which extract (A, B, C, D or E) does each statement (1—8) refer to?
· For each statement (1—8), make one letter (A, B, C, D or E) on your Answer Sheet.
· You will need to use some of these letters more than once.

1. Marketers should already be familiar with how to communicate their messages across a variety of mediums.
2. Marketing managers also develop pricing strategies to help firms maximize profits and market share while ensuring that the firms' customers are satisfied.
3. In collaboration with sales, product development, and other managers, they monitor trends that indicate the need for new products and services and they oversee product development.
4. In the United States alone 9 out of 10 people carry a mobile device according to research done by MobiThinking.
5. So marketers should build their awareness of different cultures and respective sensitivities.
6. Specifically we have something to learn from Hollywood, which I believe may serve us

as a kind of laboratory.

7. At present, SMS marketing is considered to be one of the more direct and personal forms of marketing.

8. So marketers have something to learn from non marketers.

A. SMS marketing is marketing using a mobile phone. SMS stands for short message server, otherwise known as text messaging. In short SMS marketing is done using a mobile device to transfer marketing communication to interested consumers. It's an area that is gaining a great deal of interest by businesses both small and large.

B. In a perfect world, every brand would contain a variety of meanings, the better to speak to a variety of consumers. The trouble with stuffing the brand this way is that the meaning that works for one consumer can bewilder or antagonize the next. Building a brand with many meanings can sometimes fail spectacularly. Everyone creating popular culture is trying to solve this question.

C. Marketing managers work with advertising and promotion managers to promote the firm's or organization's products and services. With the help of lower level managers, including product development managers and market research managers, marketing managers estimate the demand for products and services offered by the firm and its competitors and identify potential markets for the firm's products.

D. Marketers should also be aware of the competition that they will face when pursuing a position at a media company. Typically, marketers must have a plethora of solid experience and a vast understanding of the media industry and the specific changes impacting the industry they are looking to work in.

E. Convergence has significantly blurred the lines between print, internet, television and radio. Messaging that used to be tailored for one outlet will now have to be adjusted for a wider audience. Further, the accessibility of the internet has created a very diverse and global customer base.

PART TWO
Questions 9—14
· Read the text about the difference between Marketing & Advertising
· Choose the best sentence to fill each of the gaps.
· For each gap (9—14), mark one letter (A-H) on your Answer Sheet.
· Do not use any letter more than once.

Marketing vs. Advertising: What's the Difference?

You will often find that many people confuse marketing with advertising or vice versa. (9)... Knowing the difference and doing your market research can put your company on the path to substantial growth.

(10)... and then I'll go into the explanation of how marketing and advertising differ from one another:

Advertising: The paid, public, non-personal announcement of a persuasive message by an identified sponsor; the non-personal presentation or promotion by a firm of its products to its existing and potential customers.

Marketing: The systematic planning, implementation and control of a mix of business activities intended to bring together buyers and sellers for the mutually advantageous exchange or transfer of products.

(11)... that people think of them as one-in-the same, so lets break it down a bit.

Advertising is a single component of the marketing process. It's the part that involves getting the word out concerning your business, product, or the services you are offering. It involves the process of developing strategies such as ad placement, frequency, etc. Advertising includes the placement of an ad in such mediums as newspapers, direct mail, billboards, television, radio, and of course the Internet. (12)... with public relations following in a close second and market research not falling far behind..

The best way to distinguish between advertising and marketing is to think of marketing as a pie, inside that pie you have slices of advertising, market research, media planning, public relations, product pricing, distribution, customer support, sales strategy, and community involvement. (13)... (14)... Marketing is a process that takes time and can involve hours of research for a marketing plan to be effective. Think of marketing as everything that an organization does to facilitate an exchange between company and consumer.

A. Let's start off by reviewing the formal definitions of each

B. All of these elements must not only work independently but they also must work together towards the bigger goal.

C. Advertising only equals one piece of the pie in the strategy

D. While both components are important they are very different

E. Advertising is the largest expense of most marketing plans

F. Advertising can be defined as a way to publicize the information consumers need

G. After reading both of the definitions it is easy to understand how the difference can be confusing to the point

H. We can come a conclusion that all the elements are important for advertisers to note

PART THREE
Questions 15—20

· Read the following article on the reasons why customers don't buy from you.

· For each question (15—20) mark one letter (A, B, C or D) on your Answer Sheet for the answer you choose.

Are you spending time marketing your product, but still not selling as much as you would like? The truth is consumers have needs and steps that they go through and that persuades them to buy. If your marketing is not meeting those requirements it is probably the reasons your product is not selling. As consumers we are not just persuaded by the "price" of a product, we are moved by the benefits of the product and what it can do for us; that's our reason for purchasing. If you are finding that you are having difficulty in selling your product you may want to consider the following reasons why consumers don't buy and evaluate how you can do better at marketing your products in a way that converts consumers into your customers. They are not aware of your product.

Consumers cannot purchase products they are not aware of. If you are marketing, but consumers still don't know about your product it may be time to evaluate why it's not working. Are you targeting the right market with your message? Is your message reaching those that would have an interest in your product? It's important to remember that the solution is not always more marketing, because the problem may lie with where you are marketing at, and what marketing vehicles you are using. They don't understand the benefits of your product. Consumers don't buy products solely based on price. Now, this does not mean that they don't factor in price, they do. Consumers buy based on the benefits your product brings them. If you asked your customers what the benefits of your product are, would they know? This is important. Your marketing must be centered on the benefits for your product in order for consumers to take an interest in purchasing your product. Create a list of the top three benefits of your product and use those in your marketing message. They don't feel your product has perceived value. Consumers will not buy products that they perceive as having no value. Why should customers value your product? You can use the benefits of your product to create a perceived value and it is that perceived value that helps in the sales of your product. If a customer cannot see value they will simply pass your product by. You must create that perceived value in your marketing message. They don't see how your product meets their needs.

We've talked about benefits and perceived value, now let's talk about needs. Do consumers know how your product meets their needs? Does it make their life easier, save them time, and make them feel better? What need does your product satisfy? You have to tell consumers that, don't make them guess or come up with the answer on their own, tell them and help educate them on why they need your product.

15. Which is not one of the main reasons that the consumers do not buy your products?

A. The consumers don't find the way to know your product.

B. The practicability of the product is not obvious.

C. The product of other marketer has a more favorable price.

D. Consumers don't buy anything which they think is of no value.

16. What do we learn about from the first paragraph?

A. The consumers don't want to buy from you because you applied inappropriate ways in marketing the product.

B. It is the benefits of the product that attract the customers to pay for it.

C. A marketer should learn to summarize the reasons from the failure marketing.

D. Meeting the customers' requirements appears to be of most importance in marketing techniques.

17. What does the author mean by saying "create a perceived value in your marketing message"?

A. It means that you should create a seductive message about the product to attract the consumers' attention.

B. It refers to the benefits and requirements that consumers want from the product.

C. It advises the marketers to use the benefits of your product to advertise.

D. It is the only way that the customers can see how your product meets their needs.

18. Which is the essential concern that a customer buy a product?

A. The customer really need it.

B. It has a perceived value.

C. It has a favorable price.

D. The benefit of it sounds good.

19. A success product marketing is determined by_____.

A. where the consumers get them.

B. the way the consumers get them.

C. the sales volume in the different sales locations.

D. the awareness of your product.

20. To convert consumers into your customers, you should

A. improve your marketing tools and strategies.

B. learn about the needs and requirements of the consumers.

C. pay more attention to the product itself, not the marketing.

D. take more into consideration rather than simply marketing.

PART FOUR
Questions 21—30

- Read the article below about the five W's of marketing.
- Choose the correct word to fill each gap from A, B, C or D.
- For each question (21—30), mark one letter (A, B, C or D) on your Answer Sheet.

The Five W's of Marketing

You've heard of the Five W's: who, what, when, where, and why. They're the elements of information needed to get the full story, whether it's a journalist (21)... a scandal, a detective investigating a crime, or a customer service representative trying to resolve a (22)... There's even an old PR formula that uses the Five W's as a template for how to write a news release.

Most of the time it doesn't matter in what order the (23)... is gathered, as long as all five W's are ultimately (24)... The customer service rep's story may begin with who was offended, while the journalist may follow a lead based on what happened. The detective may start with where a crime was committed while details of who and what (not to mention when and why) are still (25)... The Five W's are helpful in marketing planning as well. But unlike in other (26)..., the development of an effective marketing program requires that they be answered in a specific order: why, who, what, where, and when. The reasons may not be obvious, but by following this pathway you can avoid a great deal of confusion, trial and error, and blind (27)..., preserving your company's precious time and (28)...

Many marketers instinctively begin with questions about what and where, as in "what" their advertising should say or "where" it should appear. That's what gets them into (29)... To (30)... their marketing efforts, think why, who, what, where, and when. The order makes all the difference.

21. A. reporting   B. uncovering   C. exposing   D. unmasking
22. A. problem   B. dispute   C. complaint   D. issue
23. A. information   B. statistics   C. intelligence   D. data
24. A. introduced   B. proposed   C. addressed   D. raised
25. A. sketchy   B. rough   C. curt   D. unshaped
26. A. fields   B. occupations   C. industries   D. professions
27. A. alleys   B. paths   C. valleys   D. tunnels
28. A. money   B. efforts   C. resources   D. vigor
29. A. dilemma   B. trouble   C. puzzle   D. uncertainty
30. A. improve   B. perfect   C. advance   D. optimize

PART FIVE
Questions 31—40

· Read the article below about being different in your marketing.

· For each question 31—40, write one word in CAPITAL LETTERS on your Answer Sheet.

Dare to Be Different In Your Marketing

Do you want to attract the attention of (31)... potential clients and customer? Then it's time to dare to be different. Over the last five years our marketing departments have become complacent. (32)... than come up (33)... new concepts, ideas, and marketing plans, we only revisit someone else's idea, (34)... a few things and call it our own. Do you want to create buzz (35)... your products and services? Would you like people to take a look at (36)... it is that you have to offer over your competitor? If you answered yes to (37)... of these questions then this year I dare you to be different. Develop new ideas, actually spend time brainstorming to firm up your own company's marketing message. Stop looking at what everyone else is doing. Quit comparing your creative ideas with others. It's (38)... we learn that adopting the tactics and strategies of another company is just simply not (39)... It's still important to do your research regarding your competitors. However, it's more important to listen to the needs of prospects and current clients. When did it become ok to quit paying attention to our markets? We want a quick fix, a fast campaign, an instaneous idea. Daring to be (40)... doesn't have to be difficult, often enough it's as simple as getting back to the basics.

PART SIX
Questions 41—52

· Read the text below from a report about brand management.

· In most lines (41—52), there is one extra word. It either is grammatically incorrect or does not fit in with the sense of the text. Some lines, however, are correct.

· If a line is correct, write CORRECT on your Answer Sheet.

· If there is an extra word in the line, write the extra word in CAPITAL LETTERS on your Answer Sheet.

Brand Management

41. Believe it or not, your company is already being facing just that type of situation. Oh, you may not

42. have realized it, and if that's the case you probably haven't been responding as you should do.

43. The challenge you're facing, like the one above all, is complicated. It, too, has long-term

44. implications. It's also expensive, and it's public—very public. Worse, if you're mishandling things, you're already damaging the health of your company. What is it? It's your branding program.

45. Don't roll up your eyes. Think about it. Companies often mismanage their brands by neglect,

46. and doing so harms their top lines, their bottom lines, and their prospects for long-term

47. success. Just because someone else hasn't dropped a bombshell on you in a breathless phone

48. call doesn't make it any less true. Like the subtle movement of the hands of a clock going, brand neglect happens slowly, almost imperceptibly, which makes it even more sinister.

49. What makes it so nonsensical is that your brand is the ultimate assct—or they should be. Your

50. brand, unlike a building, inventory, or furniture, fixtures, and equipment, needs never depreciate.

51. Quite on the contrary—brands can increase in value indefinitely as long as they're well-managed.

52. Consulting firm Interbrand estimates the market value of Coca-Cola (KO)—not means the secret formula, not the factories, not the trucks, but the brand alone—to be more than $70 billion. The McDonald's (MCD) brand is worth more than $33 billion. Disney (DIS), $28 billion.

第5单元 广告和促销
Unit 5 Advertising and Promotion

Text A

Ⅰ. 课文导读

广告是针对大量潜在消费者的一种付费的非人员沟通行为。对于公司而言,在促销组合中,广告是一种最有效的非人员促销方式。广告主要可以分为产品广告和机构广告。对于市场营销人员而言,必须学会如何在众多广告媒介中做出选择,从而恰当地配置有限的广告预算,达到最佳的广告效果。广告成本是媒介选择中需要考虑的重要因素之一。广告可以选择的媒介包括:报纸杂志、电视电台、户外展板、网络等。

Ⅱ. Text

Of the elements of the promotional mix, advertising is the most visible form of nonpersonal promotion and the most effective for many firms. Advertising refers to paid nonpersonal communications usually targeted at large numbers of potential buyers. Although U. S. citizens often think of advertising as a typical American function, it is a global activity. One-third of the top 15 advertisers in the U. S. are headquartered in other countries. Each of these companies spends billions of dollars a year on advertising in an attempt to build brand awareness and inform, persuade, or remind current and potential customers about its product offerings. Advertising expenditures can vary considerably from industry to industry, from company to company, and from one advertising medium to another. For television, the top advertising spenders are manufacturers of cars and light trucks; automobile dealers spend the most on newspaper ads. On the radio, the leading industry is telecommunications, followed by advertising for broadcast and cable television. Among individual companies, giants like Ford and McDonald's have the financial resources needed to buy ＄2 million 30-second ads on the television broadcast of the annual Super Bowl①. In contrast, small companies may be able to achieve their promotional objectives by spending a few thousand dollars on carefully targeted ads in local newspapers or coupon② packages mailed to consumers. The two basic types of ads are product and institutional advertisements. Product advertising consists of messages designed to sell a particular good or service. Advertise-

---

① The Super Bowl: 美国国家美式足球联盟(也成为国家橄榄球联盟)的年度冠军赛
② coupon: 赠券

ments for Snapple① drinks, T-Mobile② wireless phones, and Capital One credit cards are examples of product advertising. Institutional advertising involves messages that promote concepts, ideas, philosophies, or goodwill for industries, companies, organizations, or government entities. The Michigan Economic Development Corporation created the ad in an effort to attract more technologically based businesses to the state.

Marketers must choose to allocate their advertising budgets among various media. All media offer advantages and disadvantages. Cost is an important consideration in media selection, but marketers must also choose the media best suited for communicating their message. Advertising on television and in newspapers and in the form of direct mail represent the three leading media outlets③ in large part because of their flexibility. Online (Internet) advertising receives only about 2 percent of total advertising spending. Still, interactive advertising on the Internet is expected to grow far faster than the other media over the next decade. Other media expected to enjoy strong growth are cable television and out-door advertising.

Daily and weekly newspapers continue to dominate local advertising. Marketers can easily tailor④ newspaper advertising for local tastes and preferences. Advertisers can also coordinate their newspaper messages with other promotional efforts. In fact, readers rank advertising as the third most useful feature in newspapers, after national and local news. A disadvantage comes from the relatively short life span; people usually discard their papers soon after reading.

Television is America's leading national advertising medium. Television advertising can be classified as network national, local, and cable ads. The four major national networks—ABC, CBS, NBC, and Fox and relative newcomers Warner Brothers (WB) and United Paramount Network (UPN) broadcast are about one fourth of all television ads. Despite a decline in audience share and growing competition from cable, network television remains the easiest way for advertisers to reach large numbers of viewers —10 million to 20 million with a single commercial⑤. Among the heavy users of network television advertisings are auto manufacturers, financial services companies, and fast-food chains.

The average U. S. household owns five radios including those in cars—a market penetration that makes radios an important advertising medium. Advertisers like the captive audience of listeners as they commute to and from work. As a result, morning and evening drive time shows command top ad rates. In major markets, many stations serve different demographic groups with targeted programming. The potential of the Internet to deliver radio programming also offers opportunities for yet more focused targeting. Satellite transmission technology will also offer new opportunities for radio advertisers.

---

① Snapple: 斯纳普,是20世纪80年代美国纽约知名软饮料品牌
② T-mobile: 是一家跨国移动电话运营商
③ outlet: 销路;市场
④ tailor: 使适应特殊需要
⑤ commercial: (无线电或电视中的)商业广告

Magazines are a natural choice for targeted advertising. Media buyers study demographics① of subscribers and select magazines that attract the desired readers. A company with a product geared to young women would advertise in *Glamour*② and *Cosmopolitan*③; one with a product that appeals to entrepreneurs might choose *Entrepreneur*④.

The average American household receives about 550 pieces of direct mail each year, including 100 catalogs. The huge growth in the variety of direct-mail offerings combined with the convenience they offer to today's busy, time-pressed shoppers has made direct-mail advertising a multibillion-dollar business. Today this medium is tied with news-paper advertising in second place, trailing only television advertising, among the leading media alternatives. Although the cost per person reached via direct mail is high, a small business may be able to spend less on a limited direct-mail campaign than on a television or radio ad. For businesses with a small advertising budget, a carefully targeted direct-mail effort with a message that interests recipients can be highly effective.

Outdoor advertising, such as billboards and illuminated or animated designs or displays accounts for about 2 percent of total advertising expenditures. The majority of spending on outdoor advertising is for billboards⑤, but spending for other types of outdoor advertising, such as signs in transit stations, stores, airports, and sports stadiums, is growing faster. Advertisers are exploring new forms of outdoor media, many of which involve technology: computerized paintings, video billboards, trivision⑥ that displays three revolving images on a single billboard, and moving billboards mounted on trucks. Other innovations include displaying ads on the Goodyear blimp⑦, using an electronic system that offers animation and video.

Outdoor advertising suffers from several disadvantages, however. The medium requires brief messages, and mounting concern for aesthetic and environmental issues is raising opposition. The High-way Beautification Act regulates placement of outdoor advertising near interstate highways. And debates still rage about whether billboards should be allowed at all. But they can be an effective way to reach a large number of people in one geographical location and can even promote important causes, such as providing information about missing children

Ranging from Web sites and compact discs (CDs) to information kiosks⑧ in malls and financial institutions, interactive media are changing the nature of advertising. Although it currently commands only 2 percent of media spending, interactive advertising is the fastest-growing media segment.

---

① demographics of subscribers: 订户的人口数据统计
② Glamour: 英国女性杂志
③ Cosmopolitan:《时尚》,美国版时尚杂志。
④ Entrepreneur:《企业邦》,美国杂志
⑤ billboard: 广告牌
⑥ trivision: 立体摄影
⑦ blimp: 软式小飞船
⑧ kiosks: 户外报刊亭

Online advertising has changed dramatically in recent years. Companies first began experimenting with advertising on this medium in the mid-1990s. At that time, the Web was a novelty for most users. Today, successful interactive advertising adds value by offering the audience more than the product-related information contained in the early banner ads. Nike has embraced this type of advertising as one of its premier strategies. Within its Web site, consumers can visit dedicated sites tailored to each sport for which Nike has products. They can go to Nike Lab.com for the company's most cutting-edge① products—like its new running jacket that contains a built-in light, compass watch, and MP3 player.

Just like spam②, many consumers resent the intrusion of pop-up③ ads that suddenly appear on their computer screen. These ads can be difficult to ignore, remove, or pass by. Some Internet service providers, like EarthLink④, have actually turned this problem into a marketing advantage by offering service that comes without pop-ups. "You'll never log-on and be greeted by an EarthLink pop-up ad. Your address comes with spam-reducing tools and eight mailboxes," its ads promise.

III. Notes

1. The Super Bowl (美式橄榄球冠军赛). It is the championship game of the National Football League (NFL), the highest level of professional American football in the United States, culminating a season that begins in the late summer of the previous calendar year. The Super Bowl uses Roman numerals to identify each game, rather than the year in which it is held. For example, Super Bowl I was played on January 15, 1967, following the regular season played in 1966, while Super Bowl XLV was played on February 6, 2011, to determine the champion of the 2010 regular season.

2. Snapple (斯纳普,美国饮料品牌). It is a brand of tea and juice drinks which is owned by Dr Pepper Snapple Group and based in Plano, Texas. The brand was founded in 1972. The brand achieved some notoriety due to various pop-culture references including television shows.

3. Capital One Financial Corp. (第一资本金融公司). It is a U.S.—based bank holding company specializing in credit cards, home loans, auto loans, banking and saving products. A member of the Fortune 500, the company helped pioneer the mass marketing of credit cards in the early 1990s, and it is now the fourth-largest customer of the United States Postal Service and has the fifth-largest deposit portfolio in the United States.

4. T-Mobile International AG(移动电话运营商). It is a German-based holding company for Deutsche Telekom AG's various mobile communications subsidiaries outside Germany.

---

① cutting-edge: 前沿的
② spam: 垃圾邮件
③ pop-up: 突然弹出
④ EarthLink: EarthLink 公司位于美国亚特兰大市,是一家互联网服务提供商

Based in Bonn, Germany, its subsidiaries operate GSM and UMTS-based cellular networks in Europe, the United States, Puerto Rico and the US Virgin Islands. The company has financial stakes in mobile operators in both Central and Eastern Europe. Globally, T-Mobile International subsidiaries have a combined total of approximately 150 million subscribers, making the company the world's 12th-largest mobile-phone service provider by subscribers and the third-largest multinational after the UK's Vodafone and Spain's Telefónica.

5. ABC, CBS, NBC, Fox and WB(美国的五家广播公司). The American Broadcasting Company (ABC) is an American commercial broadcasting television network. Created in 1943 from the former NBC Blue radio network, ABC is owned by The Walt Disney Company and is part of Disney-ABC Television Group. CBS is a major US commercial broadcasting television network, which started as a radio network. The name is derived from the initials of the network's former name, Columbia Broadcasting System. The National Broadcasting Company (NBC) is an American commercial broadcasting television network. Fox Broadcasting Company, commonly referred to as Fox Network or simply Fox (and stylized as FOX), is an American commercial broadcasting television network owned by Fox Entertainment Group, part of Rupert Murdoch's News Corporation. The WB Television Network (commonly shortened to simply The WB) is a former television network in the United States that was launched on January 11, 1995 as a joint venture between Warner Bros. and Tribune Broadcasting.

6. United Paramount Network (UPN)(联合派拉蒙电视网). United Paramount Network (UPN) was a television network that was broadcast in over 200 markets in the United States from 1995 to 2006. UPN was originally owned by Viacom/Paramount and Chris-Craft Industries, the former of which through the Paramount Television Group produced most of the network's series. It was later owned by CBS Corporation. Its first night of broadcasting was on January 16, 1995. UPN shut down on September 15, 2006, and merged with The WB, which was shut down two days later, to form The CW Television Network.

7. The Goodyear Blimp(固特异飞艇). It is the collective name for a fleet of blimps operated by Goodyear Tire and Rubber Company for advertising purposes and for use as a television camera platform for aerial views of sporting events. The Goodyear Tire & Rubber Company was founded in 1898 by Frank Seibeiling. Goodyear manufactures tires for automobiles, commercial trucks, light trucks, SUVs, race cars, airplanes, farm equipment and heavy earth-mover machinery. Goodyear is very famous throughout the world because of the Goodyear Blimp. The first Goodyear blimp flew in 1925. Today it is one of the most recognizable advertising icons in America.

8. Highway Beautification Act(公路美化法). In the United State, this Act is passed in the Senate on September 16, 1965 and in the U. S. House of Representatives on October 8, 1965, and signed by the President on October 22, 1965. This created "23 USC 131" or Section 131 of Title 23, Unites States Code (1965), commonly referred to as "Title I of the Highway Beautification Act of 1965, as Amended". The act called for control of outdoor advertising, including removal of certain types of signs, along the nation's growing Interstate Highway System and the existing federal-aid primary highway system. It also required certain junkyard along Interstate or primary highways to be removed or screened and encouraged scenic enhancement and roadside development.

9. EarthLink, Inc.(世联科技,互联网服务提供商). It is a leading IT services, network and communications provider to more than 100,000 businesses and over one million consumers nationwide. EarthLink empowers customers with managed IT services including cloud computing, data centers, virtualization, security, applications and support services, in addition to nationwide data and voice IP services. The company operates an extensive network including 28,000 route fiber miles, 90 metro fiber rings and 4 secure data centers providing ubiquitous IP coverage across more than 90 percent of the country. Founded in 1994, the company's award-winning reputation for both outstanding service and product innovation is supported by an experienced team of professionals focused on best-in-class customer care.

Ⅳ. Useful Expressions

1. in an attempt to: 试图,力图
2. brand awareness: 品牌意识
3. in an effort to: 努力
4. rank as:(在序列中)占据
5. life span: 寿命
6. time-pressed shoppers: 时间很紧的顾客
7. transit stations: 中转车站
8. be geared to: 使适应
9. account for:(在数量上)占
10. built-in light: 内置灯

Ⅴ. Reading Comprehension

Questions

1. How many ways of advertising are mentioned in the text? Make a list.
2. What is institutional advertisement? Give two examples.
3. What are the advantages and disadvantages of outdoor advertising?
4. What changes have taken place in online advertising?
5. Apart from the above advertising, could you list other kinds of promotional tools?

Decide whether each of the following statements is true or false.

1. Advertising is a kind of nonpersonal communication targeted at potential buyers. (　　)
2. The two basic types of ads are product and institutional advertisements. (　　)
3. Cost is the only important consideration in media selection. (　　)
4. Advertising on television and in newspapers and in the form of direct mail represent the

three leading media outlets. ( )

5. Interactive advertising on the Internet is expected to grow faster than cable television and out-door advertising. ( )

6. Most useful features in newspapers are ranked as advertising, national news and local news. ( )

7. Network television remains the easiest way for advertisers to reach large numbers of viewers. ( )

8. Morning and evening drive time is essential for advertising products in the United States. ( )

9. The majority of spending on outdoor advertising is for signs in transit stations, stores, airports, and sports stadiums. ( )

10. Nike always promotes its products through online advertising. ( )

Ⅵ. Discussion

What do you think is a successful advertising in term of budget, choice of medium and the actual design of an advertisement?

Text B
BEC Reading Texts

PART ONE
Questions 1—8

- Look at the statements below and the five extracts about advertising and promotion from an article.
- Which extract (A, B, C, D or E) does each statement (1—8) refer to?
- For each statement (1—8), make one letter (A, B, C, D or E) on your Answer Sheet.
- You will need to use some of these letters more than once.

1. We should learn the concept of a promotional mix first.
2. Offering information is one of five major promotional objectives.
3. Summarizing the different types of advertising and advertising media.
4. By analyzing the target market, marketers are likely to design their proper marketing mix.
5. The ethical issues involved in promotion may arouse public concerns.
6. Identifying the factors that influence the selection of a promotional mix.
7. Direct mail accounts for a considerable proportion in advertisements
8. Describing the role of sales promotion, personal selling, and public relations in promo-

tional strategy.

A. Sales promotion accounts for greater expenditures than does advertising. Consumer-oriented sales promotions like coupons, games, rebates, samples, premiums, contests, sweepstakes, and promotional products offer an extra incentive to buy a product. Point-of-purchase advertising displays and trade shows are sales promotions directed to the trade markets, Personal selling involves face-to-face interactions between seller and buyer.

B. Advertising, the most visible form of nonpersonal promotion, is designed to inform, persuade, or remind. Product advertising promotes a good or service, while institutional advertising promotes a concept, idea, organization, or philosophy. Television, newspapers, and direct mail represent the largest advertising media categories.

C. Marketers begin by focusing on their company's target market, product value, time frame, and budget. By analyzing these factors, they develop a promotional mix and allocate resources and expenditures among personal selling, advertising, sales promotion, and public relations.

D. A company's promotional mix integrates two components: personal selling and nonpersonal selling, which includes advertising, sales promotion, and public relations, By selecting the appropriate combination of promotional mix elements, marketers attempt to achieve the firm's five major promotional objectives: provide information, differentiate a product, increase demand, stabilize sales, and accentuate the product's value.

E. Many consumers believe that advertising exerts too much influence on buyers and that it deceives customers by exaggerating product claims and consciously blurring the line between promotion and entertainment. Many consumers also question the appropriateness of marketing to children and through schools.

PART TWO
Questions 9—14

- Read the text about the Yao's career development in the U. S.
- Choose the best sentence to fill each of the gaps.
- For each gap (9—14), mark one letter (A-H) on your Answer Sheet.
- Do not use any letter more than once.

Yao's international appeal help grow our brand globally

(9)... That's saying a lot in a league where anyone under six feet five inches would be considered short. But Yao Ming (Yao is his surname) is seven feet five inches tall, a giant among giants. Just a couple of years ago, Yao left his home in China, where he played basketball for the Shanghai Sharks, to become the star center in his rookie year for the Houston Rockets. Just as quickly, (10)... Yao whose presence is hard to ignore, appeared in his first television commercial for Apple Computer, in which he promoted the firm's new PowerBook G4 computer. (His star in the advertisement was the diminutive Verne Troyer, the actor who played Mini Me in the Austin Powers films.) Viewers loved him. (11)..., which aired during a recent Super Bowl. In that ad, Yao sparred with a petite actress playing a clerk who wouldn't let him cash a check, saying, "Yo!" and pointing to a sign indicating no personal checks. A few months later, (12)..., for which he appeared in ads along with other sports celebrities like base-ball player Derek Jeter and football. Star Peyton Manning.

(13)... But Yao is different. He speaks very little English, relying heavily on a translator to help him communicate. Yet says Tom Fox, vice president of sports marketing for Gatorade, "What's truly exciting to us is Yao's ability to connect with American fans and transcend American culture. But Yao's international appeal and the NBA's international marketing strength present potential opportunities to also help grow our brand globally." (14)... As they develop their promotional strategy, they can incorporate this strength into the overall plan. "Gatorade does have aspirations around the world, and there is application for Yao if we choose to go that way," notes Fox.

A. But his slam dunk came in a commercial for Visa

B. Marketers view him as a global spokesperson rather than someone who reaches only the U. S. market

C. Yao signed an exclusive deal with Gatorade.

D. Yao Ming is the National Basketball Association's tallest player

E. Being an advertising star makes him more popular in the U. S.

F. he became a U. S. media celebrity-and a sought-after advertising spokesperson

G. Hiring sports celebrities as part of a promotional campaign is nothing new

H. Many advertisers strive to invite him to be the spokesperson of their product

PART THREE
Questions 15—20

· Read the following article on the pop-up ads online.

· For each question (15—20) mark one letter (A, B, C or D) on your Answer Sheet for the answer you choose.

When you go online, are you peppered with pop-up ads? If you are annoyed by them and find yourself chasing them around with your mouse until you can zap them off the screen, here's a new twist. The next generation of pop-ups may be implanted in your PC soft-ware. When you turn on your computer, a "silent" software program slips on also, tracking the Web sites you visit and collecting information about any purchases you make. Then, when you visit other Web sites, targeted ads pop up on your screen-the ones for goods and services that you might be interested in buying. Suppose you initially browse through a site for outdoor gear and buy a fleece jacket. Two days later, your screen might show pop-ups for adventure travel, airline tickets, outdoor clothing, and the like. You might not even be aware of it, but these pop-ups are the result of the embedded software that some people call *spyware*.

The largest creator of this software, Gator, recently teamed up with Yahoo to send such pop-ups to 43 million computer screens worldwide. In one year the agreement generated 28 million in advertising fees that were split by the two companies, and industry experts expect that figure to increase. While Yahoo insists that it is providing a service to its customers by offering more advertising choices, many consumers are less than pleased by the software or the ads. Concerned about invasion of privacy, some who discover the programs on their PCs ask service technicians to remove it. Gator, whose advertising customers include Verizon and American Express, presents itself as a way for consumers to "find bargains." Marketing head Scott Eagle says that Gator's model of targeting ads to specific consumers is far more efficient than "spraying ads across everybody." However, companies such as Hertz and The Washington Post Inc. filed lawsuits against Gator for infringement of copyright and trademark laws, claiming that its ads were getting a "free ride" on their sites.

Not surprisingly, surveys focusing on the Internet experience typically list pop-up ads as the most annoying online experience. So marketers at Atlanta-based EarthLink came up with an idea: offer subscribers software to block them. Although EarthLink, the No. 3 U. S. Internet service provider with about five million subscribers, is small change in an industry dominated by industry giant AOL, the company has based its recent market growth strategy on offering a solution to the estimated 4. 8 billion ads that pop up on computer screens worldwide every month.

Why do marketers continue to rely on such a disliked form of online advertising? The answer is cost. Pop-up ads are inexpensive to produce and cost nearly nothing to send. But they are so annoying to some computer users that dozens of special programs have been written to block them from appearing on the screen during Internet use.

15. What are "pop-up ads"?
A. The pictures chasing the PC users around.
B. The pages the PC users can zap off.
C. The online bursting advertising.
D. The ads tracking the Web sites.

16. By the word "twist"(line 3, paragraph1), the author probably means _____.
A. A curve.
B. A change.
C. improvement.
D. degeneration.

17. What is NOT the "twist" of next generation of pop-ups?
A. Targeting ads pop up on your screen.
B. The software program slips silently.
C. The screen might show more pop-ups.
D. Collecting information about the purchases.

18. What is the attitude of companies like Hertz and The Washington Post Inc. towards Ga-

tor?

A. They insist that it is providing a service to its customers by offering more advertising choices.

B. They ask service technicians to remove pop ups.

C. They think pop-ups are far more efficient.

D. They filed lawsuits against Gator for infringement.

19. How does Atlanta-based EarthLink solve the problem of pop-up ads?

A. By charging the pop-ups' companies.

B. By offering subscribers software to block pop-up ads.

C. By removing them through certain techniques.

D. By putting on more pop-up ads.

20. The author's attitude toward pop-up ads can best be described as _____.

A. skeptical.

B. objective.

C. critical.

D. indifferent.

PART FOUR
Questions 21—30

· Read the article below about the promotion.

· Choose the correct word to fill each gap from A, B, C or D.

· For each question (21—30), mark one letter (A, B, C or D) on your Answer Sheet.

What is Promotion

Promotion is one of the four elements of marketing (21)... (product, price, promotion, place). It is the communication link between sellers and buyers for the purpose of influencing, informing, or persuading a potential buyer's purchasing decision.

The (22)... of five elements creates a promotional mix or promotional plan. These elements are personal selling, advertising, sales promotion, direct marketing, and publicity. A promotional mix specifies how much attention to pay to each of the five subcategories, and how much money to (23)... for each. A promotional plan can have (24)... range of objectives, including: sales increases, new product acceptance, creation of brand equity, positioning, competitive retaliations, or creation of a corporate image. (25)..., however there are three basic objectives of promotion. These are: 1, to present information to consumers as well as others; 2, to increase demand; 3, to (26)... a product.

There are different ways to (27)... a product in different areas of media. Promoters use internet advertisement, special events, endorsements, and newspapers to advertise their product. Many times with the purchase of a product there is an (28)... like discounts, free (29)..., or a contest. This is to increase the sales of a given product.

Promotion includes several communications activities that attempt to provide added value or incentives to consumers, wholesalers, retailers, or other organizational customers to (30)... immediate sales. These efforts can attempt to stimulate product interest, trial, or purchase. Examples of devices used in promotion include coupons, samples, premiums, point-of-purchase (POP) displays, contests, rebates, and sweepstakes.

21. A. blend	B. mixture	C. combination	D. mix
22. A. qualification	B. amplification	C. description	D. specification
23. A. spend	B. settle	C. budget	D. figure
24. A. different	B. various	C. long	D. wide
25. A. Frankly	B. Fundamentally	C. Actually	D. Virtually
26. A. create	B. advertise	C. differentiate	D. introduce
27. A. sell	B. promote	C. inform	D. present
28. A. incentive	B. reason	C. impulse	D. desire
29. A. items	B. products	C. activities	D. goods
30. A. improve	B. stimulate	C. activate	D. increase

PART FIVE
Questions 31—40

· Read the article below about public service advertising.

· For each question 31—40, write one word in CAPITAL LETTERS on your Answer Sheet.

Public Service Advertising

The advertising techniques used to (31)... commercial goods and services can be used to inform, educate and motivate the public about non-commercial issues, such as HIV/AIDS, political ideology, energy conservation and deforestation. (32)..., in its non-commercial guise, is a powerful educational tool capable (33)... reaching and motivating large audiences. "Advertising justifies its existence when used in the public interest—it is much (34)... powerful a tool to use solely for commercial purposes." Attributed to Howard Gossage by David Ogilvy. Public (35)... advertising, non-commercial advertising, public interest advertising, cause marketing, and social marketing are different terms for (or aspects of) the use of sophisticated advertising and marketing communications techniques (generally associated with commercial enterprise) on (36)... of non-commercial, public interest issues and initiatives. In the United States, the granting of television and radio licensed by the FCC is contingent upon the station broadcasting a certain amount of public service advertising. To (37)... these requirements, many broadcast stations in America air the bulk of their required public service announcements (38)... the late night or early morning when the smallest percentage of viewers are watching, leaving more day and prime time commercial slots available for high-paying advertisers. Public service advertising reached (39)... height during World Wars I and II under the direction of more than one government. During WWII President Roosevelt commissioned the creation of The War Advertising

Council (now known as the Ad Council) (40)... is the nation's largest developer of PSA campaigns on behalf of government agencies and non-profit organizations, including the longest-running PSA campaign, Smokey Bear.

PART SIX
Questions 41—52

· Read the text below from a report about foreign public messaging.

· In most lines (41—52), there is one extra word. It either is grammatically incorrect or does not fit in

with the sense of the text. Some lines, however, are correct.

· If a line is correct, write CORRECT on your Answer Sheet.

· If there is an extra word in the line, write the extra word in CAPITAL LETTERS on your Answer Sheet.

Foreign Public Messaging

Foreign governments, particularly those that own marketable commercial products or services,

41. often promote their interests and positions through the advertising of those goods because the

42. target audience is not only largely unaware of the forum as well vehicle for foreign messaging but also

43. willing to receive the tour message while in a mental state of absorbing information from

44. advertisements during watching television commercial breaks while reading a periodical, or while passing by billboards in public spaces. A prime example of this messaging technique is

45. advertising campaigns how to promote international travel. While advertising foreign destinations

46. and services may stem from the typical goal of increasing revenue by drawing more tourism, some travel campaigns carry the additional or alternative intended purpose of promoting good

47. sentiments or improving existing ones whether among the target audience towards a given nation or

48. region. It is in common for advertising promoting foreign countries to be produced and distributed by

49. the tourism ministries of those countries, so these ads often carry out political statements and/or depictions of the foreign government's desired international public perception. Additionally,

50. a wide range of foreign airlines and travel-related services which advertise separately

from the destinations, themselves, are owned by their respective governments. By depicting their

51. destinations, airlines, and other services in a favorable and pleasant light, to countries market

52. themselves to populations from abroad in a manner that could mitigate by prior public impressions.

第6单元　商业合同
Unit 6　Business Contract

Text A

Ⅰ. 课文导读

在现代经济社会,商务合同已经成为我们生活中不可或缺的一部分。合同是双方意思达成一致的结果,它构成了各项经济活动的基础。诚实信用和公平交易原则是合同交易的指导性原则。合同的达成一般需要经过要约邀请、要约、反要约和接受四个环节,其中要约和接受是两个必经阶段。合同一经达成,将对双方当事人的行为产生拘束力。在普通法系国家,合同有效与否还必须考虑对价和意图两方面因素。

Ⅱ. Text

Early in history the importance of contracts was recognized as beneficial to the development of business and trade. Modern society could not exist without contracts as they are the foundation for almost all commercial activities in the world. We could not go about our daily life without contracts; in fact, most of us engage in a contract every day without even knowing it. For example, when you buy clothes at a plaza or live at a hotel, you enter into a simple contract. Generally, a contract is the result of some sort of agreement between two or more individuals of groups, and the agreement creates some obligations among the parties involved.

A simple definition of contract is an agreement that is enforceable or binding, which is the result of business negotiations. Some contracts are simple and can be formed very easily, but others are more complicated and may require many documents or pages of a written agreement. Not every contract has to be in writing, but it may be wise to put some contracts in writing to avoid disputes as to what the exact terms of the contract are.

A business contract is an agreement which sets forth binding① obligations of the relevant parties for an exchange of goods or services that are of value. It is enforceable by law, and any party that fails to fulfill his contractual obligations may be sued② and forced to make compensation③, though most contracts do not give rise to disputes.

---

① binding: 约束的
② sue: 起诉
③ make compensation: 做出赔偿

Business contracts are often used in various kinds of business activities, including hiring or being employed as an independent contractor, buying or providing services or goods, leases and real estate, selling your business, partnerships and joint ventures, franchising①, confidentiality② agreements, and so on.

To be honest and fair is very important in the business transaction. In every business contract there is an implied covenant③ that neither party shall do anything, which will have the effect of destroying or injuring the right of the other party to receive the fruits of the contract, which means that in every contract there exists an implied covenant of good faith and fair dealing. It is a general presumption that the parties to a contract will deal with each other honestly, fairly, and in good faith, so as not to destroy the right of the other party or parties to receive the benefits of the contract. It is implied in every contract in order to reinforce the expressed covenants or promises of the contract. A lawsuit based upon the breach④ of the covenant may arise when one party to the contract attempts to claim the benefit of a technical excuse for breaching the contract, or when he or she uses specific contractual terms in isolation in order to refuse to perform their contractual obligations, despite the general circumstances and understandings between the parties.

The conclusion⑤ of a satisfactory business contract results largely from the careful and meticulous⑥ business negotiation between the seller and the buyer. They are in order to reach an agreement on the terms in respect of name of commodity, brand, specification, quality, quantity, packing, price, shipment, insurance, payment, inspection, force majeure⑦, claims and disputes, arbitration, etc, which constitute the major final clauses in the contract.

Generally, there are four phases to reach an agreement in the contract. That is, invitation for offer, offer, counter-offer, and acceptance. In practice, it is not necessary for every transaction to cover these four phases. In some cases, only offer and acceptance will serve the purpose. It is stipulated in the laws of some countries that only offer and acceptance are two indispensable⑧ factors, lack of either will make no contract.

The first phase is invitation for offer (it also be called enquiry⑨). When a businessman intends to import, he may send out an enquiry to an exporter, inviting a quotation or an offer for the goods he wishes to buy or simply asking for some general information about these goods by

---

① franchise: 给予特许
② confidentiality: 保密性
③ covenant: 契约
④ breach: 违反;破坏
⑤ conclusion: 缔结,订立(合同)
⑥ meticulous: 严密的
⑦ force majeure: 不可抗力
⑧ indispensable: 必不可少的
⑨ enquiry: 询盘

mail or by telegram or telex or in the form of quotation sheets①. The exporter, on receiving the enquiry, will make a reply to it. In this way, the negotiation is getting started. A reply to enquiry from a regular customer is normally fairly brief, and does not need to be more than polite and direct.

The second phase is offer. Every business contract under United Nations Convention on Contracts for International Sale of Goods (CISG), and under most national laws, as well, requires an offer. According to the CISG, a proposal for concluding a contract addressed to one or more specific persons constitutes an offer if it is sufficiently definite and indicates the intention of the offeror② to be bound in case of acceptance. The party addressed is called offeree③. In other words, an offer is actually a proposal of certain trade terms and an expression of a willingness to make a contract according to the terms proposed. Every offer must meet the following requirements: 1) a serious intent by the offeror to be bound by the offer, for example, an offer is made without serious intent when it is made in obvious anger or as a joke, 2) reasonably certain or definite terms, such as price, and 3) communication of the offer by the offeror to the offeree. Otherwise, it just can be called invitation for offer.

The third phase is counter-offer④. When the buyer finds that the terms and conditions in the offer are acceptable, he may probably place an order promptly. However, in most cases, the party who has received the offer and is not in a position to fully accept the business terms offered may make a counter-offer. It indicates a revision of the price or other terms with the purpose of bargaining. On receiving the counter-offer, the offeror may weigh the advantages and disadvantages and decide to accept or decline it according to the specific situation. He may also make a re-offer to put forward some new terms or conditions. This is called an "anti-counter-offer". In this way, through times of negotiations, agreement is reached upon, contract singed and business concluded.

The fourth phase is acceptance. An offeree can transform an offer into an agreement by acceptance. Acceptance is merely the voluntary act by the offeree that shows consent to the terms of an offer. In general, an acceptance must be both unequivocal⑤ and communicated to the offeror. Only the offeree or the offeree's agent (an agent is someone who is authorized⑥ to act for someone else) can accept an offer. Under the CISG, Article 18, and in many countries, like the United States under the UCC and at common law, silence by the offeree cannot be an acceptance, even if the offer says that silence will be seen as an acceptance. Moreover, an offeree is usually required to say something or to do some affirmative act to show his acceptance, even if it

---

① quotation sheet: 报价单
② offeror: 要约人;发盘人
③ offeree: 受要约人;受盘人
④ counter-offer: 反要约,还盘
⑤ unequivocal: 明确的
⑥ authorize: 授权,委托;准许

is just a nod of the head to communicate "Yes". For an acceptance to be unequivocal, absolute and unconditional, it must exactly match the terms of the offer. There can be no variation from the offer nor can there be alternative① terms or conditions. Otherwise, the offer will be seen as rejected, and it is not an acceptance but a counter-offer.

In common law②, it requires other two elements for a business contract to be valid. One is consideration. For a contract to be enforceable something of value must be given, for example, a price, event if it is of nominal value, say £ 1. The other is intention. It is assumed that contracting parties intend to create legal relations, particularly in commercial circumstances. This is, however, a rebuttal presumption③—an assumption that can be contradicted④—if there is contrary evidence.

Ⅲ. Notes

1. Implied covenant of good faith and fair dealing（诚实信用和公平交易原则）. It is a general assumption of the law of contracts, that people will act in good faith and deal fairly without breaking their word, using shifty means to avoid obligations, or denying what the other party obviously understood. A lawsuit (or one of the causes of action in a lawsuit) based on the breach of this covenant is often brought when the other party has been claiming technical excuses for breaching the contract or using the specific words of the contract to refuse to perform when the surrounding circumstances or apparent understanding of the parties were to the contrary.

2. Force majeure（不可抗力）. It is a common clause in contracts that essentially frees both parties from liability or obligation when an extraordinary event or circumstance beyond the control of the parties, such as a war, strike, riot, crime, or an event described by the legal term "act of God" (such as flooding, earthquake, or volcanic eruption), prevents one or both parties from fulfilling their obligations under the contract. However, force majeure is not intended to excuse negligence or other malfeasance of a party, as where non-performance is caused by the usual and natural consequences of external forces, or where the intervening circumstances are specifically contemplated.

3. CISG: United Nations Convention on Contracts for the International Sale of Goods（联合国国际货物买卖合同公约）. It is a treaty offering a uniform international sales law that, as of August 2010, has been ratified by 76 countries that account for a significant proportion of world trade, making it one of the most successful international uniform laws. The CISG was developed by the United Nations Commission on International Trade Law (UNCITRAL) and

---

① alternative: 供选择的,供替换的
② Common law: 普通法是独立于国家制定法之外,依据某种社会权威和社会组织,具有一定强制性的行为规范的总和
③ rebuttal presumption: 可推翻的推定
④ contradict: 反驳;指出矛盾之处

was signed in Vienna in 1980. It allows exporters to avoid choice of law issues as the CISG offers "accepted substantive rules on which contracting parties, courts, and arbitrators may rely". The CISG has been regarded as a success for UNCITRAL as the Convention has since been accepted by States from "every geographical region, every stage of economic development and every major legal, social and economic system".

4. UCC: The Uniform Commercial Code（美国统一商法典）. It is first published in 1952 as one of a number of uniform acts that have been promulgated in conjunction with efforts to harmonize the law of sales and other commercial transactions in all 50 states within the USA. The goal of harmonizing state law is important because of the prevalence of commercial transactions that extend beyond one state. For example, goods may be manufactured in State A, warehoused in State B, sold from State C and delivered in State D. The UCC therefore achieved the goal of substantial uniformity in commercial laws and, at the same time, allowed the states the flexibility to meet local circumstances by modifying the UCC's text as enacted in each state. The UCC deals primarily with transactions involving personal property (movable property), not real property (immovable property).

5. Common law（普通法）. Also known as case law or precedent, it is law developed by judges through decisions of courts and similar tribunals rather than through legislative statues or executive branch action. In cases where the parties disagree on what the law is, an idealized common law court looks to past presidential decisions of relevant courts. If a similar dispute has been resolved in the past, the court is bound to follow the reasoning used in the prior decision (this principle is known as stare decisis). If, however, the court finds that the current dispute is fundamentally distinct from all previous cases (called a "matter of first impression"), judges have the authority and duty to make law by creating precedent. Thereafter, the new decision becomes precedent, and will bind future courts.

Ⅳ. Useful Expressions

1. set forth: 提出
2. avoid disputes: 避免争端
3. contractual obligation: 合同义务
4. give rise to: 引发
5. in respect of: 在……方面
6. in a position to: 能够；有做……的条件
7. in general: 一般来说
8. weigh the advantages and disadvantages: 权衡利弊

Ⅴ. Reading Comprehension

Questions

1. What is the definition of a business contract?
2. What activities will a business contract need?

3. What clauses does a business contract cover?
4. What does breaching mean in a contract?
5. What are the four phases to reach an agreement?

Decide whether each of the following statements is true or false.

1. A contract is an enforceable or binding agreement resulted from business negotiations. (   )
2. Every contract has to be in the form of writing. (   )
3. In every contract there exists an implied covenant of good faith and fair dealing. (   )
4. The conclusion of a satisfactory business contract results mostly from the honesty and integrity of both sellers and buyers. (   )
5. Generally, there are three stages to reach an agreement in the contract: offer, counter-offer, and acceptance. (   )
6. According to the laws of some countries, only offer and acceptance are two indispensable factors in a contract. (   )
7. A reply to enquiry from a regular customer should be in great detail and formality. (   )
8. Under CISG and most national laws, every business contract requires an invitation for offer. (   )
9. Only the offeror's agent can accept an offer. (   )
10. Common law requires other two factors for a valid business contract: consideration and intention. (   )

VI. Discussion

How do you understand the implied covenant of good faith and fair dealing? Illustrate it.

Text B
BEC Reading Texts

PART ONE

Questions 1—8

· Look at the statements below and the five extracts about international transaction from an article.
· Which extract (A, B, C, D or E) does each statement (1—8) refer to?
· For each statement (1—8), make one letter (A, B, C, D or E) on your Answer Sheet.
· You will need to use some of these letters more than once.

1 International transaction for the sale of goods has its own particular features.

2 Besides basic information of goods, a number of other factors should be considered for the protection of two parties from potential problems in a contract of international business.

3 The process of shipment of goods has some risks due to distance.

4 International commercial businesses and organizations have taken some measures to spread the predictable risks to both parties.

5 To ensure an effective international trade, the payment process should be satisfactory to both parties.

6 A couple of factors are involved in an international transaction that distinguishes it from a domestic one.

7 Both the buyer and the seller have their specific concerns in an international trade.

8 Distance imposes some problems in international transactions, and other assistance is required to minimize the risks to both parities.

A. Anyone involved in an international business transaction must have some knowledge not only to protect one's rights, but also to be effective and successful in international trade. Since the basic purpose of international trade is for the seller (exporter) to obtain payment for goods sold and the foreign buyer to obtain the merchandise he ordered, the payment process must satisfy both parties. Exporters want to get paid as quickly as possible, while importers usually prefer delaying payment at least until they have received the merchandise. Depending on the negotiating strength of the parties and upon the credit and business reputation of each, several different types of payment methods can be chosen.

B. However, because of the distance between them, the buyer and seller in most international transactions requiring the shipment of goods will discover that it will be impossible both to have the seller paid upon shipment and to allow the buyer to delay payment until after inspection once the goods have arrived. Thus, the help of others is required to reduce the risk to both the buyer and the seller. The seller and the buyer often do not want to be involved in lawsuits as a result of misunderstanding in the sale of goods contract since such lawsuits are often expensive and may involve foreign legal proceedings with unfamiliar laws and different regulations to at least one of the parties.

C. The contract for the sale of goods between two or more international businesses, thus, will involve more than just the price, quantity, and quality of goods. Many other factors must be taken into account to protect both the buyer and the seller from potential problems over such long distances involving foreign customs and rules. The seller's primary risk in an international transaction is not being paid for his goods. The buyer, in contrast, does not want to pay unless he is assured that the goods have arrived at his location, or at least been shipped. He also is concerned about whether the goods are of the quality and quantity as required in the contract between the parties; therefore, the buyer often wants to inspect the goods before paying for them.

D. Some parts of an international transaction are unique and unlike a domestic transaction for the sale of goods. For example, an international transaction usually involves a geographic separation of the parties, sometimes involving organizations on different continents, therefore, requiring long-distance transportation of goods. The international transaction may involve more than one legal system and perhaps different currencies. Extra regulations may be imposed on an international transaction, such as licensing requirements on exports, customs duties or tariffs, and sometimes also quotas. Moreover, the buyer and seller may not know each other and may not wish to trust each other to comply with mutual promises in a transaction involving a lot of money.

E. To avoid or minimize some of these problems, international commercial businesses and organizations, as a result of years of experience and custom, have tried to set up ways to spread the foreseeable risk to the buyer and seller through the use of specialized language of certain commercial terms (FOB, CFR, CIF, bill of lading, bill of exchange or draft, and irrevocable letter of credit) and through setting up the international transaction as a series of smaller transactions, where the risks are smaller and identifiable to each party.

PART TWO
Questions 9—14
· Read the text about classification of contracts.
· Choose the best sentence to fill each of the gaps.
· For each gap (9—14), mark one letter (A-H) on your Answer Sheet.
· Do not use any letter more than once.

Classification of Contracts

A more complete definition of a contract is a promise or set of promises for which the law will provide a remedy in the event of a breach. (9)...

A binding contract must meet the following requirements: 1) It is in the form required by the law; 2) It is between parties with the capacity to contract—that is, legally capable to contract—or made by agents or representatives of the contracting parties with the authority to act; 3) It is enforceable in the event that one of the contracting parties fails to perform the contract. (10)... However, the law does require that some agreements are made in writing.

(11)... Example of agreements to be made in writing include: contracts for the sale of land; contracts of guarantee; contracts for transfer of shares; contracts which muse be made by deed, for instance, a lease for more than three years. (12)... In contrast, a contract by deed does not require consideration.

(13)... For example, a deed may need to be affixed with a seal—a printed company stamp—if one party is a limited company. Common law requires that a deed is delivered. This determines the date from which the parties are bound. It must be clear on the face of a deed that it is executed by the parties as a deed. (14)... For instance: this document is executed as a deed and is delivered and has effect at the date written at the beginning of it.

A. Deeds may contain standard wording about execution.

B. A binding contract may be made in writing or orally, and implied from conduct, that is, by the behavior of the contracting parties.

C. A deed has different formal execution requirements depending on the contracting parties.

D. As an oral contract is not as valid as a written one.

E. A simple contract require consideration—the price in exchange for a promise to do something—and becomes effective on execution, generally when it is singed.

F. This is usually because registration is required for the agreement to be effective and the relevant registry requires a written agreement.

G. There some generally two forms of contracts: binding contract and simple contract.

H. Both simple contract and binding contract demand reconsideration.

PART THREE
Questions 15—20

· Read the following article on the reasons and solutions of complaints or claims in a sales contract.

· For each question (15—20) mark one letter (A, B, C or D) on your Answer Sheet for the answer you choose.

In foreign trade, it is ideal that the seller delivers the goods conforming to the contract in respect of quality, specification, quantity and packing, and hands over the documents concerning the goods at the right time and place stipulated in the contract. And the buyer makes payment for the goods and takes delivery of them in the same manner specified in the contract. However, there always exists a gap between ideal and reality. Complaints or claims may sometimes arise in spite of our well-planned and careful work in the performance of a sales contract. In practice, it is not infrequent that the exporter or the importer neglects or fails to perform any of his obligations, thus giving rise to breach of contract and various trade disputes, which, subsequently, leads to claim, arbitration, or even litigation.

Breach of contract means the refusal or failure by a party to a contract to fulfill an obligation imposed on him under that contract, resulting from, e. g., repudiation of liability before completion, or conduct preventing proper performance. The contract is discharged where the breach results in the innocent party treating it as rescinded and where it has the effect of depriving the party who has further undertakings still to perform of substantially the whole benefit which was the intention of the parties as expressed in the contract as the consideration for performing those undertaking.

There are two kinds of complaints or claims made by buyers:

(1) The genuine complaint or claim, which arises from such situation as the following:

a. The wrong goods may have been delivered.

b. The quality may not be satisfactory.

c. The shipment may have been found damaged, short or late.

(2) The false complaint or claim, which is made by buyers who find fault with the goods as an excuse to escape from the contract, because they no longer want the goods or because they have found that they can buy them cheaper elsewhere. Suppose you are the buyer and are suffering from someone's mistake. If a complaint or claim has to be made, the matter should be investigated in detail and these details should be laid before the party charged. Sometimes, a reference to the previously satisfactory deliveries and services may help to win more sympathetic consideration of the present complaint or claim. We must handle complaint or claims in accordance with the principle of "on the first ground to our advantage and with restraint" and settle them amicably to the satisfaction of all parties concerned. It is necessary to study the case in question and ascertain what the real cause is and who is the party to be held responsible. We must also be careful in choosing the wording in our correspondence so as to avoid any misunderstandings.

15. What is the first paragraph mainly about?

A. Sellers deliver goods through ideal.

B. Buyers make payment according to the contract.

C. Complaints or claims may sometimes appear in the performance of a sales contract.

D. There is a big gap between ideal and reality in business practice.

16. Which is the worst consequence of breach of contract?

A. arbitration   B. litigation   C. claim   D. negotiation

17. The genuine complaint or claim may arise from such situations EXCEPT

A. shipment may have been found damaged

B. The wrong goods may have been delivered.

C. The quality may not be satisfactory.

D. The price of the goods is too high.

18 What is the real motivation for a false complaint or claim?

A. The buyer have found goods at more competitive price.

B. The quality of the goods may be undesirable.

C. The seller has broken the contract.

D. The delivery process disobeys rules.

19. Why a reference to previous sound practice is made in case of a complaint?

A. to set a good example for other sellers.

B. to prevent further mistakes.

C. to escape possible punishment.

D. to gain more sympathetic attitude of the buyer.

20. For what proper wording is used in the correspondence?

A. for the sake of formalism

B. for politeness

C. for avoidance of misapprehension

D. for mutual benefit

PART FOUR
Questions 21—30

· Read the article below about the role of contracts.

· Choose the correct word to fill each gap from A, B, C or D.

· For each question (21—30), mark one letter (A, B, C or D) on your Answer Sheet.

The Role of Contracts

Each of us enters into many contracts every day without giving the matter any thought. On the way to work, you stop at a newsstand and buy a newspaper and a pack of gum. You also go into a dinner and buy a cup of coffee and a doughnut. Afterwards, you stop at a discount ticket counter and purchase two tickets to a Broadway show. Finally, you arrive at the subway station and buy a token. In each of these examples, a contract was made. In each case, there was a valid (21)... and acceptance, consideration, mutual assent, and legality. No documents were (22)..., and no contract (23)... took place, yet (24)... contracts were formed giving each party certain rights and imposing on each some responsibilities as well. Most contracts are (25)... completed without a problem and without the interested parties giving the matter much thought. Problems arise when parties to a contract (26)... to live up to their agreements or misunderstand what it is they agreed to do. The law of contracts is called upon to (27)... the dispute between the parities in accordance with established rules of law that determine each party's rights and (28)... under a valid contract. Parties can avoid many misunderstandings and disagreements between contracting parties, as well as (29)..., time-consuming litigation, if they have a basic (30)... of the law of contracts.

21.	A. demand	B. offer	C. requirement	D. purchase
22.	A. discussed	B. revealed	C. signed	D. produced
23.	A. negotiation	B. debate	C. check	D. review
24.	A. legal	B. available	C. effective	D. valid
25.	A. basically	B. routinely	C. generally	D. eventually
26.	A. fail	B. decide	C. refuse	D. has
27.	A. determine	B. end	C. settle	D. finish
28.	A. expense	B. obligation	C. benefit	D. opportunities
29.	A. favorable	B. cheap	C. advantageous	D. costly
30.	A. rule	B. idea	C. understanding	D. notion

PART FIVE
Questions 31—40

· Read the article below about the importance of contract.

· For each question 31—40, write one word in CAPITAL LETTERS on your Answer Sheet.

The Importance of Contract

Contract law is (31)... great importance in business and in everyday life. Even though most of us are unaware of it, we enter into a (32)... number of binding contracts every day. Ordinary business transactions such as buying a pack of gum at the corner grocery store, purchasing a ticket at a movie theater, or ordering a meal at a restaurant all involve valid contracts that provide the concerned parties (33)... certain rights and duties.

A contract is a legally enforceable promise between two or more people. (34)... all contracts contain enforceable promises, not all promises between people result in contracts. There are many promises made (35)... people that the courts will not enforce.

For example: Tom invites Lily to dinner and Lily (36)... Tom is looking (37)... to the date and can think of little else all day long. A half hour before Tom was to pick her up, Lily calls him and tells him that she will not be able to keep their date since Rose has (38)... her to go dancing and she has accepted. Tom is upset, hurt, and quite angry. He'd (39)... to sue her for breach of contract, since she has clearly broken a promise made to him earlier that day. Will he succeed?

Lily may not be a very nice person; she has broken a promise to a friend and needlessly hurt his feelings in the process. She may have had a moral obligation to attend the dinner date; nevertheless, she had no legal obligation to do so. The agreement she breached was not a contract, (40)... merely a social obligation that the courts will not enforce.

PART SIX
Questions 41—52

· Read the text below from a report about oral and written contracts.

· In most lines (41—52), there is one extra word. It either is grammatically incorrect or does not fit in with the sense of the text. Some lines, however, are correct.

· If a line is correct, write CORRECT on your Answer Sheet.

· If there is an extra word in the line, write the extra word in CAPITAL LETTERS on your Answer Sheet.

Oral and Written Contracts

41. An oral contract is a spoken agreement that is as valid as a written contract. For
42. example, if you have a promise that a job will be complete for monetary or any
43. other compensation, you have created an oral contract. Oral contracts are mostly
44. legally enforceable, although they are frequently subject to misinterpretation and they can be difficult to prove in court because they often come down to one
45. person's word against the other one. Moreover, some types of contracts must be in
46. writing, for example, contracts for the purchase or sale of any interest in that real property.

47. Written contracts are produced on paper or electronically. Legally, a written

48. business contract is easier to uphold than an oral contract is because there is a reference for the agreement. With a written contract, it's "easier to prove the terms

49. between the parties and to eliminate arguments over who said what ," says Jack

50. Cummins of Chicago-based Cummins & Associates, for which represents small businesses. He adds that it's often easier for businesses to recognize potential points of contention in the language because the agreement is detailed in writing. Whether

51. your small business is providing with or offering services, you should consider

52. using a written business contract and including certain specific details about the agreement.

第 7 单元　企业管理
Unit 7　Corporate Management

Text A

Ⅰ. 课文导读

公司管理制度是公司为了员工规范自身的建设,加强考勤管理,维护工作秩序,提高工作效率,经过一定的程序严格制定相应的制度,是公司管理的依据和准则。公司管理制度大体上可以分为规章制度和责任制度。规章制度侧重于工作内容、范围和工作程序、方式,如管理细则、行政管理制度、生产经营管理制度。责任制度侧重于规范责任、职权和利益的界限及其关系。一套科学完整的公司管理制度可以保证企业的正常运转和职工的合法利益不受侵害,加强考勤管理,维护工作秩序,提高工作效率。

Ⅱ. Text

In our increasingly complex and rapidly changing world, intelligent management is needed more than ever before. Effective management is the key to a better world, but mismanagement squanders① our resources and jeopardizes② our well-being.

Management is the process of working with and through others to achieve organizational objectives in a changing environment. Central to this process is the effective and efficient use of limited resources. Five components of this definition require closer examination:

1. Working with and through others. Management is, above all else, a social process. Many collective purposes bring individuals together-building cars, providing emergency health care, publishing books, and on and on. But in all cases, managers are responsible for getting things done by working with and through others.

2. Achieving organizational objectives. An objective is a target to be strived for, and one hopes, attained. Like individuals, organizations are usually more successful when their activities are guided by challenging, yet achievable, objectives. Although personal objectives are typically within the reach of individual effort, organizational objectives or goals always require collective③ action. Collective action necessitates systematic management, and organizational objectives

---

① squander: 挥霍
② jeopardize: (使)处于危险境地
③ collective: 集体的

give purpose and direction to the management process. Organizational objectives also serve later as measuring sticks for performance. Without organizational objectives, the management process, like a trip without a specific destination, would be aimless and wasteful.

3. Balancing effectiveness and efficiency. Effectiveness entails achieving a stated objective. Efficiency enters the picture when the resources required to achieve an objective are weighed against what was actually accomplished. Managers are responsible for balancing effectiveness and efficiency. Too much emphasis in either direction leads to mismanagement. A balance between effectiveness and efficiency is the key to competitiveness today. On the one hand, managers must be effective, and those who are too stingy① with resources will not get the job done. On the other hand, managers need to be efficient by containing costs as much as possible and conserving limited resources.

4. Making the most of limited Resources. We live in a world of scarcity. Those who are concerned with such matters worry not only about running out of nonrenewable energy and material resources but also about the lopsided② use of those resources. In productive organizations, managers are the trustees of limited resources, and it is their job to see that the basic factors of production—land, labor, and capital— are used efficiently as well as effectively. Management could be called "applied economics".

5. Coping with a changing environment. Managers face the difficult task of preparing for and adapting to change rather than being passively swept along by it. An awareness of the major sources of change is an excellent starting point for today's and tomorrow's managers. At this point, it is instructive to identify three overarching③ sources of change for today's managers: globalization, environmentalism, and ethics④.

Management is much more, for example, than the familiar activity of telling employees what to do. Management is a complex and dynamic mixture of systematic techniques and common sense. Currently, there are two differently approaches to dividing the management process: one is to identify managerial functions; a second focuses on managerial roles.

For most of this century, the most popular approach to describing what managers do has been the functional view. It has been popular because it characterizes the management process as a sequence of rational and logical steps. Management operates through various functions often classified as:

Planning. Commonly referred to as the primary management function, planning is the formulation of future courses of action. Plan and the objectives on which they are based give purpose and direction to the organization its subunits, and contributing individuals.

Decision Making. Managers choose alternative courses of action when they make deci-

---

① stingy: 吝啬的
② lopsided: 不平等的
③ overarching: 包罗万象的
④ ethics: 道德准则,行为准则

sions. Making intelligent and ethical decisions in today's complex world is a major management challenge.

Organizing. Structural considerations such as the chain of command, division of labor, and assignment of responsibility are part of the organizing function. Careful organizing helps ensure the efficient use of human resources.

Staffing①. Organizations are only as good as the people in them. Staffing consists of recruiting, training, and developing people who can contribute to the organized effort.

Communicating. Today's managers are responsible for communicating to their employees the technical knowledge, instructions, rules, and information required to get the job done. Recognized that communication is a two-way process, managers should be responsive to feedback and upward communication②.

Motivating. An important aspect of management today is motivating individuals to pursue collective objectives by satisfying needs and meeting expectations with meaning work and valued rewards.

Leading. Managers become inspiring leaders by serving as role models and adapting their management style to the demands of the situation. The idea of visionary③ leadership is popular today.

Controlling. When managers compare desired results with actual and take the necessary corrective action, they are keeping things on track through the control function. Deviations from past plans should be considered when formulating new plans.

During the 1970s, a researcher named Henry Mintzberg criticized the traditional functional approach as unrealistic. From his firsthand observation of managers and similar studies conducted by others, he concluded that functions "tell us little about what managers actually do. At best they indicate some vague objectives managers have when they work." Mintzberg characterizes the typical manager as follows: "The manager is overburdened with obligations; yet he cannot easily delegate④ his tasks. As a result, he is driven to overwork and is forced to do many tasks superficially. Brevity, fragmentation⑤, and verbal communication characterize his work."

Mintzberg and his followers have suggested that a more fruitful way of studying what mangers do is to focus on the key roles they play.

Interpersonal Roles. Because of their formal authority and superior status, managers engage in a good deal of interpersonal contact, especially with subordinates and peers. The three interpersonal roles that managers play are those of figurehead⑥, leader, and liaison.

---

① staff: 人员配备
② upward communication: 上行沟通
③ visionary: 有远见的
④ delegate: 移交
⑤ fragmentation: 破裂；分裂
⑥ figurehead: 有名无实的领导人

Informational Roles. Every manager is a clearinghouse① for information relating to the task at hand. Informational roles are important because information is the lifeblood of organizations. Typical roles include acting as nerve center, disseminator②, and spokesperson.

Decisional Roles. In their decisional roles, managers balance competing interests and make choices. Through decisional roles, strategies are formulated and put into action. Four decisional roles are those of entrepreneur, disturbance handler, resource allocator, and negotiator.

Both the functional approach and the role approach to explaining management are valuable. Managerial functions are a useful categorization of a manager's tasks. It is important for future managers to realize that planning and staffing, for example, require different techniques and perspectives. The role approach is valuable because it injects③ needed realism, emphasizing that the practice of management is less rational and systematic than the functional approach implies.

III. Notes

1. Applied Economics(应用经济学). It is a term that refers to the application of economic theory and analysis. While not a field of economics, it is typically characterized by the application of economic theory and econometrics to address practical issues in a range of fields including labor economics, industrial organization, development economics, health economics, monetary economics, public economics and economic history.

2. Upward Communication(上行沟通). It is a process of information flowing from the lower levels of a hierarchy to the upper levels. This type of communication is becoming more and more popular in organizations as traditional forms of communication are becoming less popular. It is concerned with the employees' comments about their own performance or work, their responses about others, about the policies and the rules of the companies, feedback and participation in decision-making. The companies which want their employees to be loyal with the company usually increase the participation of the employees by increasing upward communication.

3. Henry Mintzberg. Professor Henry Mintzberg, born in Montreal, September 2, 1939, is an internationally renowned academic and author on business and management. He is currently the Cleghorn Professor of Management Studies at the Desautels, Faculty of Management of McGill University in Montreal, Quebec, Canada, where he has been teaching since 1968. Henry Mintzberg writes prolifically on the topics of management and business strategy, with more than 150 articles and fifteen books to his name. His seminal book, *The Rise and Fall of Strategic Planning*, criticizes some of the practices of strategic planning today.

IV. Useful Expressions

1. be responsible for (to): 为……承担责任

---

① clearinghouse: (情报等的)交换所,交流中心
② disseminator: 传播者
③ inject: 注射;引入,投入

2. strive for: 为……奋斗

3. be stingy with: 吝啬

4. within the reach of: 在能力范围之内

5. be concerned with: 参与,与……有牵连

6. nonrenewable energy: 不可再生的能量

7. be responsive to: 对……产生回应

8. keep things on track: (使)保持正常

9. firsthand observation: 第一手观察

10. put into action: 实施

V. Reading Comprehension

Questions

1. What is the definition of management?

2. How do you understand the "social process" of management?

3. How do you understand the view that 'a balance between effectiveness and efficiency is the key to competitiveness today'? Use an example to illustrate your point.

4. How did Mintzberg criticize the functional approach?

5. What does it mean by 'the role approach injects needed realism'?

Decide whether each of the following statements is true or false.

1. Effective managers concentrate on the task, rather than the relationship with their subordinates. ( )

2. The role of the managers is more facilitative than directive, guiding the conversation and helping to resolve differences. ( )

3. What managers do is to tell employees what to do. ( )

4. The most vivid way to describe managers' role is that managers plan on Monday, organize on Tuesday, coordinate on Wednesday, and so on. ( )

5. One of the concerns to managers is the relationship between effectiveness and efficiency, which seem a never-ending dilemma. ( )

6. The manager's role can be described in terms of various "roles", or organized sets of behaviors identified with a position. ( )

7. Managers are responsible for the work of the people of their unit. ( )

8. The average manager is a reflective planner and precise "orchestra leader". ( )

9. By virtue of interpersonal contacts, both with subordinates and with a network of contacts, the manager emerges as the nerve center of the organizational unit. ( )

10. Mintzberg's study on management focuses on managerial function. ( )

VI. Discussion

What do you think is the most difficult thing to do as a manager? Why?

Text B
BEC Reading Texts

PART ONE
Questions 1—8

· Look at the statements below and the five extracts about management from an article.
· Which extract (A, B, C, D or E) does each statement (1—8) refer to?
· For each statement (1—8), make one letter (A, B, C, D or E) on your Answer Sheet.
· You will need to use some of these letters more than once.

1. There is a tendency of computerized coaching and electronic monitoring.
2. It is the birth of the dynamic work force.
3. Technology convergence is transforming education, medicine, materials, core competencies, whole enterprises and even the definition of industries.
4. It can be predicted that electronic systems will decease employees' dependence on managers for coaching, training, and performance feedback and help make self-directed learning a reality.
5. There are new linkages everywhere as traditional boundaries erode and markets are redefined.
6. Outsourcing payroll has become immensely popular.
7. Handling resumes electronically speeds up the process.
8. One impact of the new trend is that managerial performance will be based less on the ability to direct and coordinate work functions and more on improving key work processes.

A. Over the next 10 years, there will be a dramatic increase in the use of electronic systems to accelerate employee learning, augment decision making, and monitor performance. Proponents of these systems argue that they enable employees to learn their jobs faster, provide workers and managers with immediate performance feedback.

B. Today, college grads and professionals are just as likely to send in an electronic resume as a traditional paper-based document. And HR departments often squirrel the information in a database, which allows them to later search for applicants based on specific criteria—education or skills set, for example. The entire process-without paper, mail and filing-is faster and far more efficient.

C. Work methods and functions are no longer permanent and immutable structures; they are fluid processes that require workers to adapt continuously. Organizations will be forced to question many of the "stable state" assumptions under which they've traditionally operated, such as who their competitors are and who their potential customers may be.

D. Multimedia combining voice, image, text, and data redefines industries and competitors and creates new markets. Suppliers can act alone or in combination to market and sell goods in new ways directly to customers while bridging cultures, improving service, and collapsing cycle time.

E. Now payroll and tax processing is entering the world of electronic commerce. Thanks to the Internet, companies now can zap financial data off to a bureau. Once there, the service can handle payroll calculations, spit out transaction reports, issue paychecks or manage direct deposits, complete year-end tax filing and more.

PART TWO
Questions 9—14

· Read the text about managing priorities.

· Choose the best sentence to fill each of the gaps.

· For each gap (9—14), mark one letter (A-H) on your Answer Sheet.

· Do not use any letter more than once.

Managing Priorities

Most of us are kept so busy managing our own lives that we can't imagine how top executives manage the work of thousands of people and millions of dollars and still have time to eat, sleep, and live. (9)... But in talking about how they run their lives and companies, they do tend to focus on common themes.

Unfortunately, popular time management courses are not the answer. Even the founder of the time management movement, Alec Mackenzie, agrees that few people who take his courses stick with the techniques and really benefit from them.

(10)... Like many other company executives, Alcoa's CEO, Paul O'Neill, lists "quality" among his highest priorities. But at the very top of his list is a surprise, "safety." Alcoa leads its industry in safety and has been cutting its injury records by 50% every five years. O'Neill feels that to make an operation truly safe, you must understand it perfectly and make sure that the operation isn't inefficient in any way that would encourage dangerous shortcuts. (11)...

One principle that works for many busy managers is the 80/20 rule, (12)... —20% of its customers. A business that can identify the 20% and what they order can focus attention on those products. Illinois Tool Works, for example, used the 80/20 rule to identify which of its thousands of products it should concentrate on as it realigned its manufacturing processes. In another instance, Office Club, a discount office-supplies supermarket, decided to carry 2,200 items instead of its competitors' 5,000 because it found that 85% of its sales came from only 650 core items.

Every CEO has techniques for making time in a hectic schedule, (13)... Some count on expert secretaries to arrange their time; others learn to walk out of a meeting if participants are late. According to management expert, Peter Drucker, (14)...

A. You will find different things at the top of CEOs' priority lists

B. Establishment of priorities is a key factor in managerial and organizational effectiveness

C. There is no one secret that successful executives share

D. the most important skill for setting priorities and managing time is simply learning to say No

E. In other words, quality and safety go hand in hand

F. doing important thinking while jogging or showering or flying to meetings

G. Defined as a ranking of goals, objectives, or activities in order of importance, priorities play a special role in planning

H. which states that 80% of a company's business generally comes from a small group

PART THREE
Questions 15—20

· Read the following article on what a management trainee is.

· For each question (15—20) mark one letter (A, B, C or D) on your Answer Sheet for the answer you choose.

In every industry there is a need for managerial staff. From first-line supervisors to top executives, managers plan and direct the work of the organization, set policy, establish channels of communication, and evaluate the work that is done. These functions require knowledge, skills, and judgment that are most effectively developed on the job.

To prepare individuals for management responsibilities, many companies use Management Trainee positions. These positions are most often found in finance, trade, manufacturing, and in government agencies. Depending on the business, the position may also be referred to as marketing trainee, purchasing trainee, accounting trainee, or management intern. Whatever the title, the purpose of the position is the same: to qualify individuals for management functions within the organization. Specific duties of a Management Trainee vary widely according to the nature of the industry and the individual firm employing the trainee. Very often, a trainee's assignments are rotated among the various departments in order to develop familiarity with the whole organization and its functions. Trainees may also get classroom instruction in subjects related to their rotational experience. Instruction may include lectures, guest speakers, projects, and oral presentations. Some organizations evaluate with tests or exams to move to another level.

A Management Trainee hired by a department store may spend several months working as a clerk in one or more of the sales departments, followed by additional time working in customer services, purchasing, merchandising, and personnel departments, for example.

Many firms have formal written training programs which lay out the instruction and types programs which lay out the instruction and types of assignments the trainee will receive. They also specify times for periodic evaluation of the trainee's performance. Management traineeships may range in length from six months to two or more years. Some programs are set up, where based on the trainee's knowledge and skill set, the trainee will progress to more challenging projects or finish the program early with incentives.

The idea of a management trainee job is to evaluate the trainee's leadership, decision-making, problem-solving, communication and organization skills, then find their niche in the company. Basically, trainees will progress and succeed based on how hard they work and the area where they excel. A permanent placement is not always guaranteed but is highly possible. A management trainee role is a great way to obtain an overview of an organization and of various kinds of jobs within the o organization.

15. Which of the following is not managers' function?

A. Managers need to communicate with the employees about technical knowledge, instructions, and information.

B. Managers have to consider many things such as the chain of command, division of labor, assignment of responsibility.

C. Managers are responsible for training the trainees.

D. Managers can make decisions who to be hired on the spot.

16. What is the purpose of Management Trainee Position?

A. To train qualified managerial individuals.

B. To familiarize with the organization of the company.

C. To make progress on trainee's knowledge and skills.

D. To employ qualified men for vacant positions

17. Which is not right about management trainees?

A. Management trainees need to learn knowledge from different departments.

B. It takes management trainees a week to work in each department.

C. Management trainees will receive lectures in classroom and be tested by examinations.

D. Management trainees have already worked in the company for a period of time.

18. Which statement is not true about the paragraph 4?

A. Management trainees have many training programs, including oral programs and written programs.

B. Training period often lasts at least half a year.

C. Many training programs are set up according to the organization's policy and strategy.

D. The trainee will be awarded for finishing the work in advance.

19. What can be guaranteed after management training?

A. A permanent position.

B. Valuable experience.

C. A certification.

D. Modest salary

20. What is a management trainee?

A. An individual who receives managerial training for management work in the future.

B. A leader in the company.

C. An employee of the company

D. An applicant for interview

PART FOUR

Questions 21—30

· Read the article below about the employee selection techniques

· Choose the correct word to fill each gap from A, B, C or D.

· For each question (21—30), mark one letter (A, B, C or D) on your Answer Sheet.

Employee Selection Techniques That Are Too Good to Be True

Selecting future employees is one of the most important and difficult processes for (21)... human resource managers are responsible. The time-honored approach of interviewing, investigating an applicant's experience and education, and talking with references, although time-consuming, may still be the best method. (22)..., interviewing today is a minefield of legal do's and don'ts. You may ask an applicant about (23)... convictions but not about arrests. You may ask about medical background but not about race and (24)... And, (25)..., if you hire a person who then hurts a customer, you can be sued for not having known about his or her prior arrest record. Faced with such difficulties, many companies buy quick-and-easy solutions to the selection (26)... Many of these solutions are, in fact, too good to be true.

Take the 1980s, for example, Polygraph—lie detector-tests seemed at that time to be the wave of the future. Companies began relying on machines and polygraph experts to screen applicants. Disturbed by this trend and by the (27)... of many of the best results, Congress severely restricted polygraph use.

In the 1990s, equally questionable selection techniques are being offered as the human resource manager's best friend. Some companies borrow a technique from country fairs and try to (28)... applicants on the basis of their (29)... Others turn to "honesty tests" which claim to be able to uncover applicants who would be problem employees. Some pencil-and-paper tests do provide (30)... managers with useful information, but many tests now being marked simply do not live up to their claims.

21. A. which   B. what   C. who   D. that
22. A. except   B. apart from   C. besides   D. despite
23. A. prior   B. previous   C. before   D. former
24. A. politics   B. religion   C. interest   D. education
25. A. practically   B. ironically   C. unfortunately D. actually
26. A. fix   B. issue   C. matter   D. dilemma
27. A. inaccuracy   B. mistakes   C. accuracy   D. error
28. A. select   B. evaluate   C. judge   D. interview
29. A. appearance   B. knowledge   C. character   D. handwriting
30. A. personal   B. personnel   C. person   D. human

PART FIVE
Questions 31—40

· Read the article below about management ethics.

· For each question 31—40, write one word in CAPITAL LETTERS on your Answer Sheet.

A Fair Day's Pay?

How much is a good CEO worth? The high pay of (31)... executives can create employee distrust and sometimes outright hostility, especially during times of financial hardship. More and more companies are facing the question of (32)... to set ethical pay standards for their top brass.

How can anyone judge whether Walt Disney's Michael Eisner is (33)... the $40 million in total compensation he received in 1988? One way to make (34)... of such figures is to compare them with wages earned by the company's lowest paid workers. Does Disney do work equivalent to that of more than 2,000 people who run rides and pick up trash at Disney World? The question (35)... confined to Walt Disney. A study showed that the (36)... CEO was making 93 times the salary of an average factory worker, 72 times that of a teacher, and 44 times that of an engineer. Moreover, executives can now take advantage of many more tax breaks than they could 30 years ago.

Some corporations—including a number of well respected and very successful ones-understand how much resentment such figures can create in employees. They have put a ceiling on the amount their top executives can make. The pretax income of office furniture maker Herman Miller's CEO is limited to 20 times that of the company's manufacturing (37)... Ben & Jerry's limits its executives' pay to 5 times that of its (38)...—paid employees.

Most American corporations still scoff at such ideas and continue to widen the gap between their best-and (39)...—paid employees. But before too long, such well-paid executives may start getting some of the blame for the problems American companies have competing in the (40)... economy.

PART SIX
Questions 41—52

· Read the text below from a report about management's global agenda.

· In most lines (41—52), there is one extra word. It either is grammatically incorrect or does not fit in with the sense of the text. Some lines, however, are correct.

· If a line is correct, write CORRECT on your Answer Sheet.

· If there is an extra word in the line, write the extra word in CAPITAL LETTERS on your Answer Sheet.

Management's Global Agenda for the 1990s, According to GE's Jack Welch

41. The pace of change in the nineties will make the eighties look more like a picnic-a

walk in the

42. park. Competition will be relentless. The bar of excellence in everything we do it will be raised every day. The pace of change will be felt in several areas. Globalization is now no longer an

43. objective but an imperative, as markets open and geographic barriers become increasingly

44. blurred and even irrelevant. Corporate alliances, whether joint ventures or acquisitions, will increasingly be driven out by competitive pressures and strategies rather than finical structuring.

45. Technological innovation and the translation of that innovation into marketplace advantage will be accelerating ever faster. And in the coming decade year, we're going to see increasing demands

46. for sensitivity to the environment. Only a total number commitment of everyone in the company can provide the level of responsibility that will be acceptable to governments, employees, and customers.

47. Simply doing more of what had worked in the eighties—the restructuring, the delayering, the mechanical, top-down measures that we took—will be too incremental. More than that, it will be too

48. slow. The winners of in the nineties will be those who can develop a culture that allows them to

49. move faster, communicate with more clearly, and involve everyone in a focusing effort to serve

50. ever more demanding customers. To move toward that winning culture we've got to create

51. what we call a "boundary less" company. Then we no longer have the time to climb over barriers between

52. functions like engineering and marketing, or between people-hourly, salaried, management, and something the like.

第8单元 物 流
Unit 8　Logistics

Text A

Ⅰ. 课文导读

物流管理是商业运作中非常重要的一环,也是供应链中最富挑战性的一环。消费者们对物流有相当高的期望和要求。物流的实质是用最少的成本对原材料、半成品和成品的运输和储存进行管理。它包括订单处理、库存管理、运输配置和入库、装卸、包装等。从物流系统的角度出发,成本、速度和准确度是运输中最基本的因素。入库、装卸、包装则是和存货、运输联系在一起的。此外,设施和网点需根据业务数量和地理情况来建立,从而高效整合货物信息和运载能力。

Ⅱ. Text

No other area of business operations involves the complexity or spans① the geography of logistics. All around the globe, 24 hours of every day, 7 days a week, during 52 weeks a year, logistics is concerned with getting products and services where they are needed at the precise time desired. It is difficult to visualize② accomplishing any marketing, manufacturing, or international commerce without logistics. Most consumers in highly developed industrial nations take a high level of logistical competency for granted. When they purchase goods—at a retail store, over the telephone, or via the Internet—they expect product delivery will be performed as promised. In fact, their expectation is for timely, error-free logistics every time they order, even during the busiest periods. They have little or no tolerance for failure to perform.

Although logistics has been performed since the beginning of civilization, implementing 21st century best practices is one of the most exciting and challenging operational areas of supply chain management③. Because logistics is both old and new, we choose to characterize the rapid change taking place in best practice as a renaissance④.

---

① span: 跨越
② visualize: 设想
③ supply chain management: 供应链管理
④ renaissance: 重生,复活

Logistics involves the management of order processing①, inventory, transportation, and the combination of warehousing, materials handling, and packaging, all integrated throughout a network of facilities. The goal of logistics is to support procurement②, manufacturing, and customer accommodation supply chain operational requirements③. Within a firm the challenge is to coordinate functional competency into an integrated supply chain focused on servicing customers. In the broader supply chain context, operational synchronization④ is essential with customers as well as material and service suppliers to link internal and external operations as one integrated process.

Logistics refers to the responsibility to design and administer systems to control movement and geographical positioning of raw materials, work-in-process⑤, and finished inventories at the lowest total cost. To achieve lowest total cost means that financial and human assets⑥ committed to logistics must be held to an absolute minimum. It is also necessary to hold operational expenditures⑦ as low as possible. The combinations of resources, skills, and systems required to achieve superior logistics are challenging to integrate, but once achieved, such integrated competency is difficult for competitors to replicate⑧.

It is through the logistical process that materials flow into the manufacturing capacity of an industrial nation and finished products are distributed to consumers. The recent growth in global commerce has expanded the size and complexity of logistical operations.

Logistics adds value to the supply chain process when inventory is strategically positioned to achieve sales. Creating logistics value is costly. Although difficult to measure, most experts agree that the annual expenditure to perform logistics in the United States in 2007 was approximately 10.1 percent of the ＄13.84 billion Gross Domestic Product (GDP), or ＄1,398 billion. Expenditure for transportation in 2007 was ＄857 billion, which represented 61.3 percent of total logistics cost.

Despite the sheer size of logistical expenditure, the excitement about logistics is not cost containment⑨ or reduction. The excitement generates from understanding how select firms⑩ use logistical competency to help achieve competitive advantage. Firms having world-class logistical competency enjoy competitive advantage as a result of providing their most important customers superior service. Leading performers typically utilize information technology capable of monito-

---

① order processing: 订单处理
② procurement: 采购
③ customer accommodation supply chain operational requirements: 客户服务供应链业务要求
④ synchronization: 同步性
⑤ work-in-process: 半成品
⑥ human assets: 人力资产,指通过人力投资所形成的资本
⑦ operational expenditures: 业务费用
⑧ replicate: 复制
⑨ containment: 控制,遏制
⑩ select firms: 杰出的公司

ring global logistical activity on a real-time basis. Such technology identifies potential operational breakdowns and facilitates① corrective action prior to delivery service failure. In situations where timely corrective action is not possible, customers can be provided advance notification of developing problems, thereby eliminating the surprise of an unavoidable service failure. In many situations, working in collaboration with customers and suppliers, corrective action can be taken to prevent operational shutdowns② or costly customer service failures. By performing at above industry with respect to inventory availability, speed and consistency of delivery, and operational efficiencies, logistically sophisticated firms are ideal supply chain partners.

In the context of supply chain management, logistics exists to move and position inventory to achieve desired time, place, and possession benefits at the lowest total cost. Inventory has limited value until it is positioned at the right time and at the right location to support ownership transfer or value-added creation③. If a firm does not consistently satisfy time and location requirements, it has nothing to sell. For a supply chain to realize the maximum strategic benefit from logistics, the full range of functional work must be integrated.

Order Processing

The importance of accurate information to achieving superior logistical performance has historically been underappreciated. While many aspects of information are critical to logistics operations, the processing of orders is of primary importance. Failure to fully comprehend this importance resulted from not fully understanding how distortion and operational failures in order processing impact④ logistical operations.

In most supply chains, customer requirements are transmitted in the form of orders. The processing of these orders involves all aspects of managing customer requirements, including initial order receipt⑤, delivery, invoicing⑥, and collection. The logistics capabilities of a firm can only be as good as its order processing competency.

Inventory

The inventory requirements of a firm are directly linked to the facility network and the desired level of customer service. Theoretically, a firm could stock every item sold in every facility dedicated to servicing each customer. Few business operations can afford such a luxurious inventory strategy because the risk and total cost are prohibitive. The objective of an inventory strategy is to achieve desired customer service with the minimum inventory commitment. Excessive inventories may compensate for deficiencies in basic design of a logistics system but will ultimately result in higher-than-necessary total logistics cost.

---

① facilitate: 促进
② shutdown: 关闭；停工
③ value-added creation: 增值创造
④ impact: 冲击；对……有不良影响
⑤ initial order receipt: 初始订单收据
⑥ invoicing: 发票

Logistical strategies should be designed to maintain the lowest possible financial investment in inventory. The basic goal is to achieve maximum inventory turn① while satisfying service commitments. A sound inventory strategy is based on a combination of five aspects of selective deployment: (1) core customer segmentation②, (2) product profitability, (3) transportation integration, (4) time-based performance, and (5) competitive performance.

Transportation

Transportation is the operational area of logistics that geographically moves and positions inventory. Because of its fundamental importance and visible cost, transportation has traditionally received considerable managerial attention. Almost all enterprises, big and small, have managers responsible for transportation.

Transportation requirements can be satisfied in three basic ways. First, a private fleet of equipment may be operated. Second, contracts may be arranged with dedicated transport specialists. Third, an enterprise may engage the services of a wide variety of carriers that provide different transportation services as needed on a per shipment basis. From the logistical system viewpoint, three factors are fundamental to transportation performance: (1) cost, (2) speed, and (3) consistency.

Warehousing, Materials Handling, and Packaging

The first three functional areas of logistics—order processing, inventory, and transportation—can be engineered into a variety of different operational arrangements. Each arrangement has the potential to contribute to a specified level of customer service with an associated total cost. In essence, these functions combine to create a system solution for integrated logistics. The fourth functionality of logistics— warehousing, materials handling, and packaging—also represents an integral part of a logistics operating solution. However, these functions do not have the independent status of those previously discussed. Warehousing, materials handling, and packaging are an integral part of other logistics areas. For example, inventory typically needs to be warehoused at selected times during the logistical process. Transportation vehicles require materials handling for efficient loading and unloading. Finally, the individual products are most efficiently handled when packaged together into shipping cartons③ or other unit loads.

Facility Network Design

Classical economics neglected the importance of facility location and overall network design efficient business operations. In business operations, however, the number, size, and geographical relationship of facilities used to perform logistical operations directly impacts customer service capability and cost. Facility network design is a primary responsibility of logistical management, since a firm's facility structure is used to ship products and materials to customers.

Facility network design is concerned with determining the number and location of all types

---

① inventory turn: 库存周转
② customer segmentation: 客户细分
③ shipping cartons: 运输纸板箱

of facilities required to perform logistics work. It is also necessary to determine what inventory and how much to stock at each facility as well as the assignment of customers. The facility network creates a structure from which logistical operations are performed. Thus, the network integrates information and transportation capabilities. Specific work tasks related to processing customer orders, warehousing inventory①, and materials handling are all performed within the facility network.

Ⅲ. Notes

1. Renaissance（文艺复兴）. The Renaissance was a cultural movement that spanned roughly the 14th to the 17th century, beginning in Italy in the Late Middle Ages and later spreading to the rest of Europe. The term is also used more loosely to refer to the historical era, but since the changes of the Renaissance were not uniform across Europe, this is a general use of the term. As a cultural movement, it encompassed a flowering of literature, science, art, religion, and politics, and a resurgence of learning based on classical sources, the development of linear perspective in painting, and gradual but widespread educational reform.

2. Gross Domestic Product（GDP）（国内生产总值）. Gross domestic product (GDP) refers to the market value of all final goods and services produced within a country in a given period. GDP per capita is often considered an indicator of a country's standard of living. Gross domestic product is related to national accounts, a subject in macroeconomics. GDP can be determined in three ways, all of which should, in principle, give the same result. They are the product (or output) approach, the income approach, and the expenditure approach.

Ⅳ. Useful Expressions

1. have no tolerance for: 不容忍……
2. in the context of: 在……方面
3. hold sth. to an absolute minimum: 将...保持在最低值
4. on a real-time basis: 在实时基础上
5. prior to: 在……之前
6. in collaboration with: 与……合作
7. with respect to: 关于
8. in essence: 本质上
9. logistical process: 物流处理
   logistical operations: 物流运营
   logistical expenditure: 物流费用
   logistical competency: 物流能力
   logistical activity: 物流活动
   logistical strategies: 物流策略

---

① warehousing inventory: 仓库库存

logistically sophisticated firms: 物流先进的企业

logistical management: 物流管理

V. Reading Comprehension
Questions

1. What is logistics?
2. What does it mean by 'the complexity or spans the geography of logistics'?
3. Why is logistics an essential part of the business?
4. What does 'the logistical competency of the select firms' refer to?
5. Could you explain the statement of "Creating logistics value is costly"?

Decide whether each of the following statements is true or false.

1. Logistics is a small part in business which manages the distribution of the cargo. (　　)
2. The more developed the nation is, the higher its logistical competency is. (　　)
3. Logistics is one of the most exciting and challenging operational areas of supply chain management. (　　)
4. The main functions of logistics include order processing, inventory, transportation, and the combination of warehousing, materials handling, and packaging. (　　)
5. Logistics is a channel of the supply chain which adds the value of time and place utility. (　　)
6. Logistics as a business concept evolved in the 1950s, the beginning of the renaissance. (　　)
7. It is necessary to hold operational expenditures as low as possible. (　　)
8. Companies with a lower logistical competency enjoy a competitive advantage. (　　)
9. Logistical strategies should be planned to maintain a high financial investment in inventory. (　　)
10. Logistics combines all its functions to meet customer and legal requirements. (　　)

VI. Discussion

If you are a customer or supplier, how do you choose an ideal logistics company?

Text B
BEC Reading Texts

PART ONE
Questions 1—8

· Look at the statements below and the five extracts about a logistics strategy from an article.

- Which extract (A, B, C, D or E) does each statement (1—8) refer to?
- For each statement (1—8), make one letter (A, B, C, D or E) on your Answer Sheet.
- You will need to use some of these letters more than once.

1. What is involved in developing a logistic strategy?
2. The logistics strategy should examine the structural issues of the logistics organization, such as the optimum number of warehouses and distribution centers.
3. The key to developing a successful logistics strategy is how it is to be implemented across the organization.
4. Why shall we implement a logistics strategy?
5. The supply chain constantly changes and that will affect any logistics organization.
6. When a company creates a logistics strategy it is defining the service levels at which its logistics organization is at its most cost effective.
7. Any strategy should review how each separate function in the logistics organization is to achieve functional excellence.
8. What are the components to examine when we develop the logistics strategy?

A. The plan for implementation will include development or configuration of an information system, introduction of new policies and procedures and the development of a change management plan.

B. Because supply chains are constantly changing and evolving, a company may develop a number of logistics strategies for specific product lines, specific countries or specific customers.

C. To adapt to the flexibility of the supply chain, companies should develop and implement a formal logistics strategy. This will allow a company to identify the impact of imminent changes and make organizational or functional changes to ensure service levels are not reduced.

D. A company can start to develop a logistics strategy by looking at four distinct levels of their logistics organization. By examining the company's objectives and strategic supply chain decisions, the logistics strategy should review how the logistics organization contributes to those high-level objectives.

E. When examining the four levels of logistics organization, all components of the operation should be examined to ascertain whether any potential cost benefits can be achieved. There are different component areas for each company but the list should at least include the following: transportation, outsourcing, logistics system, competitors and information.

PART TWO
Questions 9—14

- Read the text about the logistical operating arrangements.
- Choose the best sentence to fill each of the gaps.

- For each gap (9—14), mark one letter (A-H) on your Answer Sheet.
- Do not use any letter more than once.

Logistical Operating Arrangements

The potential for logistical services to favorably impact customers is directly related to operating system design. The many different facets of logistical performance requirements make operational design a complex task, as an operating structure must offer a balance of performance, cost, and flexibility. (9)..., it is astonishing that any structural similarity exists. But keep in mind that all logistical arrangements have two common characteristics. First, they are designed to manage inventory. Second, the range of logistics alternatives is limited by available technology. (10)... Three widely utilized structures are echelon, direct, and combined.

Echelon systems utilize warehouses to create inventory assortments and achieve consolidation economies associated with large-volume transportation shipments. Inventories positioned in warehouses are available for rapid deployment to meet customer requirements. (11)... A break-bulk facility typically receives large-volume shipments from a variety of suppliers. Inventory is sorted and stored in anticipation of future customer requirements. Food distribution centers operated by major grocery chains and wholesalers are examples of break-bulk warehouses. (12)... Consolidation is typically required by manufacturing firms that have plants at different geographical locations. Products manufactured at different plants are consolidated at a central warehouse facility to allow the firm to ship full-line assortments to customers. Major consumer product manufacturers are prime examples of enterprises using echeloned systems for full-line consolidation.

(13)... Direct distribution typically uses the expedited services of premium transport combined with information technology to rapidly process customer orders and achieve delivery performance. This combination of capabilities, designed into the order delivery cycle, (14)... Examples of direct shipments are plant-to-customer truckload shipments, direct store delivery, and various forms of direct-to-consumer fulfillment required to support Internet shopping. Direct logistical structures are also commonly used for inbound components and materials to manufacturing plants because the average shipment size is typically large.

A. In contrast to inventory echeloning are logistical systems designed to ship products direct to customer's destination from one or a limited number of centrally located inventories

B. proceeds through a common arrangement of firms and facilities as it moves from origin to final destination

C. A consolidation warehouse operates in a reverse profile

D. reduces time delays and overcomes geographical separation from customers

E. The use of echelons usually implies that total cost analysis justifies stocking some level of inventory or performing specific activities at consecutive levels of a supply chain

F. When one considers the variety of logistical systems used throughout the world to service widely diverse markets

G. These two characteristics tend to create commonly observed operating arrangements

H. Typical echelon systems utilize either break-bulk or consolidation warehouses

PART THREE
Questions 15—20

· Read the following article on just-in-time techniques.

· For each question (15—20) mark one letter (A, B, C or D) on your Answer Sheet for the answer you choose.

Just-in-Time (JIT) techniques have received considerable attention and discussion in recent years in all areas related to supply chain management. Sometimes referred to as just-in-time purchasing, and frequently referred to as just-in-time delivery, the goal of JIT is to time-phase activities so that purchased materials and components arrive at the manufacturing or assembly point just at the time they are required for the transformation process. Ideally, raw material and work-in-process inventories are minimized as a result of reducing or eliminating reserve stocks. The key to JIT operations is that demand for components and materials depends on the finalized production schedule. Requirements can be determined by focusing on the finished product being manufactured. Once the production schedule is established, just-in-time arrival of components and materials can be planned to coincide with those requirements, resulting in reduced handling and minimal inventories. The implications of JIT are numerous. Obviously, it is necessary to deal with suppliers who have high and consistent levels of quality, as their components will go directly in to the finished product. Absolutely reliable logistical performance is required and eliminates, or at least reduces, the need for buffer stocks of materials. JIT generally requires more frequent deliveries of smaller quantities of purchased inputs, which may require modification of inbound transportation. Clearly, to make JIT work, there must be very close cooperation and communication between manufacturers' purchasing organization and suppliers. In JIT operations, companies attempt to gain the benefits of backward vertical integration but avoid the formal tie of ownership. They achieve many of the same ends through coordination and process integration with suppliers.

Originally, JIT was applied to manufacturing processes characterized as MTP, since the effective functioning of the system is dependent upon a finalized production schedule. However, as manufacturing strategies have evolved with more emphasis on flexibility, reduced lot-size production quantities, and quick changeovers, JIT concepts have evolved to accommodate ATO and MTO manufacturing as well and in manufacturing is now referred to as *lean*, as discussed above. In many situations, lead suppliers are used by manufacturers to sort, segregate, and sequence materials as they flow into assembly operations. The goal is to reduce handling and facilitate continuous JIT.

Some organizations, seeing the benefits of JIT systems and recognizing the benefits of supplier integration, have gone so far as to bring their suppliers' personnel into their production plants. The supplier personnel are empowered to use the customer's purchase orders, have full access to production schedules, and have responsibility for scheduling arrival of materials.

15. By the word "work-in-process" (line 5, paragraph 1), the author means _____.

　A. partly completed products

　B. products being assembled

　C. semi-manufactured products

　D. made-up products

16. What do JIT operations depend on?

　A. Reserve stocks

　B. The finalized production schedule

　C. Manufacturing or assembly point

　D. The efficiency of manufacturers

17. Which of the following is NOT the description of Just-in-Time(JIT) techniques?

　A. It is to time-phase activities.

　B. Suppliers' components go directly in to the finished product.

　C. JIT generally requires more frequent deliveries of smaller quantities of purchased inputs.

　D. In JIT operations, companies attempt to gain the benefits of backward vertical integration.

18. Which of the following term is mentioned in the passage?

　A. MTP

　B. ATO

　C. MTO

　D. FOB

19. Which of the following is NOT right?

　A. MTP is concerning manufacturing processes.

　B. ATO is the item used for suppliers.

　C. The effective functioning of JIT is dependent upon a finalized production schedule.

　D. JIT has numerous implications.

20. What might be the most appropriate title of the passage?

　A. The Goal of JIT.

　B. Just-in-Time Techniques.

　C. The Implications of JIT.

　D. The Advantages of JIT.

PART FOUR

Questions 21—30

· Read the article below about the importance of inventory.

· Choose the correct word to fill each gap from A, B, C or D.

- For each question (21—30), mark one letter (A, B, C or D) on your Answer Sheet.

Inventory in Logistics

Inventory typically represents the second largest component of logistics cost to transportation. The risks associated with (21)... inventory increase as products move down the supply chain closer to the customer because the potential of having the product in the wrong place or form increases and costs have been (22)... to distribute the product. In addition to the risk of lost sales due to (23)... because adequate inventory is not available, other risks include obsolescence, pilferage, and damage. Further, the cost of carrying inventory is significantly influenced by the cost of the capital (24)... up in the inventory. Geographic specialization, decoupling, supply/demand balancing, and buffering uncertainty provide the basic rationale for maintaining inventory. While there is (25)... interest in reducing overall supply chain inventory, inventory does add value and can result in lower overall supply chain costs with appropriate trade-offs.

From a supply chain logistics perspective, the major (26)... inventory elements are replenishment cycle stock, safety stock, and in-transit stock. The appropriate replenishment cycle stock can be determined using an EOQ formula to reflect the trade-off between storage and ordering cost. Safety stock depends on the mean and variance of demand and the replenishment cycle. In-transit stock depends on the transport (27)...

Inventory management uses a combination of reactive and planning logics. Reactive logic is most appropriate for items with low volume, high demand, and high performance cycle uncertainty because it (28)... the risk of inventory speculation. Inventory planning logic is appropriate for high-volume items with relatively (29)... demand. Inventory planning methods offer the potential for effective inventory management because they take (30)... of improved information and economies of scale.

21. A. holding   B. supporting   C. maintaining   D. keeping
22. A. caused   B. incurred   C. aroused   D. leaded
23. A. stockouts   B. stakeouts   C. deficiency   D. shortage
24. A. appended   B. added   C. bound   D. tied
25. A. essential   B. significant   C. substantial   D. real
26. A. available   B. controllable   C. convertible   D. viable
27. A. category   B. vehicle   C. tool   D. mode
28. A. postpones   B. removes   C. overcomes   D. ignores
29. A. invariable   B. stable   C. static   D. fixed
30. A. account   B. charge   C. advantage   D. care

PART FIVE
Questions 31—40

- Read the article below about processes in logistics.
- For each question 31—40, write one word in CAPITAL LETTERS on your Answer Sheet.

What is Logistics?

Logistics is the management of the flow of goods (31)... the point of origin and the point of destination in order to meet the (32)... of customers or corporations. Logistics involves the integration of information, transportation, inventory, warehousing, material handling, and packaging, and often security.

Logistics as a business concept evolved in the 1950s (33)... to the increasing complexity of supplying businesses with materials and shipping out products in an increasingly globalized supply chain, leading to a call for experts called supply chain logisticians. Business logistics can be defined as "having the right item in the right quantity at the right (34)... at the right place for the right price in the right condition to the right customer", and is the science of process and incorporates all industry sectors. The goal of logistics work is to manage the fruition of project life cycles, supply chains and resultant efficiencies.

In business, logistics may have (35)... internal focus, or external focus covering the flow and storage of materials (36)... point of origin to point of consumption. The (37)... functions of a qualified logistician include inventory management, purchasing, transportation, warehousing, consultation and the organizing and planning of these activities. Logisticians combine a professional knowledge of each of these functions (38)... coordinate resources in an organization. There are two fundamentally different forms of logistics: one optimizes a steady flow of material through a network of transport links and storage nodes; the (39)... coordinates a sequence of resources to (40)... out some project.

PART SIX
Questions 41—52

· Read the text below about logistics value generation.
· In most lines (41—52), there is one extra word. It either is grammatically incorrect or does not fit in with the sense of the text. Some lines, however, are correct.
· If a line is correct, write CORRECT on your Answer Sheet.
· If there is an extra word in the line, write the extra word in CAPITAL LETTERS on your Answer Sheet.

Logistics Value Generation

41. The key to achieving logistical leadership is to master the art of matching with operating competency and commitment to key customer expectations and requirements. This customer

42. commitment, while in an exacting cost framework, is the logistics value proposition. It is a unique

43. commitment of a firm to either an individual or selected customer groups. The typical enterprise

44. seeks to develop and implement an overall logistical competency that satisfies customer

expectations at a realistic total cost expenditure. Very seldom will either the lowest total cost or

45. the highest attainable customer service constitutes the appropriate logistics by strategy. Likewise,

46. the desired combination will be more different for different customers. A well-designed logistical

47. effort must provide high customer impact while is controlling operational variance and minimizing

48. inventory commitment. And, most of all, it must have relevancy to specific customers. Significant advances have been made in the development of tools to aid management in the measurement

49. of cost/service trade-offs. Formulation of a sound strategy requires a capability due to estimate

50. operating cost required to achieve alternative service levels. Likewise, alternative levels of system performance are meaningless unless viewed in terms of overall business unit customer

51. accommodation, manufacturing, and procurement strategies. Leading to firms realize that a well-designed logistical system can help achieve competitive advantage. In fact, as a general

52. rule, firms that obtain a strategic advantage based on logistical competency establish against the nature of their industry's competition.

第9单元 商业道德和社会责任
Unit 9　Business Ethics and Social Responsibility

Text A

Ⅰ. 课文导读

商业道德和企业的社会责任一直是一个有争议的话题。随着经济的不断发展,企业对经济利益的单纯追求对社会造成了种种负面影响。人们逐渐意识到企业在保证经济利益的同时,也必须对人们生活质量的提高和环境保护承担相应的责任。事实上,社会与企业活动之间一直都存在着一种隐性的"社会契约",它制约着我们的企业,也就是说企业在做出任何商业决策时,都必须考虑整个社会系统将因这些决策而受到什么样的影响。

Ⅱ. Text

　　The rival position to that of Friedman and Levitt is simply that business has other obligations in addition to pursuing profits. The phrase "in addition to" is important. Critics of the narrow view do not as a rule believe there is anything wrong with corporate profit. They maintain, rather, that corporations have other responsibilities as well—to consumers, to their employees, and to society at large①. If the adherents② of the broader view share one belief, it is that corporations have responsibilities beyond simply enhancing their profits because, as a matter of fact, they have such great social and economic power in our society. With that power must come social responsibility. As professor of business administration Keith Davis puts it③:

　　One basic proposition is that social responsibility arises from social power. Modern business has immense social power in such areas as minority employment and environmental pollution. If business has the power, then a just relationship demands that business also bear responsibility for its actions in these areas. Social responsibility arises from concern about the consequences of business's acts as they affect the interests of others. Business decisions do have social consequences. Businessmen cannot make decisions that are solely economic decisions, because they are interrelated with the whole social system. This situation requires that businessmen's thinking be broadened beyond the company gate to the whole social system. Systems thinking is re-

---

① society at large: 整个社会
② adherent: 支持者;跟随者
③ As sb. puts it: 正如某人所说

quired.

Social responsibility implies that a business decision maker in the process of serving his own business interests is obliged to take actions that also protect and enhance society's interests. The net effect is to improve the quality of life in the broadest possible way, however quality of life is defined by society. In this manner, harmony is achieved between business's actions and the larger social system. The businessman becomes concerned with social as well as economic outputs and with the total effect of his institutional actions on society.

Adherents of the broader view, like Davis, stress that modern business is intimately① integrated with the rest of society. Business is not some self-enclosed world, like a private poker party. Rather, business activities have profound ramifications throughout society. As a result, although society expects business to pursue its economic interests, business has other responsibilities as well.

Melvin Anshen has cast the case for the broader view in a historical perspective. He maintains that there is always a kind of "social contract" between business and society. This contract is, of course, only implicit, but it represents a tacit understanding within society about the proper goals and responsibilities of business. In effect, in Anshen's view, society always structures the guidelines within which business is permitted to operate in order to derive certain benefits from business activity. For instance, in the nineteenth century society's prime interest was rapid economic growth, which was viewed as the source of all progress, and the engine of economic growth was identified as the drive for profits by unfettered②, competitive, private enterprise. This attitude was reflected in the then-existing③ social contract.

Today, however, society has concerns and interests other than rapid economic growth—in particular, a concern for the quality of life and for the preservation of the environment. Accordingly, the social contract is in the process of being modified. In particular, Anshen writes, "It will no longer be acceptable for corporations to manage their affairs solely in terms of the traditional internal costs of doing business, while thrusting④ external costs on the public."

In recent years we have grown more aware of the possible deleterious⑤ side effects of business activity, or what economists call externalities⑥. Externalities are the unintended negative (or in some cases positive) consequences that an economic transaction between two parties can have on some third party. Industrial pollution provides the clearest illustration. Suppose, for example, that a factory makes widgets⑦ and sells them to your firm. A byproduct of this economic transaction is the waste that the rains wash from the factory yard into the local river, waste that dama-

---

① intimately: 紧密地
② unfettered: 不受约束的
③ then-existing: 当时存在的
④ thrust: 强使接受
⑤ deleterious: 有害的
⑥ externalities: 外部性
⑦ widget: 小机械玩意儿

ges recreational and commercial fishing interests downstream. This damage to third parties is an unintended side effect of the economic transaction between the seller and buyer of widgets.

Defenders of the new social contract, like Anshen, maintain that externalities should no longer be overlooked. In the jargon① of economists, externalities must be "internalized." That is, the factory should be made to absorb the cost, either by disposing of its waste in an environmentally safe (and presumably more expensive) way or by paying for the damage the waste does downstream. On the one hand, basic fairness requires that the factory's waste no longer be dumped onto third parties. On the other hand, from the economic point of view, requiring the factory to internalize② the externalities makes sense, for only when it does so will the price of the widgets it sells reflect their true social cost. The real production cost of the widgets includes not just labor, raw materials, machinery, and so on but also the damage done to the fisheries downstream. Unless the price of widgets is raised sufficiently to reimburse③ the fisheries for their losses or to dispose of the waste in some other way, then the buyer of widgets is paying less than their true cost. Part of the cost is being paid by the fishing interests down stream. Some advocates of the broader view go beyond requiring business to internalize its externalities in a narrow economic sense. Keith Davis maintains that, in addition to considering potential profitability, a business must weigh the long-range social costs of its activities as well. Only if the overall benefit to society is positive should business act.

For example, a firm that builds row upon row of look-alike houses may be saving $5,000 on each house and passing along $4,000 of the saving to each buyer, thus serving consumer interests. In the long run④, however, this kind of construction may encourage the rapid development of a city slum⑤. In this instance, the lack of long-range outlook may result in serious social costs.

In sum⑥, the expectation of the social responsibility model is that a detailed cost or benefit analysis will be made prior to⑦ determining whether to proceed with an activity and that social costs will be given significant weight in the decision-making process. Almost any business action will entail some social costs. The basic question is whether the benefits outweigh the costs so that there is a net social benefit. Many questions of judgment arise, and there are no precise mathematical measures in the social field, but rational and wise judgments can be made if the issues are first thoroughly explored.

---

① jargon: 行话
② internalize: 内在化
③ reimburse: 补偿
④ in the long run: 从长远看来
⑤ slum: 贫民窟
⑥ in sum: 总之
⑦ prior to: 之前

III. Notes

1. Melvin Anshen. Melvin Anshen has published a series of books on business, including: *Management and Corporations* (1985), *An Introduction to Business* (1942), *Private Enterprise and Public Policy* (1954), *Corporate Strategies for Social Performance* (1980), *Managing the Socially Responsible Corporation* (1974).

2. Externalities (外在性). In economics, an externality (or transaction spillover) is a cost or benefit, not transmitted through prices, incurred by a party who did not agree to the action causing the cost or benefit. The benefits of externalities, in this case, are called a positive externality or external benefit, while its cost is called a negative externality or external costs. In these cases of both negative and positive externalities, in a competitive market, prices do not reflect the full costs or benefits of producing or consuming a product or service. Also, producers and consumers may neither bear all of the costs nor reap all of the benefits of the economic activity, and too much or too little of the goods will be produced or consumed in terms of overall costs and benefits to society.

IV. Useful Expressions

1. in addition to: 加上
2. society at large: 整个社会
3. as a matter of fact: 事实上
4. be interrelated with: 与……相联系
5. be integrated with: 与……形成整体
6. tacit understanding: 默契
7. in effect: 实际上
8. side effect: 副作用
9. dispose of: 处置
10. in the long run: 从长远看来
11. in sum: 总之

V. Reading Comprehension

Questions

1. Why does Keith Davis think "Systems thinking is required?"
2. How should a corporation internalize its externalities?
3. What dose Melvin Anshen mean by "social contract"?
4. What is the difference between the traditional and new social contract?
5. What is the expectation of the social responsibility model?

Decide whether each of the following statements is true or false.

1. The narrow viewers maintain that a company must lay emphasis on both social responsibility and economic interests.　　　　　　　　　　　　　　　　　　　　　　　(　　)

2. Since business has immense social power, it has the responsibility to bear the negative consequences of economic development. (   )

3. Systems thinking is required because business decisions are interrelated with the whole society. (   )

4. Businessman has responsibility solely to their company, to their customers and to their employees. (   )

5. Social responsibility refers to remedial measure that a company makes to remedy the damage during the process of serving its own profits. (   )

6. The social contract represents an implicit understanding that the business should be progressed with a goal of charity. (   )

7. Social contract is being modified according to the concerns for the quality of life and the preservation of the environment. (   )

8. Externalities are the unexpected negative consequences to some third party. (   )

9. A factory should internalize the externality to realize its social value. (   )

10. There are many questions in building a precise mathematical measure to judge the commercial activities. (   )

Ⅵ. Discussion

Share your opinions with your partners about how a corporation can balance the social responsibility and the benefits of its own?

Text B
BEC Reading Texts

PART ONE
Questions 1—8

- Look at the statements below and the five extracts about business ethics from an article.
- Which extract (A, B, C, D or E) does each statement (1—8) refer to?
- For each statement (1—8), make one letter (A, B, C, D or E) on your Answer Sheet.
- You will need to use some of these letters more than once.

1. Business ethical norms reflect the norms of each historical period. As time passes norms evolve, causing accepted behaviors to become objectionable.

2. The range and quantity of business ethical issues reflects the interaction of profit-maximizing behavior with non-economic concerns.

3. In recent years, the issue of business ethics has garnered increased attention.

4. Ethics implicitly regulates areas and details of behavior that lie beyond governmental

control.

5. Business ethics applies to all aspects of business conduct and is relevant to the conduct of individuals and entire organizations.

6. A firm's employees should practice business ethics, which involves following a set of principles when conducting business.

7. Quite apart from the issue of rightness and wrongness, the fact is that ethical behavior in business serves the individual and the enterprise much better in the long run.

8. As part of more comprehensive compliance and ethics programs, many companies have formulated internal policies pertaining to the ethical conduct of employees.

A. Each firm has a social responsibility, which is the firm's recognition of how its business decision can affect society. The term social responsibility is sometimes used to describe the firm's responsibility to its community and to the environment. However, it may also be used more broadly to include the firm's responsibility to its customers, employees, stockholders, and creditor. Although the business decisions a firm makes are intended to increase its value, the decisions must not violate its ethics and social responsibilities.

B. Business ethics is a form of applied ethics or professional ethics that examines ethical principles and moral or ethical problems that arise in a business environment. It has both normative and descriptive dimensions. As a corporate practice and a career specialization, the field is primarily normative. Governments use laws and regulations to point business behavior in what they perceive to be beneficial directions.

C. The term 'business ethics' came into common use in the United States in the early 1970s. By the mid-1980s at least 500 courses in business ethics reached 40,000 students, using some twenty textbooks and at least ten casebooks along supported by professional societies, centers and journals of business ethics. The Society for Business Ethics was started in 1980. European business schools adopted business ethics after 1987 commencing with the European Business Ethics Network (EBEN).

D. Organizations can manage ethics in their workplaces by establishing an ethics management program. Corporate research and watchdog groups such as the Ethics Resource Center and the Council on Economic Priorities point out that the number of corporations that engage in ethics training and initiate socially responsive programs has increased dramatically over the course of the past two decades.

E. If a business owner treats employees, customers, and competitors in a fair and honest manner—and suitably penalizes those who do not perform in a similar fashion—he or she is far more likely to have an ethical work force of which he or she can be proud. "It is perfectly possible to make a decent living without compromising the integrity of the company or the individual," wrote business executive William R. Holland.

PART TWO
Questions 9—14

- Read the text about the ethical dilemmas that U. S. firms faced in global business.
- Choose the best sentence to fill each of the gaps.
- For each gap (9—14), mark one letter (A-H) on your Answer Sheet.
- Do not use any letter more than once.

Global Business, Global Ethics

U. S. firms typically have a code of ethics that provides guidelines for their employees. (9)... Consider a U. S. firm that sells suppliers to foreign manufacturers. Both its code of ethics and the U. S. Foreign Corrupt Practices Act prevent the firm from offering payoffs ("kickbacks") to any employees of the manufacturing companies that order its suppliers. Competitors based in other countries, however, may offer payoffs to employees of the manufacturing companies. (10)... Thus, the U. S. supplier is at a disadvantage because its employees are required to follow a stricter code of ethics. This is a common ethical dilemma that U. S. firms face in a global environment. (11)...

Another ethical dilemma that U. S. firms may face involves their relationship with certain foreign governments. (12)... Officials of some foreign governments commonly accept bribes from firms that need approval for various business activities. For example, a firm may need to have its products approved for safety purposes, or its local manufacturing plant may need to be approved for environmental purposes. (13)... Those firms that pay off government officials may receive prompt attention from the local governments. Employees of Lockheed Martin were charged with bribing Egyptian government officials to win a contract to build new aircraft. Executives of IBM's Argentina subsidiary were charged with bribing Argentina subsidiary were charged with bribing Argentine government officials to generate business from the government.

Many U. S. firms attempt to follow a worldwide code of ethics that is consistent across countries. (14)... Although a worldwide code of ethics may place a U. S. firm at a disadvantage in some countries, it may also enhance the firm's credibility.

A. Firms that conduct business in foreign countries are subject to numerous rules imposed by the global government

B. American business ethics are based around the idea that it is possible to maximize wealth and profit while also being committed to upholding values and laws

C. However, these guidelines may be much more restrictive than those generally used in some foreign countries

D. The process of approving even minor activities could take months and prevent the firm from conducting business

E. The employees of U. S. firms must either ignore their ethical guidelines or be at a disadvantage in certain foreign countries

F. In some countries, this type of behavior is acceptable

G. This varies from place to place, based on countries' specific cultural or societal beliefs

H. This type of policy reduces the confusion that could result from using different ethical standards in different countries

PART THREE
Questions 15—20

· Read the following article on the reasons why so many companies do not adhere to business ethics.

· For each question (15—20) mark one letter (A, B, C or D) on your Answer Sheet for the answer you choose.

Business ethics are the behaviors that a business adheres to in its daily dealings with the world. They apply not only to how the business interacts with the world at large, but also to their one-on-one dealings with a single customer.

Business ethics are also the principles of conduct by which a company operates. This includes how the company owners want to manage the business and how the owners expect the employees to conduct themselves. Actions that result in civil lawsuits, criminal liability, or that simply damage the reputation of a business can all be considered examples of bad business ethics.

Dishonesty is a common example of bad business ethics. For example, if a company makes false claims in its advertising, the company is being dishonest to its customers. Making false advertising claims and failing to replace damaged or defective products or to refund their purchase price are examples of bad business ethics that can give a company a poor reputation and that can lead to civil lawsuits.

Many businesses have gained a bad reputation just by being in business. To some people, businesses are interested in making money, and that is the bottom line. It could be called capitalism in its purest form. Making money is not wrong in itself. It is the manner in which some businesses conduct themselves that brings up the question of ethical behavior.

Many global businesses, including most of the major brands that the public use, can be seen not to think too highly of good business ethics. Many major brands have been fined millions for breaking ethical business laws. Money is the major deciding factor.

Many companies have broken anti-trust, ethical and environmental laws and received fines worth millions. The problem is that the amount of money these companies are making outweighs the fines applied. Billion dollar profits blind the companies to their lack of business ethics, and the dollar sign wins.

A business may be a multi-million seller, but does it use good business ethics and do people care? Business ethics should eliminate exploitation, from the sweat shop children who are making sneakers to the coffee serving staff who are being ripped off in wages. Business ethics can be applied to everything from the trees cut down to make the paper that a business sells to the ramifications of importing coffee from certain countries.

In the end, it may be up to the public to make sure that a company adheres to correct business ethics. If the company is making large amounts of money, they may not wish to pay too close attention to their ethical behavior. There are many companies that pride themselves in their correct business ethics, but in this competitive world, they are becoming very few and far between.

15. Which of the following is not true about the business ethics?

A. It is the behavior that a business adheres to in its daily dealings with the world.

B. It includes the moral principles or codes a company implements to ensure that all individuals working in the company act with acceptable behavior.

C. It is the principles of conduct by which a company operates.

D. It has nothing to do with advertising and a reasonable cost for the quality of the product.

16. Why does the author say "many businesses have gained a bad reputation just by being in business" in the 4th paragraph?

A. Because the business ethics is considered to be an oxymoron.

B. Because making money is not wrong in itself.

C. Because a company can not make money and simultaneously adhere to the business ethics.

D. Because many companies did not mean to violate the business ethics.

17. Which is main reason why so many companies do not adhere to business ethics?

A. Billion dollar profits blind the companies to their lack of business ethics

B. Making money and profits should ignore the business ethics.

C. The amount of the fines is not even worth mentioning when compared with profits.

D. Many companies lack the consciousness of the business ethics.

18. What is considered to be a dishonesty?

A. Companies received fines because it makes false claims in its advertising.

B. Companies recall the defective products or to refund their purchase price.

C. Companies conceal the deficiency of products.

D. Companies become the link in the chain of unethical businesses.

19. What does the author suggest to deal with the ethics violation?

A. Business ethics should eliminate exploitation

B. The authority is urged to give stricter levels of punishment.

C. Companies should pride themselves in their correct business ethics.

D. Public should put pressure on those bad business ethics.

20. Which is not one of the phenomena in the present business world?

A. Many popular companies have been fined time and time again.

B. It is considered that businesses are interested in making money.

C. The issue of business ethics has garnered increased attention.

D. Those which adhere to business ethics are becoming very few and far between.

PART FOUR
Questions 21—30

- Read the article below about the ethical standards of behavior in small business.
- Choose the correct word to fill each gap from A, B, C or D.
- For each question (21—30), mark one letter (A, B, C or D) on your Answer Sheet.

Establishing Ethical Standards of Behavior in a Small Business

Entrepreneurs and small business owners (21)... great influence in determining the ethical philosophies of their business enterprises. Employees often follow the lead of the owner in (22)... their duties and (23)... to their responsibilities, so it is incumbent on the owner to establish a work environment that embraces moral standards of behavior. Business experts and ethicists alike point to a number of actions that owners and managers can take to help (24)... their company down the path of ethical business behavior. Establishing a statement of organizational values, for example, can provide employees—and the company as a whole—with a specific framework of expected (25)... Such statements offer employees, business associates, and the larger community (26)... a consistent portrait of the company's operating principles—why it (27)..., what it believes, and how it intends to act to make sure that its activities (28)... with its professed beliefs. Active reviews of strategic plans and objectives can also be undertaken to make certain that they are not in conflict with the company's basic ethical standards. In addition, business owners and managers should (29)... standard operating procedures and performance measurements within the company to ensure that they are not structured in a way that encourages unethical behavior. As Ben & Jerry's Ice Cream founders Ben Cohen and Jerry Greenfield stated, "a values-led business seeks to maximize its impact by (30)... socially beneficial actions into as many of its day-to-day activities as possible. In order to do that, values must lead and be right up there in a company's mission statement, strategy and operating plan."

21.	A. employ	B. implement	C. wield	D. execute
22.	A. executing	B. performing	C. fulfilling	D. exerting
23.	A. presiding	B. attending	C. devoting	D. participating
24.	A. navigate	B. steer	C. drive	D. lead
25.	A. standard	B. scene	C. action	D. behavior
26.	A. together	B. similarly	C. alike	D. equally
27.	A. appears	B. exists	C. occurs	D. arises
28.	A. tally	B. coherent	C. dovetail	D. match
29.	A. read	B. guarantee	C. test	D. review
30.	A. integrating	B. completing	C. gathering	D. putting

PART FIVE
Questions 31—40

- Read the article below about pressures on ethical principles.

· For each question 31—40, write one word in CAPITAL LETTERS on your Answer Sheet.

Competitive Pressures on Ethical Principles

American society places a great emphasis on success, (31)... in and of itself is not a bad thing. It is perfectly justifiable to want to make full (32)... of one's talents and provide for oneself and one's family. People involved in the world of business, (33)..., often face situations in which advancement—whether in position, influence, or financial stature—can be gained, but only by hurting other individuals or groups. Small business owners are confronted (34)... these choices even more often than other people of the business world because of the greater degree of autonomy in decision-making that they often enjoy. Moreover, the ethical decisions of small business owners are likely to impact far greater numbers of people (35)... are the ethical decisions of that business owner's employees. Very often, an employee's ethical choices (to claim credit for the work done by another, to falsify number of hours worked, etc.) have (36)... impact on a relatively small number of people, usually co-workers or his or her employer. The ethical choices of business owners, however—whether to use inferior materials (37)... preparing goods for customers, whether to place employees in a poor HMO, whether to lay off a dozen workers (38)... of careless personal financial expenditures, etc. often have far more wide-ranging repercussions. Indeed, the pressure to make morally compromised choices on behalf of the company you lead can be quite powerful, (39)... the enterprise is a lone clothing store or a regional chain of record stores, especially when you feel the health and vitality of your enterprise may be at (40)...

PART SIX
Questions 41—52

· Read the text below from a report about ethical dilemmas.

· In most lines (41—52), there is one extra word. It either is grammatically incorrect or does not fit in with the sense of the text. Some lines, however, are correct.

· If a line is correct, write CORRECT on your Answer Sheet.

· If there is an extra word in the line, write the extra word in CAPITAL LETTERS on your Answer Sheet.

Ethical Dilemmas

41. Most of people involved in business—whether functioning as a small business owner, employee,

42. or chief executive officer of a multinational company—eventually face ethical or moral dilemmas

43. in the workplace. Such dilemmas are usually complex, for they force the person making the wrong

44. decision to weigh out the benefits that various business decisions impart on individuals

him or

45. herself and groups with the negative repercussions that those same decisions they usually have on other individuals or groups. LaRue Hosmer, a business ethics expert who teaches at the

46. University of Michigan, observed that reaching at a "right" or "just" conclusion when faced with moral problems can be a bewildering and vexing proposition. But he contended that business

47. people are likely to reach and act on morally appropriate decisions if only they do not lose sight of

48. the fundamental issue of fairness. Those who get sidetracked by issues of profitability and legality

49. in gauging the morality of a business decision making, on the other hand, often reach ethically

50. skewed choices. As has been proven time and again in the business world, the legality of a course

51. of action may be utterly irrelevant to its "rightness." In addition, any such discussion of business

52. ethics is a subjective one, for everyone brings in different concepts of ethical behavior to the table.

These moral standards are shaped by all sorts of things, from home environment to religious upbringing to cultural traditions.

第10单元 电子商务
Unit 10 Electronic Business①

Text A

I. 课文导读

随着互联网的普及,人们的交际活动越来越频繁。通过互联网接收和发送邮件进行网上购物,已经成为很多人的日常行为。与此同时,一些公司利用互联网开始了和他们与顾客的第一次沟通,而另外一些公司则运用互联网和他们的客户进行着交易。网络市场的高效性和低廉的交易成本使大量买家和卖家在此聚集,形成了电子商务。互联网在减少公司开支,全方位的向客户提供服务,帮助公司进入新的市场等方面提供了很大的便利。在当今社会,如果一个公司不能及时实现业务网络化,那么他们将会有可能在激烈的市场竞争中被淘汰。

II. Text

In five years' time, says Andy Grove, the chairman of Intel, all companies will be Internet companies, or they won't be companies at all. The Internet is said to be both over-hyped② and undervalued. Internet is the most transforming invention in human history. It has the capacity to change everything—the way we work, the way we learn and play, even, maybe, the way we sleep or have sex. What is more, it is doing so at far greater speed than the other great disruptive③ technologies of the 20th century, such as electricity, the telephone and the car.

Everybody loves e-mail; if you are a teenage girl, chat is cool; and the ability to retrieve information about so many things is truly miraculous, even if search engines are a bit clunky④. Despite early misgivings about credit-card security, buying certain kinds of things on the web—for example, books, CDs and personal computers—is convenient and economical, and has become popular. All these things are certainly nice to have, but they could hardly be called revolutionary.

But while the media have concentrated on just a few aspects of the web—the glamorous

---

① 电子商务可为 e-business 或者 e-commerce
② over-hype: 夸张
③ disruptive: 颠覆性的
④ clunky: 笨拙的

consumer side of content① and shopping on the one hand, and the seamy② end of pornography and extremist rantings③ on the other—something much more important is happening behind the scenes: e-business. The Internet is turning business upside down and inside out. It is fundamentally changing the way companies operate, whether in high-tech or metal-bashing④. This goes far beyond buying and selling over the Internet, or e-business, and deep into the processes and culture of an enterprise.

Some companies are using the Internet to make direct connections with their customers for the first time. Others are using secure Internet connections to intensify relations with some of their trading partners, and using the Internet's reach and ubiquity⑤ to request quotes or sell off perishable stocks of goods or services by auction. Entirely new companies and business models are emerging in industries ranging from chemicals to road haulage⑥ to bring together buyers and sellers in super-efficient new electronic marketplaces.

The Internet is helping companies to lower costs dramatically across their supply and demand chains, take their customer service into a different league, enter new markets, create additional revenue streams⑦ and redefine their business relationships. What Mr. Grove was really saying was that if in five years' time a company is not using the Internet to do some or all of these things; it will be destroyed by competitors who are.

Most senior managers no longer need convincing. A recent worldwide survey of 500 large companies carried out jointly by the Economist Intelligence Unit (a sister company of The Economist) and Booz Allen Hamilton Inc., a consultancy⑧, found that more than 90% of top managers believe the Internet will transform or have a big impact on the global marketplace by 2001.

That message is endorsed by Forrester Research, a fashionable high-tech consultancy. It argues that e-business in America is about to reach a threshold from which it will accelerate into "hyper-growth". Inter-company trade of goods over the Internet, it forecasts, will double every year over the next five years, surging from $43 billion last year to $1.3 trillion in 2003. If the value of services exchanged or booked online were included as well, the figures would be more staggering⑨ still.

That makes Forrester's forecasts of business-to-consumer e-business over the same period—rise from $8 billion to $108 billion—look positively modest. There are two explanations: business-to-business spending in the economy is far larger than consumer spending, and businesses

---

① content: 满意
② seamy: 丑恶的
③ rantings: 咆哮
④ metal-bashing: 金属敲击——舆论界的这种叫法是指撞击废铜烂铁而制作成的音乐
⑤ ubiquity: 无所不在
⑥ road haulage: 公路运输
⑦ revenue stream: 收益来源
⑧ consultancy: 顾问公司
⑨ staggering: 令人惊愕的

are more willing and able than individuals to use the Internet.

Forrester expects Britain and Germany to go into the same hyper-growth stage of e-business about two years after America, with Japan, France and Italy a further two years behind. And just as countries will move into e-business hyper-growth at different times, so too will whole industries. For example, computing and electronics embraced the Internet early and will therefore reach critical mass earlier than the rest. Aerospace, telecoms and cars are not far behind. Other conditions for early take-off include the ready availability of the right kind of software, computing platforms and systems-integration expertise①.

Just as crucial is the impact of so-called "network effects" as online business moves from a handful of evangelizing② companies with strong market clout③, such as Cisco Systems, General Electric, Dell, Ford and Visa, to myriad④ suppliers and customers. As both buyers and sellers reduce their costs and increase their efficiency by investing in the capacity to do business on the Internet, it is in their interest to persuade more and more of their business partners to do the same, thus creating a self-reinforcing circle.

However, even within particular industries companies are moving at different speeds. Much depends on the competition they are exposed to, both from fast-moving traditional rivals and from Internet-based newcomers. But nobody can afford to be complacent⑤. Successful new e-businesses can emerge from nowhere. Recent experience suggests it takes little more than two years for such a start-up to formulate⑥ an innovative business idea, establish a web presence and begin to dominate its chosen sector. By then it may be too late for slow-moving traditional businesses to respond.

For evidence of how far most companies still have to go in developing their Internet strategies, look no further than their corporate websites. A few pioneers—such as Charles Schwab in stock broking and Dell in the PC business—have successfully transferred many of their core activities to the web, and some others may be trying their hand at a few web transactions, with an eye on developing their site as an extra distribution channel later. But more often than not, those websites are stodgily⑦ designed billboards, known in the business as "brochure⑧ ware", which do little more than provide customers and suppliers with some fairly basic information about the company and its products.

Most managers know perfectly well that they have to do better. The Yankee Group, another technology consultancy, earlier this year questioned 250 large and medium-sized American com-

---

① expertise: 专业技能
② evangelize: 传福音
③ clout: 影响力
④ myriad: 无数的
⑤ complacent: 自满的
⑥ formulate: 规划
⑦ stodgily: 死板地
⑧ brochure: 小册子

panies across a broad range of industries about their views on e-business, and found that 58% of corporate decision makers considered the web to be important or very important to their business strategy. Only 13% thought it not important at all. A large majority (83%) named "building brand awareness" and "providing marketing information" as key tasks for their websites, and almost as many (77%) thought the web was important for generating revenue. A smaller majority (57%) also saw its potential for cutting costs in sales and customer support. Yet despite all this positive talk, three-quarters did not yet have websites that would support online transactions or tie in with their customer databases and those of their suppliers, although many were working on it.

In other words, most bosses know what they should be doing, but have not yet got around to it. It is easy to understand why. Knowing that you need a coherent e-business strategy is one thing, getting one is altogether more difficult. And until you decide precisely what your strategy should be, it will not be clear what kind of IT infrastructure investments① you will need to make.

Ⅲ. Notes

1. Intel(英特尔公司). Intel Corporation is an American multinational semiconductor chip maker corporation headquartered in Santa Clara, California, United States and the world's largest semiconductor chip maker, based on revenue. It is the inventor of the x86 series of microprocessors, the processors found in most personal computers. Intel was founded on July 18, 1968, as Integrated Electronics Corporation (though a common misconception is that "Intel" is from the word intelligence). Intel also makes motherboard chipsets, network interface controllers and integrated circuits, flash memory, graphic chips, embedded processors and other devices related to communications and computing.

2. The Economist Intelligence Unit (《经济学人》情报部 EIU). It is part of the Economist Group. It is a research and advisory company providing country, industry and management analysis worldwide and incorporates the former Business International Corporation, a U. S. company acquired by the parent organization in 1986. It is particularly well known for its monthly country reports, five-year country economic forecasts, country risk service reports and industry reports. The company also specializes in tailored research for companies that require analysis for particular markets or business sectors. 2006 marked the 60th anniversary of the Economist Intelligence Unit's inception.

3. The Economist(《经济学家》). The Economist is an English-language weekly news and international affairs publication owned by The Economist Newspaper Ltd. and edited in offices in the City of Westminster, London, England. Continuous publication began under founder James Wilson in September 1843. While The Economist refers to itself as a newspaper, each print edition appears on glossy paper, like a news magazine. In 2009, it reported an average cir-

---

① infrastructure investments: 基础设施投资

culation of just over 1.6 million copies per issue, above half of which are sold in North America and English speaking countries.

4. Booz Allen Hamilton Inc. (BAH) (博思艾伦管理和技术咨询公司). It is an American public consulting firm headquartered in McLean, Fairfax County, Virginia, with 80 other offices throughout the United States. The firm was founded by Edwin Booz in Chicago circa 1914. It is listed as number 438 in the 2011 Fortune 500 and is listed as the 9th largest US Government contractor (the largest for consulting services) by Washington Technology magazine in 2011.

5. Forrester Research (美国福雷斯特研究公司). An independent technology and market research company that provides its clients with advice about technology's impact on business and consumers. Forrester Research has five research centers in the US. It also has four European research centers. The firm has 27 sales locations worldwide. It offers a variety of services including syndicated research on technology as it relates to business, quantitative market research on consumer technology adoption as well as enterprise IT spending, research-based consulting and advisory services, events, workshops, teleconferences, and executive peer-networking programs.

6. Cisco Systems (思科系统公司). Cisco Systems, Inc. is an American multinational corporation headquartered in San Jose, California, United States, that designs and sells consumer electronics, networking, voice, and communications technology and services. Cisco has more than 70,000 employees and annual revenue of US $40.0 billion as of 2010. Cisco's current portfolio of products and services is focused upon three market segments-Enterprise and Service Provider, Small Business and the Home.

7. General Electric (通用电气公司). GE is an American multinational conglomerate corporation incorporated in Schenectady, New York and headquartered in Fairfield, Connecticut, United States. The company operates through four segments: Energy, Technology Infrastructure, Capital Finance and Consumer & Industrial.

8. Dell (戴尔公司). Dell, Inc. is an American multinational information technology corporation which develops, sells and supports computers and related products and services. Bearing the name of its founder, Michael Dell, the company is one of the largest technological corporations in the world, employing more than 103,300 people worldwide. Dell is listed at number 41 in the Fortune 500 list.

9. Visa (维萨公司). Visa Inc. is an American multinational financial services corporation headquartered on 595 Market Street, Financial District in San Francisco, California, United States, although much of the company's staff is based in Foster City, California. It facilitates electronic funds transfers throughout the world, most commonly through Visa-branded credit card and debit cards.

10. The Charles Schwab Corporation (嘉信理财集团). An American brokerage and banking company, based in San Francisco, California., It was founded in 1971 by Charles R. as a traditional, brick and mortar brokerage firm and investment newsletter publisher. In 1973, the company name changed from First Commander Corporation to Charles Schwab & Co., Inc. The company started offering discount brokerage on May 1, 1975, and would become one of the world's largest discount brokers. In 2009, Chairman Charles R. Schwab received the inaugural Tiburon CEO Summit award for Maintaining a Focus on Consumer Needs.

11. Yankee Group(扬基集团). A Massachusetts company, sells advice and market-research information relating to information technology. Founded in 1970, the Yankee Group emerged as the first independent technology research and consulting firm. Launched by Howard Anderson and focused on market research surrounding major telecommunications service providers, the Yankee Group went through a re-branding in 2005 after it was acquired from Reuters by Emily Nagle Green and Alta Communications. Yankee Group believes that the emergence of a seamless, ever-present, high capacity, highly-capable network will transform social and business interactions over the next 20 years.

Ⅳ. Useful Expressions

1. concentrate on: 集中精力做某事
2. a handful of: 少量
3. a self-reinforcing circle: 自我强化的循环圈
4. be exposed to: 暴露于
5. corporate website: 公司网站
6. distribution channel: 分销渠道
7. more often than not: 经常,往往
8. get round to: 着手做某事（包含拖延之意）

Ⅴ. Reading Comprehension

Questions

1. In what ways does Internet turn business upside down and inside out?
2. What are the complaints about Internet?
3. What can we infer from the difference between the two forecasts of inter-company trade of goods and business-to-consumer e-business?
4. What are the main functions of the Internet for companies?
5. What does it mean by 'evangelizing companies with strong market clout'?

Decide whether each of the following statements is true or false.

1. Internet, as the most transforming invention, has changed the traditional way of business. (   )
2. Buying and selling on Internet can be called revolutionary. (   )
3. Nowadays, some companies are using the Internet to sell stocks by auction. (   )
4. Electronic business can lower the cost of a company but increase the risks. (   )
5. In future five years, a company which does not use Internet to do business could fail in competition. (   )
6. Individuals are less willing and unable to shop on Internet. (   )

7. Computing and electronics have a closer relationship with the Internet than others.   (   )

8. It costs much time and money to build a company on Internet to do business.   (   )

9. Transferring many of their core activities to the web makes the success of Charles Schwab and Dell.   (   )

10. Brochure ware provides customers with all of information about the product and the suppliers.   (   )

Ⅵ. Discussion

What do you think are the advantages and disadvantages of e-business?

Text B
BEC Reading Texts

PART ONE
Questions 1—8

- Look at the statements below and the five extracts about e-commerce from an article.
- Which extract (A, B, C, D or E) does each statement (1—8) refer to?
- For each statement (1—8), make one letter (A, B, C, D or E) on your Answer Sheet.
- You will need to use some of these letters more than once.

1. The acceleration of e-commerce is in want of relative regulations or rules.

2. Discussion continues to revolve around whether e-commerce should be considered as trade in goods or in services.

3. E-commerce is becoming more social and more connected to the offline world.

4. In the last decade, many startup e-commerce accelerates the development of telecom products.

5. The Internet has created a new economic ecosystem, the e-commerce marketplace.

6. Doing business on the Internet is becoming the indispensable part of people's daily life.

7. The development of e-commerce, in turn, has motivated the growing of global economy.

8. Many e-commerce service providers stand to gain as e-commerce traffic accelerates.

A. The e-commerce market has become the virtual main street of the world. Providing a quick and convenient way of exchanging goods and services both regionally and globally, e-commerce has boomed. Today, e-commerce has grown into a huge industry with US online retail generating ＄175B in revenues in 2007. With more than 70% of Americans using the Internet on a daily basis for private and/or business use and the rest of the world also beginning to catch on, e-commerce's global growth curve is not likely to taper off anytime soon.

B. Global Internet penetration rates have an enormous impact on e-commerce growth rates. Currently, more than 30.2% of the world has access to the internet, and hence, e-commerce. Reduced Internet surfing charges, Internet technology development covering expanded bandwidth, and increased speeds & reliability could make e-commerce available to a large pool of emerging market consumers. In China, the internet penetration rate is now at 29% as of June 2010.

C. Many companies interested in selling products and services through the Internet choose to contract the construction and operation of their e-commerce platforms to third-party vendors. Some of these companies, such as Volusion e-commerce, GSI Commerce (GSIC), Web Cube and Digital River (DRIV) offer comprehensive, integrated packages that include software, web-hosting, order fulfillment and distribution and online marketing. Other firms offer more limited services such as Ariba (ARBA) and Akamai Technologies (AKAM).

D. Perhaps the clearest indication of the growing importance of e-commerce in the global economy is the rapidity with which Internet use has grown and spread during the last decade. The boom in e-commerce also includes increased use of other media for trade, such as the telephone, television, fax, and electronic payment. Because e-commerce became such an integral part of the global economy, the WTO has begun to consider how it fits into the multilateral trade framework, and what rules or regulations should apply.

E. Developing countries, particularly those without strong e-commerce sectors, are in favor of classifying e-commerce as trade in services. They argue that they need the flexibility of regulating e-commerce in order to nurture their own industries, and that liberalizing too soon would give an unfair advantage to the e-commerce industries in developed countries. Developing countries such as India and China who have booming e-commerce sectors are in favor of liberalizing trade in e-commerce, but would prefer to do so under the GATS so that they can begin with industries that have a comparative advantage.

PART TWO
Questions 9—14

- Read the text about the transaction on the internet.
- Choose the best sentence to fill each of the gaps.
- For each gap (9—14), mark one letter (A-H) on your Answer Sheet.
- Do not use any letter more than once.

Transacting Business via Electronic Data

The term e-commerce embraces all the ways of transacting business via electronic data. (9)..., and it is the internet that has put e-commerce near the top of the corporate agenda in the first years of the 21st century.

(10)..., but it embodies a revolutionary idea: that electronic commerce is qualitatively different from ordinary time-worn commerce, that (in the jargon) there is a paradigm shift in the way that business is conducted in the world of e-commerce. Doing business via the internet is not only much quicker and much cheaper than other methods, (11)... There is the much-vaunted death of distance: a customer 10,000 miles away becomes as accessible as one around the corner. And e-commerce has created the phenomenon of the long tail.

(12)... In its April 1999 report "Making Open Finance Pay", Forrester Research, an American research company, gave examples of the way in which the internet had altered the pricing structure of a number of industries, particularly those with high information content. Before the advent of the internet it cost $100 to make an equity market order. Afterwards it cost just $15, an 85% fall in price, far more than could ever have been gleaned from traditional economies of scale. This is a revolution for organizations whose structures and strategies have built-in assumptions about relationships between price and volume.

(13)... Online sales in the United States are reckoned to have grown by some 18% in 2007. The country's five largest online retailers (often called e-tailers) were Amazon, Staples, Office Depot, Dell and Hewlett-Packard. Dell became a market leader in computers through early use of the internet to sell goods and services direct to consumers, and to buy components from suppliers.

Financial service offerings over the internet have also sprouted like mushrooms, (14)... At Charles Schwab, an American retail brokerage firm, it took just three years for online dealing to account for more than half of all its securities trading.

A. Furthermore, economies of scale are undermined

B. although security issues have imposed some restraint on the industry

C. E-commerce is merely an elision of electronic commerce

D. E-commerce also allows unknown firms to establish new businesses cheaply and rapidly

E. Electronic commerce has grown rapidly

F. But it is most closely identified with commerce transacted over the internet

G. though the security challenges is being faced as a result of engaging in electronic commerce

H. it is also thought to overturn old rules about time, space and price

PART THREE
Questions 15—20

· Read the following article on three pillars of electronic commerce.

· For each question (15—20) mark one letter (A, B, C or D) on your Answer Sheet for the answer you choose.

An electronic business model that builds on traditional market spaces is the three pillars of electronic commerce model by Peter Fingar. At the foundation of the model is the existing market space. Three electronic pillars support open market processes: electronic information, electronic relationships, and electronic transactions. Thus, this model builds on the existing market space and utilizes electronic mechanisms as an enabler of supporting open market processes.

The first pillar is electronic information. The WWW is viewed as a "global repository" of documents and multimedia data. Constructing an electronic information pillar is easy: most word processing software packages will easily convert documents into a web-readable format. The challenge is to construct a good, solid pillar that will not crumble, or in WWW terms, the web page does not freeze-up or links do not lead the visitor to a dead-end or having them wandering through a maze of links without easily finding the necessary information. Thus, the construction of the electronic information pillar should not be conducted in a shoddy fashion, or it will not adequately support the objective of an open market. The retrieval of the desired electronic information is the cause of frustration to many web "surfers. " Search engines and other intelligent agents are increasing in popularity to assist users to more efficiently and effectively navigate the WWW.

The second pillar, electronic relationships, is the central pillar. The saying "If you build it, they will come" does not apply to web-site based electronic commerce. Placing information on products and service offerings on a web site does not mean that potential customers or guests will visit that web site a first time, and it especially does not mean that a user will return to the site. The electronic relationships pillar is about building a site that has the feeling of being a "port of entry" into a community. Having entrants pass through this port of entry on a somewhat regular basis is the key to successfully engaging in electronic commerce. In order to attract users over and over again to a site (which also means away from other sites), the site needs to have certain features; it must: (1) Be innovative; (2) Add value; (3) Provide information and interaction not otherwise available; and (4) Create forums for opinion-building activities.

The third pillar is the electronic transactions pillar. Many businesses have built an electronic information pillar and some have built or are building an electronic community pillar, but substantially fewer have constructed the electronic transaction pillar. Two impediments to constructing the pillar exist: the ability to engage in meaningful and sufficient negotiation processes and security of transaction data.

15. Which is the base of the electronic business model?
A. The electronic information.
B. The existing market space.
C. The electronic relationship.
D. The electronic transaction.
16. What is our aim to construct an electronic information pillar?
A. Converting the documentary information into a web-readable format.
B. Enabling the potential consumers easily to find the necessary information.
C. Collecting documents and multimedia data from the internet.
D. Constructing a good, solid web page which can provide the information.
17. Why is the electronic relationships the central pillar. ?

A. Because the wed page readers can't find the information by themselves.

B. Because the potential customers do not return to the site to find information.

C. Because the web site should play the role of "port of entry" into a community.

D. Because a web site won't work if only you find some way to attract and keep the consumers.

18. Which is not the information we can learn from the third pillar?

A. The electronic transaction pillar is a guarantee of a successful negotiation in the transaction.

B. There are still some obstructions in building the electronic transaction pillar.

C. The electronic transaction pillar is a system of security in transaction.

D. Building electronic transaction pillar is to make an efficient and safe transaction.

19. In order to build good customer relationships, electronic commerce web sites need to be designed to

A. be innovative and attractive.

B. provide information and interaction not otherwise available.

C. create forums for opinion-building activities. .

D. give potential customers the feeling of community and interaction they are increasingly expecting.

20. What is the main idea of the text?

A. There are three main pillars that support the e-commerce.

B. We should pay attention on making an interactive relationship.

C. E-commerce is ramping up at a good rate.

D. The internet is the substantial media in e-commerce.

PART FOUR
Questions 21—30

· Read the article below about the impact of electronic commerce on business models.

· Choose the correct word to fill each gap from A, B, C or D.

· For each question (21—30), mark one letter (A, B, C or D) on your Answer Sheet.

Impact of Electronic Commerce

Today's forward thinking CEO recognizes the (21)... of e-commerce as a strategic business issue, not just one more technical issue to be (22)... to the IS department, perhaps the existing EDI group. Although a company may have reengineered its (23)... business process and perhaps painfully installed an ERP system to bring inefficiencies to the back office, e-commerce is about reengineering outward-facing processes-industry process reengineering.

(24)..., electronic commerce is not just a technology, it is a way of (25)... business that has the potential to impact every aspect of the firm's value chain. Implementing full-scale, innovative applications of electronic commerce requires management teams to view the marketplace beyond the typical physical boundaries.

The biggest problem that electronic commerce pioneers encounter is the limited set of mental models that (26)... our thinking. We tend to think of the web in our "industrial age" (27)... — where everything must be described and related to the physical world.

If electronic commerce applications are not placed in the proper business context and the strategy (28)... with the business' overall business strategy, then the electronic commerce application is likely to fail. Thus, new business models are necessary that (29)... electronic commerce initiatives with overall business goals. So first of all, we should discuss the need to align a firm's on-line strategy with its overall business strategy. (30)... that discussion, emerging business paradigms that fully embrace the electronic commerce philosophy are going to be discussed, including a new view of the value chain.

21. A. problem   B. challenge   C. importance   D. doubt
22. A. represented   B. appointed   C. replaced   D. delegated
23. A. internal   B. external   C. inward   D. outward
24. A. Thus   B. Besides   C. However   D. Further
25. A. making   B. managing   C. running   D. conducting
26. A. bound   B. provoke   C. constrain   D. control
27. A. illusion   B. vision   C. paradigm   D. form
28. A. connected   B. linked   C. aligned   D. combined
29. A. combine   B. integrate   C. assemble   D. ally
30. A. Concerning   B. Following   C. After   D. Beside

PART FIVE
Questions 31—40

· Read the article below about the role of e-commerce as a powerful business channel.

· For each question 31—40, write one word in CAPITAL LETTERS on your Answer Sheet.

E-commerce, A Powerful Business Channel

Electronic commerce has the promise to be a very powerful business channel. Many "traditional" businesses such as General Electric, American Airlines, and US Air have (31)... successfully implemented successful web-based strategies. New businesses, such as Amazon.com, are challenging many traditional businesses to rethink the (32)... they conduct business. The success of Amazon.com has prompted many, previously "traditional" businesses, such as the bookstore retailer, Barnes and Noble, to (33)... the electronic commerce arena.

When implemented properly and when aligned (34)... the firm's overall corporate strategy, electronic commerce can significantly enhance the operations of a firm. The potential benefits of electronic commerce to businesses depend on the extent of implementation and also the industry in (35)... the firm operates. The outlook for web-based revenues is particularly (36)... for the travel, financial services, computing hardware and software industries. The primary benefits to consumers are convenience, access to information, and price comparison. All of these benefits to the consumer (37)... in more buying power.

(38)... business models and the value chain are no longer representatives of the virtual society in which electronic commerce operates. The value chain of electronic commerce-based companies places the customer as the center of focus with a sharing of data throughout all processes of the value chain and the customer.

Besides, the (39)... of electronic commerce depends on the assurance in which businesses and customers place in its underlying systems. Security is often cited as the number one impediment (40)... the growth of electronic commerce.

PART SIX
Questions 41—52

· Read the text below from a report about online shopping.

· In most lines (41—52), there is one extra word. It either is grammatically incorrect or does not fit in with the sense of the text. Some lines, however, are correct.

· If a line is correct, write CORRECT on your Answer Sheet.

· If there is an extra word in the line, write the extra word in CAPITAL LETTERS on your Answer Sheet.

Shopping Online

41. In America, women now outnumber over men online; the average age of all web surfers is
42. increasing; their level of education is decreasing; and their average spending is growing. In a
43. short, online consumers are rapidly becoming just like offline consumers. So it should be come
44. as no surprise that, just as it was on the high street, clothing was the biggest category of goods
45. sold online in America at last Christmas. Similar trends are already evident in Europe and will no
46. doubt spread to Asia. But e-commerce involves in a lot more than retail sales and services such as travel, in which more than half of all bookings are expected to move online within a few years.
47. For instance, with billions of dollars of used goods are now sold on internet auction sites, notably on the hugely successful eBay. Second-hand cars are now eBay's biggest category, sales that
48. many once thought would be impossible to conduct on the internet. Some of the big American
49. dotcoms are now finding that growth is accelerating even faster than overseas: eBay's

Chinese service, for instance, is already the biggest e-commerce site in that country. Then there are the

50. billions spent on buying everything from pornography to financial services—and this does not

51. include business-to-business (B2B) services, already worth more than ＄1 trillion a year according

52. to some estimates. Wal-Mart, for one reason, now conducts all its business with suppliers over a proprietary B2B network.

第 11 单元 信息时代的会计
Unit 11 Accounting in the Information Age

Text A

Ⅰ. 课文导读

我们生活在一个信息时代,及时获得有效和可靠的信息至关重要。会计在信息时代逐渐凸显出其不可替代的作用。根据会计信息使用的主体不同,会计可以分为管理会计和财务会计。一些国际准则和国际协会对会计信息的使用提出了具体要求。会计等式是由会计要素组成,"资产=负债+所有者权益"这一基本会计等式体现了会计要素之间的平衡关系。会计人员职业素养的形成非常重要,遵循会计职业道德应当贯穿于会计活动的各个环节。

Ⅱ. Text

Now we live in an information age, where information and its reliability greatly influence our financial well-being. Accounting is playing an increasingly important role in this age. Knowledge of accounting gives us career opportunities and the insight to take advantage of them. Accounting is also called the language of business, as all organizations set up an accounting information system to communicate data to help people make better decisions.

Accounting is defined by the American Institute of Certified Public Accountants (AICPA) as "the art of recording, classifying, and summarizing in a significant manner and in terms of money, transactions and events which are, in part at least, of financial character, and interpreting the results thereof." Accounting is a standard set of rules for measuring a firm's financial performance. Evaluating a company's financial performance is crucial for many groups.

Accounting that focuses on reporting to people inside the business entity is called management accounting① and is used to provide information to employees, managers, and auditors②. Management accounting is concerned primarily with providing a basis for making management or operating decisions.

Accounting that provides information to people outside the business entity is called financial accounting③ and provides information to present and potential shareholders, creditors, such as

---

① management accounting: 管理会计
② auditors: 审计员
③ financial accounting: 财务会计

banks or vendors①, financial analysts②, economists, and government agencies. Standard financial statements also serve as a yardstick③ of communicating financial performance to the general public. For example, monthly sales volumes released by Kentucky Fried Chicken (KFC)'s Corp. provide both its managers and the general public with an opportunity to evaluate the company's financial performance across major geographic segments④.

The purpose of accounting is to provide a means of identifying, recording and communicating relevant, reliable, and comparable information about an organization's business activities. Identifying business activities requires selecting transactions and events relevant to an organization. Recording business activities requires keeping a chronological log⑤ of transactions and events measured in dollars and classified and summarized in a useful format. Communicating business activities requires preparing accounting reports such as financial statements⑥. It also requires analyzing and interpreting such reports. In order to do this, an accounting system must be designed. A system design serves the needs of users of accounting information. Once a system has been designed, reports can be issued and decisions based upon these reports are made for various departments.

Since accounting is used by everyone in one form or another, a good understanding of accounting principles is beneficial to all. As different users have different needs, the presentation of financial accounting is very structured and subject to many more rules than management accounting. The body of rules that governs financial accounting in a given jurisdiction⑦ is called Generally Accepted Accounting Principles (GAAP). To use and interpret financial statements effectively, we need to understand these principles, which can change over time in response to the demands of users. GAAP aims to make information in financial statements relevant, reliable, and comparable. Relevant information affects the decisions of its users. Reliable information is trusted by users. Comparable information is helpful in contrasting organizations.

In today's global economy, there is increased demand by external users for comparability in accounting reports. This often arises when companies wish to raise money from lenders and investors in different countries. To that end, the International Accounting Standards Board (IASB) issues⑧ International Financial Reporting Standards (IFRS) that identify preferred accounting practices. The IASB hopes to create more harmony among accounting practices of different countries. If standards are harmonized, one company can potentially use a single set of financial statements in all financial markets. Many countries' standard setters support the IASB, and

---

① vendor: 经销商
② financial analyst: 财务分析员
③ yardstick: 标准
④ geographical segment: 地理分区
⑤ chronological log: 按时间顺序的日志
⑥ financial statement: 财务报表
⑦ jurisdiction: 管辖权;管辖范围
⑧ Issue: 颁布

differences between U. S. GAAP and IASB's practices are fading. Yet, the IASB does not have authority to impose① its standards on companies.

The basic accounting equation② is the foundation for the double-entry bookkeeping system③. It reflects two basic aspects of a company: what it owns and what it owes. For each transaction, the total debits equal the total credits.

Assets, liabilities④ and equity⑤ are the basic elements of the accounting equation. The excess of assets over liabilities is owner's equity. Thus, assets are equal to liabilities plus owner's equity at all times. Any business transaction has to affect at least one of these elements. Assets are resources with future benefits that are owned or controlled by a company. Examples are cash, supplies equipment, and land. The claims on a company's assets—what it owes—are separated into owner and nonowner claims. Liabilities are what a company owes its nonowners (creditors) in future payments, products, or services. Equity (also called owner's equity or capital) refers to the claims of its owners. In a corporation, it represents the stockholders' equity. Together, liabilities and equity are the source of funds to acquire assets.

The relation of assets, liabilities, and owner's equity is reflected in the following accounting equation:

Assets = Liabilities + Equity.

Liabilities are usually shown before equity in this equation because creditors' claims must be paid before the claims of owners. (The terms in this equation can be rearranged; for example, Assets-Liabilities = Equity.) The accounting equation applies to all transactions and events, to all companies and forms of organization, and to all points in time. For example, Lenovo's assets equal $18,650, its liabilities equal $8,450, and its equity equals $10,200 ($ in millions).

An elaborate form of this equation is presented in a balance sheet⑥ which lists all assets, liabilities, and owner's equity, as well as totals to ensure that it balances. The balance sheet is also called the statement of financial position. The purpose of this statement is to demonstrate where the company stands, in financial terms, at a specific date. The date is important, as the financial position of a business may change quickly. Every business prepares a balance sheet at the end of the year, and many companies prepare one at the end of each month.

Accounting is often confused with bookkeeping. Bookkeeping is concerned with the recording of business data, while accounting is concerned with the design, interpretation of data, and the preparation of financial reports. Three forms of business entities exist: 1) sole proprietorship⑦, 2) partnership, and 3) corporations. Corporations have the unique status of being a sepa-

---

① impose: 强制
② accounting equation: 会计等式
③ double-entry bookkeeping system: 复式记账法
④ liabilities: 负债
⑤ equity: 股票
⑥ balance sheet: 资产负债表
⑦ sole proprietorship: 独资企业

rate legal entity in which ownership is divided into shares of stock. A shareholder's liability is limited to his/her contribution to capital. Whenever a business transaction is recorded, it must be recorded to accounting records at cost. All business transactions must be recorded. All properties owned by businesses are assets. All debts are liabilities. The right of owners is equity.

We must guard against the narrow view of accounting. The most common contact with accounting is through credit approvals, checking accounts, tax forms, and payroll①. These experiences are limited and tend to focus on the recordkeeping parts of accounting. Recordkeeping, or bookkeeping, is the recording of transactions and events, either manually or electronically. This is just one part of accounting in scope. Accounting also identifies and communicates information on transactions and events, and it includes the crucial processes of analysis and interpretation.

Technology is a key part of modern business and plays a major role in accounting. Technology reduces the time, effort, and cost of recordkeeping while improving clerical accuracy②. Some small organizations continue to perform various accounting task manually, but even they are influenced by technology. As technology has changed the way we store, process, and summarize masses of data, accounting has been freed to expand. Consulting, planning, and other financial services are now closely linked to accounting. These services require sorting③ data, interpreting their meaning, identifying key factors, and analyzing their implications.

On the other hand, ethics are crucial to accounting. The goal of accounting is to provide useful information for decisions. For information to be useful, it must be trusted. This demands ethics in accounting. Ethics are beliefs that distinguish right from wrong. They are accepted standards of good and bad behavior. Providers of accounting information often face ethical choices as they prepare financial reports. These choices can affect the price a buyer pays and the wages paid to workers. They can even affect the success of products and services. Misleading information can lead to a wrongful closing of a division that harms workers, customers, and suppliers. There is an old saying: Good ethics are good business.

III. Notes

1. American Institute of Certified Public Accountants(美国注册会计师协会). Founded in 1887, AICPA is the national professional organization of Certified Public Accountants (CPAs) in the United States, with more than 370,000 CPA members in 128 countries in business and industry, public practice, government, education, student affiliates and international associates. It sets ethical standards for the profession and U.S. auditing standards for audits of private companies, non-profit organizations, federal, state and local governments. It develops and grades the Uniform CPA Examination. The AICPA maintains offices in New York City; Washington, DC; Durham, NC; and Ewing, NJ. The AICPA's founding establishes accountancy as a

---

① payroll: 工资表
② clerical accuracy: 办公准确性
③ sort: 整理

profession distinguished by rigorous educational requirements, high professional standards, a strict code of professional ethics, a licensing status, and a commitment to serving the public interest.

2. Kentucky Fried Chicken(KFC) 's Corp（肯德基公司）. It is a chain of fast food restaurants based in Louisville, Kentucky, in the United States. KFC has been a brand and operating segment, termed a concept of Yum Brands since 1997 when that company was spun off from PepsiCo as Tricon Global Restaurants Inc. KFC primarily sells chicken pieces, wraps, salads and sandwiches. While its primary focus is fried chicken, KFC also offers a line of grilled and roasted chicken products, side dishes and desserts. Outside the USA, KFC offers beef based products such as hamburgers or kebabs, pork based products such as ribs and other regional fare.

3. Lenovo（联想集团有限公司）. It is a Chinese multinational computer technology corporation that develops, manufactures and markets desktops and notebook personal computers, workstations, servers, , storage drives, IT management software, and related services. Incorporated as Legend in Hong Kong in 1988, Lenovo's executive headquarters are in Research Triangle Park, North Carolina, United States. . Lenovo's principal operations are currently located in Beijing, Morrisville, North Carolina, in the United States, and Singapore, with research centers in those locations, as well as Shanghai, Shenzhen, Xiamen, and Chengdu in China, and Yamato in Kanagawa Prefecture, Japan. Lenovo acquired the former IBM PC Company Division, which marketed the ThinkPad line of notebook PCs, in 2005 for approximately $1.75 billion.

4. Generally Accepted Accounting Principles（一般公认会计原则）. It refers to the standard framework of guidelines for financial accounting used in any given jurisdiction; generally known as Accounting Standards. GAAP includes the standards, conventions, and rules accountants follow in recording and summarizing, and in the preparation of financial statements.

5. International Accounting Standards Board（国际会计准则理事会）. It is an independent, privately funded accounting standard-setter based in London, England. The IASB was founded on April 1, 2001 as the successor to the International Accounting Standard Committee (IASC). It is responsible for developing International Financial Reporting Standards (the new name for International Accounting Standard issued after 2001), and promoting the use and application of these standards.

6. International Financial Reporting Standards（国际财务报告准则）. They are principles-based Standards, Interpretations and the Framework (1989) adopted by IASB. Many of the standards forming part of IFRS are known by the older name of International Accounting Standards (IAS). IAS were issued between 1973 and 2001 by the Board of the International Accounting Standard Committee (IASC). On 1 April 2001, the new IASB took over from the IASC the responsibility for setting International Accounting Standards. During its first meeting the new Board adopted existing IAS and SICs. The IASB has continued to develop standards calling the new standards IFRS.

7. Double-entry Bookkeeping System（复式记账法）. It is a set of rules for recording financial information in a financial accounting system in which every transaction or event changes at least two different ledger accounts. When each financial transaction is closely analyzed, it reveals two aspects. One aspect will be "receiving aspect" or "incoming aspect" or "expenses/loss aspect". This is termed as the "Debit aspect". The other aspect will be "giving aspect" or "outgoing aspect" or "income/gain aspect". This is termed as the "Credit aspect". The double entry system is so named since it records both the aspects of a transaction (as opposed to single-entry bookkeeping system) where both aspects are not always recorded).

8. Balance Sheet (资产负债表). In financial accounting, a balance sheet or statement of financial position is a summary of the financial balances of a sole proprietorship, a business partnership or a company. Assets, liabilities, and ownership equity are listed as of a specific date, such as the end of its financial year. A balance sheet is often described as a "snapshot of a company's financial condition". Of the four basic financial statements, the balance sheet is the only statement which applies to a single point in time of a business' calendar year.

Ⅳ. Useful Expressions

1. take the advantage of: 利用
2. serve as a yardstick of: 将……作为衡量标准
3. be subject to: 受...控制
4. in response to: 回应
5. impose upon/on: 强加于
6. masses of: 大量的
7. be crucial to: 对……很关键
8. credit and debit: 贷方和借方

Ⅴ. Reading Comprehension

Questions

1. What are the functions of accounting?
2. What's the difference between management accounting and financial accounting?
3. What is the accounting equation? What is the relationship between its elements?
4. What is the function of balance sheet?
5. What are the differences between accounting and bookkeeping?

Decide whether each of the following statements is true or false.

1. Accounting is a standard set of rules for measuring a firm's financial performance. (　)
2. Accounting that reports to people inside the business entity is called financial accounting. (　)
3. Communicating business activities requires preparing accounting reports such as a chronological log of transactions. (　)
4. Accounting principles will never change in the course of time. (　)

5. Assets, liabilities and equity are the basic elements of the accounting equation.   (   )
6. The accounting equation applies to most of transactions and events.   (   )
7. Every company prepares a balance sheet at the beginning of the year.   (   )
8. Accounting is indistinguishable with bookkeeping.   (   )
9. Technology plays a vital role in modern accounting.   (   )
10. Morals are of great significance to accounting.   (   )

VI. Discussion

What is your view on the saying: good ethics are good business?

Text B
BEC Reading Texts

PART ONE
Questions 1—8

- Look at the statements below and the five extracts about economic decision making from an article.
- Which extract (A, B, C, D or E) does each statement (1—8) refer to?
- For each statement (1—8), make one letter (A, B, C, D or E) on your Answer Sheet.
- You will need to use some of these letters more than once.

1. Evaluation of alternatives in economic decision making must take into account of the factor of comparability.
2. It discusses two characteristics of internal decision makers.
3. Users and accounting profession will decide whether accounting information is useful or not.
4. It distinguishes two branches of accounting corresponding to internal and external decision makers.
5. It analyzes the two parties which can determine the usefulness of accounting information
6. Internal and external decision makers play different roles in economic process.
7. It stresses the importance of comparability of accounting information in and economic decision making.
8. It introduces two categories of economic decision makers and their definition.

A. There are two parties that decide what accounting information is useful and what is not. One is the users. It is a grave mistake for economic decision makers to leave this decision up to the "experts". If the accounting profession is not providing the information users need, or is not preparing it in a way that makes sense, the users must demand a change. The second party that decides what accounting information is useful and what is not is the accounting profession—but always with the proviso that the information should be tailored to the needs of users.

B. The decisions made by internal and external decision makers are similar in some ways, but so different in other ways that two separate branches of accounting have developed to meet the needs of these two categories of user. The accounting information generated specifically for use by internal decision makers is the product of what is called management accounting, while that generated for use by external parties is the product of what is called financial accounting.

C. Much of human life revolves around economic issues. We will be better equipped to deal with these issues and their effects on our daily lives if we understand the economic decision-making process and the information that affects it. First, let's take a look at the people making economic decisions. Economic decision makers can be divided into two broad categories: internal and external. Internal decision makers are individuals within a company who make decisions on behalf of the company, while external decision makers are individuals or organizations outside a company who make decisions that affect that company.

D. The first characteristic of internal decision makers is they make decisions for the company. In other words, they act on behalf of the company. They decide such things as whether the company should sell a particular product, whether it should enter a certain market, and whether it should hire or fire employees. Note that in all of these matters, the responsible internal decision maker is not making the decision for herself of himself, but rather for the company. The second characteristic of internal decision makers is that they have greater access to the financial information of the company than do people outside the company.

E. Economic decision making involves the evaluation of alternatives. In order to be useful in such an evaluation, the accounting information for one alternative must be comparable to the accounting information for the other alternative(s). For example, assume you intend to make an investment and are considering two companies as investment alternatives. If the two companies use totally different accounting methods, you would find it very difficult to make a useful comparison. Comparability is an important quality of accounting information in many decision-making settings.

PART TWO
Questions 9—14

- Read the text about accounting.
- Choose the best sentence to fill each of the gaps.
- For each gap (9—14), mark one letter (A-H) on your Answer Sheet.
- Do not use any letter more than once.

Accounting

Many people think of accounting as a highly technical field which can be understood only by professional accountants. Actually, nearly everyone practices accounting in one form or another on an almost daily basis. (9)... Whether you are preparing a household budget, balancing your checkbook, or preparing your income tax return, you are working with accounting concepts and accounting information.

Accounting has often been called the "language of business." (10)... What are "corporate profits"? What levels of corporate profits are necessary to finance the development of new products, new jobs, and economic growth? One cannot hope to answer such questions without understanding the accounting concepts and terms involved in the measurement of income.

Since a language is a means of social communication, it is logical that a language should change to meet the changing needs of society. (11)... For example, as society has become increasingly interested in measurements more meaningful and more reliable. (12)... Although accounting has made its most dramatic progress in the field of business, the accounting functions is vital to every unit of our society. An individual must account for his or her income, and must file income tax returns. Often an individual must supply personal accounting information in order to buy a car or home, to quality for a college scholarship, to secure a credit card, or to obtain a bank loan. (13)... The federal government, the states, the cities, the school districts, all must use accounting as a basic for controlling their resources and measuring their accomplishments. Accounting is equally essential to the successful operation of a business, a university, a fraternity, a social program, or a city.

(14)... therefore, some knowledge of accounting is needed by all citizens if they are to act intelligently in meeting the challenges of our society.

A. Accounting has changed with the passage of time

B. In accounting, too, changes and improvements are continually being made

C. In very election the voters must make decisions at the ballot box on issues involving accounting concepts

D. We live in an era of accountability

E. Accounting has become an indispensable part of modern life

F. Large corporations are accountable to their stockholders, to governmental agencies, and to the public

G. In recent years, corporate profits have become a topic of considerable public interest

H. Accounting is the art of measuring, communicating, and interpreting financial activity

PART THREE
Questions 15—20

· Read the following article on some important accounting fields.

· For each question (15—20) mark one letter (A, B, C or D) on your Answer Sheet for the answer you choose.

As in many other areas of human activity during the twentieth century, a number of specialized fields in accounting have evolved as a result of technological advances and accelerated economic growth. The most important accounting fields are described briefly as follows.

Financial accounting is concerned with the recording of transactions for a business enterprise or other economic unit and the periodic preparation of various reports from such records. The reports, which may be for general purposes or for a special purpose, provide useful information for managers, owners, creditors, governmental agencies, and the general public. Of particular importance to financial accountants are the rules of accounting, and generally accepted accounting principles. Corporate enterprises must employ such principles in preparing their annual reports on profitability and financial status for their stockholders and the investing public.

Auditing is a field of activity involving an independent review of the accounting records. In conducting an audit, public accountants examine the records supporting the financial reports of an enterprise and give an opinion regarding their fairness and reliability. An important element of "fairness and reliability" is adherence to generally accepted accounting principles. In addition to retaining public accountants for a period audit, many corporations have their own permanent staff of internal auditors. Their principle responsibility is to determine if the various operating divisions are following management's policies and procedures. Cost accounting emphasizes the determination and the control of costs. It is concerned primarily with the costs of manufacturing processes and of manufactured products. In addition, one of the most important duties of the cost accountants is to gather and explain cost data, both actual and prospective.

Management uses these data in controlling current operations and in planning for the future.

Management accounting uses both historical and estimated data in assisting management in daily operations and in planning future operations. It deals with specific problems that confront enterprise managers at various organizational levels. The management accountant is frequently concerned with identifying alternative courses of action and then helping to select the best one. In recent years, public accountants have realized that their training and experience uniquely quality them to advise management personnel on policies and administration.

Tax accounting is another important area. Accountants specialized in this field, must be familiar with the tax statutes affecting their employer or clients and also must keep up to date on administrative regulations and court decisions on tax cases.

15. What has brought about the evolution of accounting?

A. City development

B. Law enforcement

C. Growth of professionals

D. Technological advancement

16. Financial report will NOT provide information for

A. non-governmental organizations

B. managers

C. creditors

D. governmental agencies

17. Why must corporate enterprises employ termed general accepted accounting principles?

A. It is a general practice in accounting.

B. To prepare their annual reports.

C. It is supervised by the government.

D. To make their work more effective.

18. What is the role of public accountant?

A. Check the enforcement of management's policies

B. Divide the management procedure

C. Examine the accounting records and give opinions

D. Evaluate the accounting of an enterprise

19. What data does management accounting use?

A. Current data

B. Historical data

C. Statistical data

D. Up-to-date data

20. Accountants specialized in tax accounting need NOT be familiar with:

A. Tax statutes

B. Administrative regulations

C. Court decisions on tax cases

D. Government policies

PART FOUR
Questions 21—30

· Read the article below about aspects of accounting.

· Choose the correct word to fill each gap from A, B, C or D.

· For each question (21—30), mark one letter (A, B, C or D) on your Answer Sheet.

Aspects of Accounting

Accounting is one of the (21)... professions on record. The art of bookkeeping has been practiced from very early times. The Romans had an elaborate system of keeping accounts, and it is said they used a system (22)... to the double entry system. A review of accounting over the ages indicates accountants have not always done the same work, but they have (23)... similar functions. For example, accountants in Roman times were responsible for recording business transactions. During the industrial (24)... of the United States, much of the (25)... came from England and Scotland and the investors insisted on sending accountants from those countries to vouch for the reported results of the undertakings. In the late 1800s a professional accountant was described as an (26)...: someone who looks for leaks, someone who detects and exposes that which is wrong, and someone who clearly reports facts as they exist, whetherthey be plainly expressed by clear and distinct records or whether they be concealed or hidden. The infrastructure that (27)... the production and delivery of accounting's information product is the accounting information system. Simply (28)..., a system is a set of resources brought together to achieve some common goal. The (29)... of an accounting information system is to collect and store data about business processes that can be used to generate a meaningful output for decision makers.

The resources (30)... to build accounting information systems include people and technologies. As you are probably aware, technologies have evolved over the years from manual resources to the advanced information technologies available today. This evolution will continue.

21. A. youngest   B. oldest   C. largest   D. smallest
22. A. akin   B. prior   C. related   D. due
23. A. done   B. achieved   C. performed   D. realized
24. A. development B. expansion   C. advancement D. progress
25. A. resource   B. power   C. relation   D. capital
26. A. investor   B. adventurer   C. investigator D. pioneer
27. A. supports   B. brings   C. causes   D. increases
28. A. said   B. argued   C. defined   D. told
29. A. effect   B. objective   C. function   D. result
30. A. possible   B. proper   C. available   D. present

PART FIVE
Questions 31—40

· Read the article below about bookkeeping and accounting.
· For each question 31—40, write one word in CAPITAL LETTERS on your Answer Sheet.

Bookkeeping and Accounting

The underlying purpose of accounting is to provide financial information (31)... an economic entity. The financial information provided by an accounting system is needed by managerial decision makers to help them plan and control the activities of the economic entity. (32)... information is also needed by outsiders— owners, creditors, potential investors, the government, and the public— (33)... have supplied money to the business or who have some other interest in the business that will be served by information about its financial position and operating results.

There is some confusion over the (34)... between "bookkeeping" and "accounting." This is partly due to the fact that the two are related.

Bookkeeping is the recording of business data (35)... a prescribed manner. A bookkeeper may be responsible (36)... keeping all of the records of a business or only a small segment, such as a portion of the customer accounts in a department store. Much of the work of the bookkeeper is clerical in nature and is increasingly (37)... handled by mechanical and electronic equipment.

Accounting is primarily (38)... with the design of the system of records, the preparation of reports based on the recorded data, and the interpretation of the reports. Accountants often direct and review the work of bookkeepers. The larger the firm, the greater is the number of levels of responsibility and authority. The work of accountants at the beginning levels may possibly include some bookkeeping. In any event, the accountant must have a (39)... higher level of knowledge, conceptual, and analytical skill (40)... is required of the bookkeeper.

PART SIX
Questions 41—52

· Read the text below from a report about evolution of accounting.

· In most lines (41—52), there is one extra word. It either is grammatically incorrect or does not fit in with the sense of the text. Some lines, however, are correct.

· If a line is correct, write CORRECT on your Answer Sheet.

· If there is an extra word in the line, write the extra word in CAPITAL LETTERS on your Answer Sheet.

Evolution of Accounting

Accounting is thousands of years old; the earliest accounting records, which
41. dates back more than 7,000 years ago, were found in Mesopotamia (Assyrians). The
42. people of that time relied on primitive accounting methods to record the growth of
43. crops and herds. Accounting is evolved, improving over the years and advancing
44. as business has advanced. Early accounts served mainly to assist the memory of
45. the businessperson and the audience as for the account was the proprietor or record
46. keeper alone. Cruder forms of accounting were not inadequate for the problems
47. created by a business entity involving in multiple investors, so double-entry bookkeeping first emerged in northern Italy in the 14th century, where trading
48. ventures began to require more capital than a single individual was able to invest
49. something. The development of joint stock companies created wider audiences for accounts, as investors without firsthand knowledge of their operations relied on
50. accounts to provide with the requisite information. This development resulted in a
51. split of accounting systems for internal (i.e. management accounting) and external (i.e. financial accounting) purposes, and subsequently also in accounting and disclosure regulations and a growing need for independent attestation of external
52. accounts by auditors. Today, accounting is even called "the language of business" because it is the vehicle for reporting financial information about a business entity to many different groups of people.

第 12 单元　知识产权
Unit 12　Intellectual Property

Text A

Ⅰ. 课文导读

在现代社会权利的保护中知识产权具有重要意义。知识产权有多种分类,在传统上一般分为两类:版权和工业产权。版权又称为文化产权,是指文学、艺术、科学作品的作者对其作品享有的权利,它涵盖了各类文化作品所涉及的各项权利。工业产权包括专利、商标、服务标志、工业设计等多项权利,专利和商标为工业产权的两项核心权利。

Ⅱ. Text

Rapid scientific and technological development all over the world has made the protection and use of innovation① an important issue in many countries. Owners of intellectual property like to enjoy the exclusive② rights to their innovations as long as possible. Broadly speaking, intellectual property means the legal rights which result from intellectual activity in the industrial, scientific, literary and artistic fields. Countries have laws to protect intellectual property for two main reasons. One is to give statutory③ expression to the moral and economic rights of creators in their creations and the rights of the public in access to④ those creations. The second is to promote, as a deliberate act of government policy, creativity and the dissemination⑤ and application of its results and to encourage fair trading that would contribute to economic and social development.

Generally speaking, intellectual property aims at safeguarding creators and other producers of intellectual goods and services by granting them certain time-limited rights to control the use made of those productions. Those rights do not apply to the physical object in which the creation may be embodied but instead to the intellectual creation as such. Intellectual property is traditionally divided into two branches, "copyright" and "industrial property."

---

① innovation: 创新
② exclusive: 专有的
③ statutory: 法定的
④ in access to: 接近,使用
⑤ dissemination: 传播

Copyright① grants to authors, artists, composers, and publishers the exclusive right to produce and distribute expressive and original work. Only expressive pieces, or writings, may receive copyright protection. A writing need not be words on paper: in copyright law, it can be a painting, sculpture, or other works of art. The writing element merely requires that a work of art, before receiving copyright protection, must be reduced to some tangible② form. This may be on paper, on film, on audiotape, or on any other tangible instrument that can be reproduced.

The writing requirement ensures that copyrighted material is capable of being reproduced③. Without this requirement artists could not be expected to know whether they were infringing④ on the original work of another person. The writing requirement also enforces the copyright rule that ideas cannot be copyrighted: only the expression of ideas can be protected.

Copyrighted material also must be original. This means that there must be something new about the work that sets it apart from previous similar works. If the variation is more than trivial⑤, the work will receive copyright protection.

Copyrighted material can receive varying degrees of protection. The scope of protection is generally limited to the original work that is in the writing. For example, assume that an artist has created a sculpture of the moon. The sculptor may not prevent others from making sculptures of the moon. However, the sculptor may prevent others from making sculptures of the moon that are exact replicas of his own sculpture.

Copyright protection gives the copyright holder the exclusive right to (1) reproduce the copyrighted work, (2) create derivative works from the work, (3) distribute the work, (4) perform the work, and (5) display the work. The first two rights are infringed whether they are violated in public or in private. The last three rights may be infringed only if they are violated in public. Public is defined under the Copyright Act as a performance or display to a "substantial number of persons" outside of friends and family.

The most important exception to the exclusive rights of the copyright holder is the "fair use" doctrine⑥. This doctrine allows the general public to use copyrighted material without permission in certain situations. These situations include educational activities, literary and social criticism, parody⑦, and news reporting. Whether a particular use is fair depends on a number of factors, including whether the use is for profit, what proportion of the copyrighted material is used, and what economic effect the user has on the copyright owner.

The major international copyright treaty is the Berne Convention for the Protection of Literary and Artistic Works (1971). There are several other international treaties which are also con-

---

① copyright: 版权
② tangible: 有形的
③ reproduce: 复制
④ infringe: 侵犯
⑤ trivial: 琐碎的
⑥ doctrine: 原则
⑦ parody: 滑稽性模仿作品

cerned with copyright protection, that is, the International Convention for the Protection of Performers, Producers of Phonograms①, and Broadcasting Organizations; the Geneva Convention for the Protection of Producers of Phonograms Against the Unauthorized Reproduction of their Phonograms; the Satellite Transmission Convention. The Berne Convention is the largest treaty with the most member-nations and is generally considered to be the most detailed and comprehensive② of the copyright treaties. Furthermore, it's recognized by both WIPO and WTO through the Agreement on Trade-Related Aspects of Intellectual Property Rights as authoritative world-wide.

Industrial property covers patents③, trademarks, service marks, industrial designs, commercial names and designations④. Here two important terms, patents and trademarks will be discussed.

A patent is a set of exclusive rights granted by a state (national government) to an inventor or their assignee⑤ for a limited period of time in exchange for the public disclosure⑥ of an invention. The procedure for granting patents, the requirements placed on the patentee, and the extent of the exclusive rights vary widely between countries according to national laws and international agreements. Typically, however, a patent application must include one or more claims defining the invention which must be new, non-obvious, and useful or industrially applicable. In many countries, certain subject areas are excluded from patents, such as business methods, treatment of the human body and mental acts. The exclusive right granted to a patentee in most countries is the right to prevent others from making, using, selling, or distributing the patented invention without permission. It is just a right to prevent others' use. A patent does not give the proprietor⑦ of the patent the right to use the patented invention, should it fall within the scope of an earlier patent.

There are chiefly two types of patent systems in the world: registration and examination. Some countries, such as France, grant a patent upon registration. Since no initial inquiry is made by the government agency at the time of filing about whether the innovation is deserving of patent protection at law, it is difficult to determine the validity of the patent under this system until an alleged infringement⑧ is made and a court of law makes a determination. Under the second type of system, examination, a patent is granted following a careful investigation by a government agency, usually, of whether the innovation is worthy of patent protection and whether any prior similar patents have been granted to another person in the nation.

The major international treaty dealing with patent are the 1970 Patent Cooperation Treaty

---

① phonogram: 录音制品
② comprehensive: 全面的
③ patent: 专利
④ designations: 名称
⑤ assignee: 代理人
⑥ disclosure: 公开
⑦ proprietor: 拥有者,所有者
⑧ alleged infringement: 涉嫌侵犯

and the 1883 Paris Convention for the Protection of Industrial Property as revised and amended several times. This convention has over 85 member countries.

Trademark is another important concept in industrial property. It's a distinctive sign or indicator used by an individual, business organization, or other legal entity to indentify that the products or services to consumers with which the trademark appears originate from a unique source, and to distinguish its products or services from those of other entities.

A trademark may be designated① by the following symbols:

1. ™ for an unregistered trademark, that is, a mark used to promote or brand goods
2. ℠ for an unregistered service mark, that is, a mark used to promote or brand services
3. ® for a registered trademark

A trademark is typically a name, word, phrase, logo, symbol, design, image, or a combination of these elements. There is also a range of non-conventional trademarks comprising marks which do not fall into these standard categories, such as those based on color, smell, or sound. The owner of a registered trademark may commence② legal proceedings for trademark infringement to prevent unauthorized use of that trademark. However, registration is not required. The owner of a common law trademark may also file suit③, but an unregistered mark may be protectable only within the geographical area within which it has been used or in geographical areas into which it may be reasonably expected to expand.

Ⅲ. Notes

1. fair use (合理使用). The term 'fair use' originated in the United States. It is a limitation and exception to the exclusive right granted by copyright law to the author of a creative work, a doctrine in the United States copyright law that allows limited use of copyrighted material without acquiring permission from the rights holders. Examples of fair use include commentary, criticism, news reporting, research, teaching, library archiving and scholarship. It provides for the legal, non-licensed citation or incorporation of copyrighted material in another author's work under a four-factor balancing test.

2. Berne Convention for the Protection of Literary and Artistic Works(保护文学和艺术作品伯尔尼公约). Usually known as the Berne Convention, it is an international agreement governing copyright, which was first accepted in Berne, Switzerland in 1886. Its 9 original member countries have now grown to 163. The Berne Convention requires its signatories to recognize the copyright of works of authors from other signatory countries (known as members of the Berne Union) in the same way as it recognizes the copyright of its own nationals. In addition to establishing a system of equal treatment that internationalized copyright amongst signatories, the agreement also required member states to provide strong minimum standards for copyright

---

① designate: 标明
② commence: 开始;启动
③ file suit: 起诉

law.

3. International Convention for the Protection of Performers, Producers of Phonograms, and Broadcasting Organizations（保护表演者、录音制品制作者和广播组织的国际公约,即"罗马公约"）. This convention was accepted by members of the World Intellectual Property Organization on October 26, 1961. The agreement extended copyright protection for the first time from the author of a work to the creators and owners of particular, physical manifestations of intellectual property, such as audiocassettes or DVDs. Currently there are 86 member countries.

4. Geneva Convention for the Protection of Producers of Phonograms Against the Unauthorized Reproduction of their Phonogram（保护录制者,防止录制品被擅自复制的日内瓦公约）. The convention was singed in 1971 at Geneva. It provides that member countries must protect producers of phonograms from the unauthorized reproduction and importation of their works for a period of no less than 20 years. The means for doing this, however, is left to each individual country.

5. Satellite Transmission Convention（发送卫星传输节目信号公约）. Sponsored jointly by WIPO and UNESCO, the convention was concluded in Brussels in 1974. It requires member countries to take "adequate measures" to prevent the unauthorized distribution in or from their territory of any program-carrying signal transmitted by satellite. The number of member countries at present is 30.

6. WIPO（世界知识产权组织）. The World Intellectual Property Organization is one of the 16 specialized agencies of the United Nations. WIPO was created in 1967 "to encourage creative activity, to promote the protection of intellectual property throughout the world." WIPO currently has 184 member states, administers 24 international treaties, and is headquartered in Geneva, Switzerland. 183 of the UN Members as well as the Holy See are Members of WIPO. Non-members are the states of Cook Islands, Kiribati, Marshall Islands, Federated States of Micronesia, Nauru, Niue, Palau, Solomon Islands, Timor-Leste, Tuvalu, Vanuatu and the states with limited recognition. Palestine has observer status.

7. Agreement on Trade-Related Aspects of Intellectual Property（与贸易有关的知识产权协定）. It is an international agreement administered by the World Trade Organization that sets down minimum standards for many forms of intellectual property regulation as applied to nationals of other WTO Members. It was negotiated at the end of the Uruguay Round of the General Agreement on Tariffs and Trade in 1994.

8. Patent Cooperation Treaty（专利合作条约）. The treaty, agreed to in 1970, establishes a mechanism for making an international application whose effect in each member countries is the same as the filing for a national patent. The goal of the treaty is the elimination of unnecessary repetition by both patent offices and applicants. Eventually, the member countries plan to establish a single international search authority. As of June 10, 2007, there were 127 member countries.

9. Paris Convention for the Protection of Industrial Property（保护工业产权巴黎公

约). The convention, signed in Paris, on March 20, 1883, was one of the first intellectual property treaties. It established a Union for the protection of industrial property. Among the member's duties is the obligation to participate in regular revisions. Three basic principles are incorporated in the convention: national treatment, right of priority and common rules.

Ⅳ. Useful Expressions

1. broadly speaking: 广义上说
2. in access to: 接近,使用
3. infringe on: 侵犯
4. fall into categories: 归入…类别
5. file suit: 起诉
6. grant a patent: 授予专利权
7. fall within the scope of: 在……范围内
8. legal entity: 法人实体

Ⅴ. Reading Comprehension

Questions

1. What is the general aim of the intellectual property?
2. What does it mean by 'tangible form' in the copyright protection?
3. What is "fair use" doctrine in copyright?
4. What is a typical patent application like?
5. How can an unregistered trademark be protected?

Decide whether each of the following statements is true or false.

1. Intellectual property is traditionally divided into two branches, "copyright" and "patent." ( )
2. In copyright law, a writing must be words on paper ( )
3. Ideas cannot be copyrighted, only the expression of ideas can be protected. ( )
4. The right of displaying the copyrighted work is infringed only if it is violated in private. ( )
5. "Fair use" doctrine allows the general public to use copyrighted material without permission in certain situations. ( )
6. The major international copyright treaty is the Satellite Transmission Convention. ( )
7. There are mainly two types of patent systems: registration and application. ( )
8. Commercial names and designations belong to industrial property. ( )
9. The symbol ™ is for a registered service mark. ( )
10. A trademark is typically a name, word, logo, symbol, design, etc. ( )

VI. Discussion

What are the similarities and differences between copyright, trademark and patent?

Text B
BEC Reading Texts

PART ONE
Questions 1—8

- Look at the statements below and the five extracts about intellectual property from an article.
- Which extract (A, B, C, D or E) does each statement (1—8) refer to?
- For each statement (1—8), make one letter (A, B, C, D or E) on your Answer Sheet.
- You will need to use some of these letters more than once.

1. Intellectual property law attempts to strike a balance between the respective demands of different parities of innovations.

2. There are chiefly two types of intellectual property and each has its own features.

3. International law and national law perform different functions for intellectual property.

4. Intellectual property law can balance competing concerns and wishes of innovators, consumers, competitors, developing nations.

5. The unique feature of intellectual property has made it rather challenging to establish and enforce laws, thus obtaining relevant national and international laws is a must for international business.

6. Artistic property and industrial property, two major branches of intellectual property, each cover some subparts.

7. Intellectual property rights may be implemented by civil remedies.

8. Intangibility of intellectual property brings about the difficulty in its protection and law design as well as heated discussion at an international level.

A. Intellectual property rights can be enforced through civil remedies, and may involve criminal sanctions. As a final remedy, the right holder can obtain financial compensation for losses caused by infringement by choosing between damages or an account of profits which the defendant made from the infringement. Other final remedies may include delivery up and destruction of infringing documents, a court order to reveal relevant information, or an injunction.

B. Intellectual property is, in essence, useful information or knowledge. It is divided, for the purposes of study (and for establishing legal rights), into two principal branches: artistic property and industrial property. Artistic property encompasses artistic, literary, and musical works. These are protected, in most countries, by copyrights and neighboring rights. Industrial property is itself divided into two categories: inventions and trademarks. Inventions include both useful products and useful manufacturing processes. They are protected in a variety of ways, the most common protection being in the form of patents, petty patents and inventors' certificates. Trademarks include "true" trademarks, trade names, service marks, collective marks, and certification marks. All of these are markings that identify the ownership rights of manufacturers, merchants, and service establishments. They are protected by trademark laws.

C. Intellectual property is a type of personal property, but it is intangible. As such, it is difficult, not only to protect, since it cannot be easily held or contained, but to define and to design laws that will govern and control it. The increasing globalization and technological development of our world often make the laws of just a few years ago obsolete in this field of study. However, the issues surrounding the acquisition, protection, and transfer of knowledge across international borders will continue to be debated intensely in the near future. Anyone involved in business internationally must, therefore, have some basic, working knowledge of the national and international laws relating to intellectual property.

D. Regardless of its form, intellectual property is a creature of national law. International law does not create it. International law does, however, set down guidelines for its uniform definition and protection, and it sets up ways that make it easier for owners to acquire rights in different countries. National law—and sometimes regional law—is also important in establishing the rules for assigning and licensing intellectual property. Recently, the international community has worked to establish international norms for the transfer of intellectual property, but so far the effort has not been fully successful.

E. Rapid technological development throughout the world has made the protection and use of innovation an important issue in the economic success of nations. Owners of intellectual property want to enjoy the exclusive rights to their innovations as long as possible. A reasonably long period of time in which the innovator can enjoy the benefits of his innovation can be a powerful means of protecting the commercial benefits of creativity as well as an incentive for more innovations, thus leading to greater benefits both economically and socially from technological advancements. Consumers, competitors, and some developing nations, however, want innovations to be made available publicly as soon as possible, to reduce prices and provide greater availability of the innovations with fewer costs to them. Thus, intellectual property law tries to balance these competing concerns and desires.

PART TWO
Questions 9—14

- Read the text about trade secrets.
- Choose the best sentence to fill each of the gaps.
- For each gap (9—14), mark one letter (A-H) on your Answer Sheet.
- Do not use any letter more than once.

Trade Secrets

Some business information or processes cannot qualify as copyrights, patents, or trademarks. (9)... Trade secrets include customer lists, pricing information, marketing techniques, management skills, production and engineering techniques, management skills, production and engineering techniques, formulas, research and development, and generally anything that makes a business unique and valuable to a competitor. (10)..., although know-how usually involves a certain type of trade secrets—those that are more technical, scientific, or managerial in a business. Once trade secrets are released or become part of the public's general knowledge, called the "public domain," they can be generally used by anyone and cannot be retrieved for the exclusive use of a business. (11)... If everyone in the public knows about a trade secret, it loses its value. A business cannot charge another for information that is easily available to the general public. (12)... (13)... Normally, a business protects its trade secrets by allowing only a select few employees to know them and by having all employees who use or know trade secrets to agree in a contract never to divulge them. If an employee wrongfully divulges a trade secret, the employer can sue the employee for damages for breach of contract and perhaps a personal injury (tort) committed against the business; the monetary award can be high. Sometimes, businesses would rather use confidentiality agreements with employees to protect trade secrets rather than go through the expense of making some trade secrets patentable since obtaining patents can be costly and time-consuming. Trade secrets can last indefinitely unlike patents; often just the filing of a patent requires disclosure of the innovation and its processes to a government agency for examination. This disclosure can result in the invention being copied illegally or "reverse engineered" by competitors. (14)...

A. A trade secret is of great significance to the growth of a business.

B. Thus, confidentiality is very important in trade secrets.

C. However, they can be protected as valuable knowledge from appropriation by competitors as trade secrets.

D. It is for that reason that Coca-cola's formula is kept a tight secret and only a few people on earth know it.

E. A trade secret, if properly kept confidential, need not ever be disclosed to the public.

F. Anyone who reveals a trade secrete to the public can be punished by law.

G. Sometimes trade secrets are called know-how

H. There are usually no registrations or filing requirements to protect a trade secret under a country's national law

PART THREE
Questions 15—20

· Read the following article on the history and development of WIPO.

· For each question (15—20) mark one letter (A, B, C or D) on your Answer Sheet for the answer you choose.

The World Intellectual Property Organization (WIPO) is one of the specialized agencies of the United Nations (UN) system of organizations. The "Convention Establishing the World Intellectual Property Organization" was signed at Stockholm in 1967 and entered into force in 1970. However, the origins of WIPO go back to 1883 and 1886, with the adoption of the Paris Convention and the Berne Convention respectively. Both of these conventions provided for the establishment of international secretariats, and both were placed under the supervision of the Swiss Federal Government. The few officials who were needed to carry out the administration of the two conventions were located in Berne, Switzerland.

Initially there were two secretariats (one for industrial property, one for copyright) for the administration of the two conventions, but in 1893 the two secretariats united. The most recent name of the organization, before it became WIPO, was BIRPI, the acronym of the French-language version of the name: United International Bureaux for the Protection of Intellectual Property (in English). In 1960, BIRPI moved from Berne to Geneva.

At the 1967 diplomatic conference in Stockholm, when WIPO was established, the administrative and final clauses of all the then existing multilateral treaties administered by BIRPI were revised. They had to be revised because member States wished to assume the position of full governing body of the Organization (WIPO), thus removing the supervisory authority of the Swiss Government, to give WIPO the same status as all the other comparable intergovernmental organizations and to pave the way for it to become a specialized agency of the United Nations system of organizations.

Most of the inter-governmental organizations now called specialized agencies did not exist before the Second World War. They were created for the specific purpose of dealing with a particular subject or field of activity at the international level. However, some inter-governmental organizations, such as the International Labor Office (ILO), the Universal Postal Union (UPU) and the International Tele-communication Union (ITU) were in existence, and had become the responsible intergovernmental organizations in their respective fields of activity long before the establishment of the United Nations. After the United Nations was established, these organizations became specialized agencies of the United Nations system. Similarly, long before the United Nations was established, BIRPI was the responsible intergovernmental organization in the field of intellectual property. WIPO, the successor to BIRPI, became a specialized agency of the United Nations when an agreement was signed to that end between the United Nations and WIPO which came into effect on December 17, 1974.

15. The origin of WIPO is related to:

A. Tokyo Convention

B. London Convention

C. Berne Convention

D. Rome Convention

16. In_____, the former name of WIPO, BIRPI moved from Berne to Geneva.
  A. 1967   B. 1960   C. 1970   D. 1974

17. Which is NOT the reason for the revision of the administrative and final clauses of all the then existing multilateral treaties administered by BIRPI?
  A. Remove the supervisory authority of the Swiss Government
  B. Give WIPO the same status as other comparable intergovernmental organizations
  C. Make WIPO a specialized agency of the United Nations system
  D. These clauses are out of date, and need revision to keep pace with the time.

18. What is the purpose of establishing specialized agencies before WWII?
  A. Cope with a particular subject of activity at the international level
  B. Deal with widespread terrorist activities around the world
  C. Respond to any emergence in a global scope
  D. Practice special personnel for different countries

19. What is the relation between member states of UN and specialized agencies?
  A. Member states are administrated by all specialized agencies
  B. Member states observe the rules and regulations of specialized agencies
  C. Member states make their own decision for whether to join a specialized agency
  D. Member states have no choice but to join all specialized agencies

20 Which organization was responsible for intellectual property before the establishment of UN?
  A. WIPO   B. BIRPI   C. UPU   D. ITU

PART FOUR
Questions 21—30
· Read the article below about copyright.
· Choose the correct word to fill each gap from A, B, C or D.
· For each question (21—30), mark one letter (A, B, C or D) on your Answer Sheet.

Copyright

Reproduction, the oldest and most common of the copyright rights, is consistently defined in the market countries of the West. For example, the German statute defines it as the "right to make copies of a work, irrespective of the method of number"; the British Copyright Act refers to "reproducing the work in any material form"; the French Copyright Law defines a work reproduction as "the material fixation of a work by any method that (21)... indirect communication to the public"; and the U.S Copyright Act refers merely to the making of "copies".

In socialist countries, although a copyright does (22)... the right of reproduction, the right can be exercised effectively only by state (23)... As a consequence, (24)... holders have to assign their rights to an agency—commonly their employer—and hope that the agency will (25)... their copyrighted work.

Of course, the development of the Internet and the World Wide Web in the past 15 years has totally changed the ease with which copyrighted works may be (26)... It is now possible—though not necessarily (27)...—to instantly send a perfect copy of a work of art, music, literature, or software to millions of people around the world with the click of a (28)... The rapid developments in (29)... have made enforcement of copyrights law much more (30)..., and business firms have been struggling to protect their intellectual property in this new age.

21. A. forbids   B. permits   C. requires   D. suggests
22. A. include   B. exclude   C. explain   D. describe
23. A. companies   B. organizations   C. agencies   D. institutions
24. A. reproduction   B. trademark   C. goods   D. copyright
25. A. develop   B. promote   C. produce   D. copy
26. A. stolen   B. downloaded   C. uploaded   D. reproduced
27. A. legal   B. available   C. beneficial   D. helpful
28. A. disc   B. monitor   C. mouse   D. speaker
29. A. society   B. religion   C. culture   D. technology
30. A. effective   B. difficult   C. confusing   D. practical

PART FIVE
Questions 31—40

· Read the article below about the concept of property.

· For each question 31—40, write one word in CAPITAL LETTERS on your Answer Sheet.

The Concept of Property

The concept of property has been the subject of much discussion and debate for philosophers, writers, politicians, and other intellectuals throughout history. James Fenimore Cooper, the popular American writer, saw (31)... as "the groundwork of moral independence"; Abraham Lincoln described it as "the fruit of labor" and " a positive good in the world'; for John Locke, the English philosopher and political theorist, it was "the reason (32)... men enter into society"; Walter Lippmann, the highly respected American journalist, (33)... it as "the only dependable foundation of personal liberty"; while Pierre J. Proudhon, the noted French anarchist, saw it as "theft", saying it represented the exploitation of the worker.

Philosophical and political definitions aside, property is a relatively (34)... concept in the eyes of the law: the right of an individual to exclusively possess, use, and dispose of anything (35)... can be owned. Broadly (36)..., there are two separate types of property: personal and real. Personal property is characterized by its portable nature; it can be carried from place to place. Furthermore, personal property can be either tangible or intangible. Tangible personal property encompasses ownership interest in things that have a physical existence and are able to be moved, or carried from place to place. Most property (37)... into this category; a car, wallet, photograph, textbook, shirt, pen, and watch are all common (38)... of tangible personal property. Intangible personal property, on the other hand, by its (39) . . . nature does not have a physical existence, but is merely a (40) . . . that can be owned, as opposed to a real, tangible object. Common examples of intangible property include copyrights, patents, trademarks, stocks, and bonds.

PART SIX
Questions 41—52

· Read the text below from a report about the protection of inventions.

· In most lines (41—52), there is one extra word. It either is grammatically incorrect or does not fit in with the sense of the text. Some lines, however, are correct.

· If a line is correct, write CORRECT on your Answer Sheet.

· If there is an extra word in the line, write the extra word in CAPITAL LETTERS on your Answer Sheet.

The Protection of Inventions

Most laws dealing with the protection of inventions do not actually define the

41. notion of an invention. A number of countries, however, define inventions as new

42. solutions to all technical problems. The problem may be old or new, but the solution, in order to merit the name of invention, must be a new one. Merely

43. discovering something that already exists in nature, such as a previously unknown

44. plant variety, is not an invention. Human intervention must be added up. So the

45. process for extraction of a new substance from a plant may be called an invention.

46. An invention is not necessarily in a complex item. The safety pin was an invention which solved an existing "technical" problem. New solutions are, in essence, ideas,

47. and are protected as such thing. Thus protection of inventions under patent law

48. does not require that the invention might be represented in a physical embodiment. Patents, also referred to as patents for invention, are the most widespread means of

49. protecting the rights of inventors. Simply put, a patent is the right that granted to an inventor by a State, or by a regional office acting for several States, which allows the inventor to exclude anyone else from commercially exploiting his invention for a

50. limited period time, generally 20 years. By granting an exclusive right, patents provide incentives to individuals, offering them recognition for their creativity and

51. material reward for their marketable inventions. These incentives encourage innovation, which in turn contributes to the continuing enhancement of the quality of

52. human life. In return for the exclusive right, the inventor must not adequately disclose the patented invention to the public, so that others can gain the new knowledge and can further develop the technology.

第 13 单元　人力资源管理
Unit 13　Staffing and Human Resource Management

Text A

Ⅰ. 课文导读

人力资源管理指根据企业发展战略的要求,有计划地对人力资源进行合理配置,通过对企业中员工的招聘、培训、使用、考核、激励、调整等一系列过程,调动员工的积极性,发挥员工的潜能,为企业创造价值,确保企业战略目标的实现。是企业的一系列人力资源政策以及相应的管理活动。这些活动主要包括企业人力资源战略的制定,员工的招募与选拔,培训与开发,绩效管理,薪酬管理,员工流动管理,员工关系管理,员工安全与健康管理等。

Ⅱ. Text

Staffing① has long been an integral part of the management process. Like other traditional management functions, such as planning and organizing, the domain② of staffing has grown throughout the years. Early definitions of staffing focused narrowly on hiring people for vacant positions. Today, staffing is defined more broadly as human resource planning, acquisition, and development aimed at providing the talent necessary for organizational success. This broader definition underscores③ the point that people are valuable resources requiring careful nurturing④. The day has long passed when management could view labor simply as a commodity to be bought, exploited to exhaustion, and discarded when convenient. Global competitive pressures have made the skillful management of human resources more important than ever.

A particularly promising development in the staffing area is the linkage of the human resource perspective with strategic management. A logical sequence of staffing activities—human resource planning, selection, performance appraisal⑤, and training —all derive from organizational strategy and structure. Without a strategic orientation, the staffing function becomes hap-

---

① staffing: 人员编制
② domain: 领域
③ underscore: 强调
④ nurture: 培养
⑤ performance appraisal: 绩效考核

hazardly① inefficient and ineffective.

Human Resource Planning. Planning enables managers to cope better with an uncertain environment and to allocate scarce resources more efficiently. In recent years, management scholars have emphasized the need to plan the human side of organized endeavor: "There continues to be in organizations a failure, particularly on the part of line managers and functional managers② in areas other than personnel, to recognize the true importance of planning for and managing human resources."

Human resource planning helps management find the right people for the right jobs at the right time. Formally defined, human resource planning is the development of a comprehensive staffing strategy for meeting the organization's future human resource needs.

Human resource planning requires a systematic approach to staffing. Staffing has suffered from a lack of continuity as people are hired and trained on an "as needed" basis. With today's rapidly changing conditions, organizations need a foresighted, systematic approach that provides specific answers to this overriding③ question: "How can the organization assure that it will have people of the right types and numbers, organized appropriately, managed effectively, and focused on customer satisfaction?" Answers to this question can be obtained through a systematic approach. First, current staffing needs are assessed. Next, future needs of human resources are forecast. Third, a comprehensive staffing strategy is formulated. Finally, evaluation and updating of the system are achieved by continually recycling through the process.

Selection. Management finds qualified people to fill available jobs through the employee selection process. Generally speaking, employee selection serves as the organization's human resource gatekeeper. Today's managers are challenged to find the best available talent without unfairly discriminating against any segment of society.

A person who has applied for a particular job is not necessarily qualified to hold it. Thus, a screening mechanism④ is required to separate those who are qualified from those who are not. Personnel management experts commonly compare the screening process to a hurdle race⑤. Typical hurdles job that applicants have to clear are psychological tests, work sampling tests, reference checks, interviews, and physical examinations. Many companies have added pre-employment drug tests to this list. Importantly, Equal Employment Opportunity (EEO) legislation in the United States and elsewhere delineates⑥ what managers can and cannot do when screening job applicants.

Performance Appraisal. Although formal performance appraisal systems are considered es-

---

① haphazardly: 随意地
② line manager and functional manager: 直线管理人员和职能管理人员
③ overriding: 最重要的
④ a screening mechanism: 筛选机制
⑤ hurdle race: 跨栏比赛
⑥ delineate: 描绘

sential in today's organizations, they are often a source of dissatisfaction, as the following survey demonstrated. In a survey of 589 personnel administrators①, 87% reportedly used formal performance appraisal systems, yet only 56% of those with such systems were satisfied with them. Performance appraisal can be effective and satisfying if systematically developed and implemented techniques replace haphazard methods. For our purposes, performance appraisal is the process of evaluating individual job performance as a basis for making objective personnel decisions. This definition intentionally excludes occasional coaching, in which a supervisor simply checks an employee's work and gives immediate feedback. Although personal coaching is fundamental to a good management, formally documented② appraisal are needed both to ensure equitable distribution of opportunities and rewards and to avoid prejudicial treatment of protected minorities.

Training. There is often a gap between what employees *do* know and what they *should* know. Filling this knowledge gap by means of training has become big business. According to U. S. government statistics, American companies spend an incredible $30 or $40 billion a year on training. An estimated one-third of the U. S. work force participated in employer-sponsored training programs③ in 1990. As the term is used here, training is the process of changing employee behavior, attitudes, or opinions through some type of guided experience.

Management development is the most common type of training today. Basic computer-skills training, now ranked fifth, has become increasingly important. Renewed competitive emphasis on customer service has elevated④ customer relations/services training to the number-seven spot. Videotape, a comparative newcomer to organizational training, has quickly become the most extensively used instructional method.

After an employee has joined the organization, part of human resource management process involves dealing with human resource problems such as sexual harassment⑤, alcohol and drug abuse⑥, and AIDS. These three problems deserve a closer look from a human resource management perspective. Each is a serious threat to individual well-being and organizational performance.

Controlling Alcohol and Drug Abuse. The statistics tell a grim story about the number-one drug problem—alcohol. Serious drinking problems afflict approximately 10% of the U. S. population. About 10.5 million American qualify as alcoholics. 25% of American polls⑦ say alcohol has been a problem in their family. Once believed to be a character disorder, alcoholism is now considered a disease in which an individual's normal social and economic roles are disrupted by

① personnel administrator: 人事管理员
② document: 记录
③ employer-sponsored training programs: 由雇主资助的培训项目
④ elevate: 提升
⑤ sexual harassment: 性骚扰
⑥ drug abuse: 滥用药物，暗指吸毒者
⑦ poll: 民意测验

the consumption of alcohol. Very few alcoholics are actually the skid-row-bum① type; the vast majority are average citizens with jobs and families.

The National Institute on Drug Abuse "estimates that if every worker from age 18 to 40 were tested for drugs on any given day, 14% to 25% would test positive②." Compared with nonabusers, alcoholic employees and drug abusers are significantly less productive, 10 times more likely to be absent and 3 times more likely either to have or to cause an accident.

Discouraging Sexual Harassment. A great deal of misunderstanding surrounds the topic of sexual harassment because of sexist attitudes, vague definitions, and inconsistent court findings. Sexual harassment, defined generally as unwanted sexual attention or conduct, has both behavioral and legal dimensions. Important among these are the following:

● Although female employees are typically the victims of sexual harassment, both women and men (in the United States) are protected under Title Ⅶ of the Civil Rights Act of 1964.

● Sexual harassment includes, but is not limited to, unwanted physical contact. Gestures, displays, joking, and language also may create a sexually offensive or intimidating③ work environment.

● It is the manager's job to be aware of and correct cases of sexual harassment. Ignorance of such activity is not a valid legal defense.

Developing a Responsible AIDS Policy. The current acquired immune deficiency syndrome (AIDS) epidemic raises two critical questions for managers: (1) How should the organization treat an individual who has tested positive for the AIDS virus? and (2) What can be done to prevent an AIDS victim's coworkers from panicking?

Equal treatment, education, and confidentiality are the three key components of a well-conceived AIDS policy. As stated in a report titled "AIDS: Corporate America Responds": treatment of employees with AIDS should be the same as that for others with a chronic④ or life-threatening illness... including eligibility⑤ for the same work privileges and medical benefits.

Coworkers of an individual who tests positive for the AIDS virus are less likely to panic if they are given the latest facts. According to the best available medical evidence, the virus is spread only through sexual contact, infected⑥ blood products, and from infected mothers to their unborn children. Other modes of transmission, such as those encountered in medical and dental settings⑦, are being investigated. Employees' fears about normal casual contact in the workplace, including the sharing of drinking fountains⑧, dining facilities, tools, and rest rooms, are

---

① skid-row-bum: 街头流浪
② positive: 呈阳性
③ intimidating: 令人紧张不安的
④ chronic: 慢性的
⑤ eligibility: 资格
⑥ infect: 传染
⑦ dental settings: 牙科器具
⑧ drinking fountains: 饮水机

unrealistic. Organizations without a responsible AIDS policy will have to cope with an even greater problem, unwarranted fear①.

Sexual harassment, alcohol and drug abuse, and AIDS are contemporary human resource problems that require top management attention and strong policies. Special care needs to be taken in each area to avoid discrimination. These three problems represent an erosion② of human potential that today's organizations cannot afford if they are to achieve a competitive edge③.

Ⅲ. Notes

1. Equal Employment Opportunity（平等就业机会）. Title Ⅶ of the Civil Rights Act of 1964 was the first federal law designed to protect most U. S. employees from employment discrimination based upon that employee's (or applicant's) race, color, religion, sex, or national origin. The Title also established the U. S. Equal Employment Opportunity Commission to assist in the protection of U. S. employees from discrimination. Equal employment opportunity was further enhanced when President Lyndon B. Johnson signed Executive Order 11246 on September 24, 1965, created to prohibit federal contractors from discriminating against employees on the basis of race, sex, creed, religion, color, or national origin.

2. National Institute on Drug Abuse（美国国家滥用药物研究所）. It is a component of the National Institutes of Health. Its mission is to lead the nation in bringing the power of science to bear on drug abuse and addiction. NIDA's work involves (1) supporting and conducting basic, clinical, and applied research across a broad range of disciplines ranging from genetics and neurobiology to behavioral and social science and (2) ensuring rapid and effective dissemination and use of research results to improve prevention and treatment and inform policy.

3. Civil Rights Act（民权法）. The Civil Rights Act of 1964 was a landmark piece of legislation in the United States that outlawed major forms of discrimination against blacks and women, including racial segregation. It ended unequal application of voter registration requirements and racial segregation in schools, at the workplace and by facilities that served the general public.

Ⅳ. Useful Expressions

1. fill the gap: 填补空白
2. by means of: 通过……方式
3. be aware of: 意识到
4. test positive: 检查呈阳性
5. a strategic orientation: 战略定位
6. cope with: 应付

---

① unwarranted fear: 不必要的恐惧
② erosion: 侵蚀，腐蚀
③ a competitive edge: 竞争优势

7. discriminate against: 歧视

8. compare... to: 将……比作

9. on any given day: 在任何给定的一天

V. Reading Comprehension

Questions

1. What is the definition of staffing?
2. Why is the staffing function a key determinant of organizational success?
3. What is the systematic approach to staffing in human resource planning?
4. What types of training are usually included in the training program?
5. Compared with traditional human resource management, what are the features of modern human resource management?

Decide whether each of the following statements is true or false.

1. Human resource is part of the strategic planning process. Much is done in the company that doesn't involve in the planning, policy or finalization stages of any deal. (   )

2. The main work of a human resource department is to select skilled people for the right jobs at the right time. (   )

3. It is unlawful to discriminate employees on the basis of race, color, sex, religion, age, national origin, handicapped status, being a disabled veteran. (   )

4. A manager is effective if he or she reaches a stated objectives and efficient if limited resources are not wasted in the process. (   )

5. Managers make hiring and other personnel decisions on the basis of ability to perform and personal taste. (   )

6. A systems approach to human resource planning will help management devise staffing strategies for future human resource needs. (   )

7. Nowadays employees are treated as valuable human resources. (   )

8. Human resources should be categorized with basic business resources (trucks, filing cabinets, etc). (   )

9. Staffing function is a key determinant of organizational success. (   )

10. There are only three human resource problems: sexual harassment, alcohol and drug abuse, and AIDS. (   )

VI. Discussion

Should someone who has tested positive for the AIDS virus be fired? Explain.

Text B
BEC Reading Texts

PART ONE
Questions 1—8

· Look at the statements below and the five extracts about Human Resources from an article.
· Which extract (A, B, C, D or E) does each statement (1—8) refer to?
· For each statement (1—8), make one letter (A, B, C, D or E) on your Answer Sheet.
· You will need to use some of these letters more than once.

1. External factors are those outside the control of the organization.
2. In ensuring such objectives are achieved, the HR Department is to implement an organization's human resource requirements effectively.
3. In simple terms, an organization's human resource management strategy should maximize return on investment in HR.
4. Development of the individual benefits the organization, the nation and its citizens.
5. HR development is the structure that allows for individual development, satisfying the organization's, or the nation's goals.
6. Human Resources Development is a framework for the expansion of human capital within an organization or a municipality, region, or nation.
7. The analysis requires consideration of the internal and external factors that can have an effect on the resourcing, development, motivation and retention of employees and other workers.
8. At the level of a national strategy, it can be a broad inter-sector approach to fostering creative contributions to national productivity.

A. Human resource managers seek to achieve this by successfully matching the supply of skilled and qualified individuals and the capabilities of the current workforce, with the organization's ongoing and future business plans and requirements to maximize return on investment and secure future survival and success.

B. These include issues such as economic climate and current and future labor market trends. On the other hand, internal influences are broadly controlled by the organization to predict, determine, and monitor—for example—the organizational culture, underpinned by management style, environmental climate, and the approach to ethical and corporate social responsibilities.

C. Human Resources Development is a combination of training and education, in a broad context of adequate health and employment policies, which ensures the continual improvement and growth of the individual, the organization, and the national human resourcefulness.

D. In organizations, it is important to determine both current and future organizational requirements for both core employees and the contingent workforce in terms of their skills/technical abilities, competencies, flexibility etc.

E. In the corporate vision, the Human Resources Development framework views employees as an asset to the enterprise, whose value is enhanced by development, "Its primary focus is on growth and employee development... it emphasizes developing individual potential and skills" Human Resources Development in this treatment can be in-room group training, tertiary or vocational courses or mentoring and coaching by senior employees with the aim for a desired outcome that develops the individual's performance.

PART TWO
Questions 9—14

· Read the text about the human resource management.
· Choose the best sentence to fill each of the gaps.
· For each gap (9—14), mark one letter (A-H) on your Answer Sheet.
· Do not use any letter more than once.

Human Resource Management

(9)... For the last 20 years, empirical work has paid particular attention to the link between the practice of HRM and organizational performance, evident in improved employee commitment, lower levels of absenteeism and turnover, (10)..., enhanced quality and efficiency. This area of work is sometimes referred to as 'Strategic HRM' or SHRM (not to be confused with the Society for Human Resource Management). Within SHRM three strands of work can be observed: Best practice, Best Fit and the Resource Based View (RBV).

The notion of best practice-sometimes called 'high commitment' HRM-proposes that the adoption of certain best practices in HRM will result in better organizational performance. These practices included: (11)..., sharing information, self-managed teams, high pay based on company performance and the reduction of status differentials. However, there is a huge number of studies which provide evidence of best practices, usually implemented in coherent bundles, and (12)...

Best fit, or the contingency approach to HRM, argues that HRM improves performance where there is a close vertical fit between the HRM practices and the company's strategy. This link ensures close coherence between the HR people processes and policies and the external market or business strategy. (13)... For example, a set of 'life cycle' models argue that HR policies and practices can be mapped onto the stage of an organization's development or life cycle. Competitive advantage models take Porter's ideas about strategic choice and map a range of HR practices onto the organization's choice of competitive strategy. Finally 'configuration models' provide a more sophisticated approach which advocates a close examination of the organization's strategy in order to determine the appropriate HR policies and practices. However, this approach assumes that the strategy of the organization can be identified-(14)...

A. Practicing good human resource management (HRM) enables managers of an enterprise to express their goals with specificity

B. providing employment security, selective hiring, extensive training

C. many organizations exist in a state of flux and development

D. therefore it is difficult to draw generalized conclusions about which is the 'best' way

E. Research in the area of Human Resource Management or HRM has much to contribute to the organizational practice of HRM

F. increasing worker comprehension of goals, providing the necessary resources

G. higher levels of skills and therefore higher productivity

H. There are a range of theories about the nature of this vertical integration

PART THREE
Questions 15—20

· Read the following article on the development of human resources.

· For each question (15—20) mark one letter (A, B, C or D) on your Answer Sheet for the answer you choose.

Human Resources Development (HRD) is not a defined object, but a series of organized processes. Specific interventions, areas of expertise and practice that fall within this definition of HRD are recognized as performance improvement, organizational learning, career management and leadership development. HRD as a structure allows for individual development, potentially satisfying the organization's goals. The development of the individual will benefit both the individual and the organization. The HRD framework views employees as an *asset* to the enterprise whose value will be enhanced by development: "Its primary focus is on growth and employee development and it emphasizes developing individual potential and skills"

An apprentice will step through the development process to become a tradesman in their field as will a white-collar trainee to become a professional in their field. Training will allow the individual to complete a task within their field today. Training provides, maintains and enhances skills to perform the job.

HRD is the framework that focuses on the organizations competencies at the first stage, training, and then developing the employee, through education, to satisfy the organizations long-term needs and the individuals' career goals and employee value. HRD can be defined simply as developing the most important section of any business by attaining or upgrading the skills and attitudes of employees at all levels in order to maximize the effectiveness of the enterprise. The people within an organization are its HR.

Compared to other disciplines within Business Economics, HR Professionals have over the years in practice had difficulties in justifying HR investment, especially during recessions. This can in many ways be argued as being based on Human Capital lacking measurability, merely because the field has followed the measurement similar to other disciplines within Business Economics. Systems have arisen such as Learning Management Systems (LMS), Human Resource Management Systems (HRMS) and Enterprise Resource Planning (ERP). LMS has had focus on HRD, but not as an integrated part of Business Economics.

Recent innovative studies and development shows that it is possible to encompass HRD as a concept of Business Economics. The concept is called HRD intelligence. HRD intelligence focuses entirely on the behavior, attitudes, skills and knowledge. When used as a concept and a system HRD intelligence has the task to collect, structure, provide, promote, pull and document information, within or outside the control of the company, which all have the characteristics to have an influence on the success of the strategies of the business, and hereby support better business decision-making.

15. By the word "asset" (line 7, paragraph 1), the author means _____.
A. an agent
B. an item of value owned
C. something useful to defeat enemy
D. economic resource

16. Which of the following is NOT what Human Resources Development focuses on?
A. Enhancing the organization's value.
B. Employees' development.
C. Developing individual potential and skills.
D. Becoming a tradesman.

17. Which of the following is the right description of HRD?
A. A series of training.
B. An framework.
C. An organized process.
D. A defined object.

18. Why does the author compare HRD to other disciplines within Business Economics?
A. To emphasize the importance of HRD.
B. To differentiate HRD from other disciplines.
C. To reveal the difficulties of HRD in practice.
D. To analyze HRD's similar measurement to other disciplines.

19. Which of the following is NOT the right description of HRD intelligence?
A. It focuses entirely on the behavior, attitudes, skills and knowledge.
B. It can help employers and bosses make better decision in business.
C. It has an influence on the performance and results of companies.
D. It is superior to HRD.

20. Why do Human Resource Professionals have difficulties in justifying HR investment?
A. Because the field has arisen many systems such as LMS, HRMS, ERP etc.

B. Because the field has many different measurement to other disciplines.

C. Because the field lacks a certain measurability.

D. Because the systems like LMS, HRMS are not integrated in Business Economics.

PART FOUR
Questions 21—30

· Read the article below about the human resource.

· Choose the correct word to fill each gap from A, B, C or D.

· For each question (21—30), mark one letter (A, B, C or D) on your Answer Sheet.

What HR is About

Human resource is a term used to describe the individuals who make up the (21)... of an organization, (22)... it is also applied in labor economics to, for example, business sectors or even whole nations. Human resource is also the name of the function within an organization (23)... with the overall responsibility for implementing strategies and policies (24)... to the management of individuals. Despite its more everyday use, terms such as "human resource" and, similarly, "human capital" continue to be perceived (25)... and may be considered insulting. They create the impression that people are merely commodities, like office machines or vehicles, despite assurances to the contrary.

Modern analysis emphasizes that human beings are not "commodities" or "resources", but are creative and social beings in a productive enterprise. The 2000 revision of ISO 9001, in contrast, requires (26)... the processes, their sequence and interaction, and to define and communicate responsibilities and authorities. In general, heavily unionized nations such as France and Germany have adopted and encouraged such approaches. (27)..., in 2001, the International Labor Organization decided to revisit and revise its 1975 Recommendation 150 on Human Resources Development. One view of these trends is that a strong social (28)... on political economy and a good social (29)... system facilitates labor mobility and tends to make the entire economy more productive, as labor can develop skills and experience in various ways, and move from one enterprise to another with little (30)... or difficulty in adapting. Another view is that governments should become more aware of their national role in facilitating human resources development across all sectors.

21. A. resource   B. workforce   C. manpower   D. staff
22. A. although   B. because   C. supposing   D. but
23. A. involved   B. associated   C. along   D. charged
24. A. according   B. belonging   C. relating   D. as
25. A. indifferently B. negatively   C. strangely   D. oddly
26. A. implementing B. identifying   C. conducting   D. assuring
27. A. However   B. Anyway   C. Also   D. Further
28. A. contact   B. capital   C. consensus   D. status

29.	A. transport	B. security	C. service	D. welfare
30.	A. controversy	B. challenge	C. doubt	D. trouble

PART FIVE
Questions 31—40

- Read the article below about applicant recruitment.
- For each question 31—40, write one word in CAPITAL LETTERS on your Answer Sheet.

Applicant Recruitment

Applicant recruitment and employee selection form a major part of an organization's overall resourcing strategies, (31)... identify and secure people needed for the organization. Recruitment activities need to be responsive to the increasingly competitive market to secure suitably qualified and capable recruits at all (32)... To be effective, these initiatives need to include how and when to source the best recruits, internally or (33)... Common to the success of (34)... are: well-defined organizational structures with sound job design, robust task and person specification and versatile selection processes, reward, employment relations and human (35)... policies, underpinned by a commitment for strong employer branding and employee engagement and on-boarding strategies. Internal recruitment can provide the most cost-effective (36)... for recruits if the potential of the existing pool of employees has been enhanced through training, development and other performance-enhancing activities such as performance appraisal, succession planning and development centers to review performance and assess employee development needs and promotional potential. (37)... many organizations, securing the best quality candidates requires external recruitment methods. (38)... changing business models demand skill and experience that cannot be sourced or rapidly enough developed from the existing employee base. It would be unusual for an organization to undertake all aspects of the recruitment process (39)... support from (40)...—party dedicated recruitment firms. This may involve a range of support services, such as: provision of CVs or resumes, identifying recruitment media, advertisement design and media placement for job vacancies, candidate response handling, short-listing, conducting aptitude test, preliminary interviews or reference and qualification verification.

PART SIX
Questions 41—52

- Read the text below about the definition of human resource development.
- In most lines (41—52), there is one extra word. It either is grammatically incorrect or does not fit in with the sense of the text. Some lines, however, are correct.
- If a line is correct, write CORRECT on your Answer Sheet.
- If there is an extra word in the line, write the extra word in CAPITAL LETTERS on your Answer Sheet.

The Definition of HRD

At the organizational level, a successful Human Resources Development program prepares the

41. individual to undertake a higher level of work, " Be organized learning over a given period of time, to provide the possibility of performance change". In these settings, Human Resources

42. Development is the framework that those focuses on the organization's competencies at the first stage, training, and then developing the employee, through education, to satisfy the

43. organization's long-term needs and the individual's career goals and employee value relating to

44. their present and future employers. Human Resources Development can be defined simply as

45. developing the most important section of any business, and its human resource, by attaining or

46. upgrading employee skills and attitudes at all levels to maximize our enterprise effectiveness.

47. The people within an organization are its human resource development. Human Resources

48. Development from a business perspective is not entirely focused on the individual's growth and

49. development; "development occurs them to enhance the organization's value, not solely for

50. individual improvement. Individual education and development is not a tool and a means to an

51. end, not the end goal itself". The broader concept of national and more strategic attention to the

52. development of human resources is beginning to emerge on as newly independent countries face strong competition for their skilled professionals and the accompanying brain-drain they experience.

第14单元 货币和银行
Unit 14　Money and Banking

Text A

Ⅰ.课文导读
现代商业银行的最初形式是资本主义商业银行,它是资本主义生产方式的产物。商业银行发展到今天,与其当时因发放基于商业行为的自偿性贷款从而获得"商业银行"的称谓相比,已相去甚远。今天的商业银行已被赋予更广泛、更深刻的内涵。特别是第二次世界大战以后,随着社会经济的发展,银行业竞争的加剧,商业银行的业务范围不断扩大,逐渐成为多功能、综合性的"金融百货公司"。

Ⅱ. Text

A bank has two essential characteristics:

It accepts demand deposits①.

It makes commercial loans.

Commercial banks obviously have these characteristics. Today, however, other financial institutions often compete directly with commercial banks in offering financial services, and terms such as "nonbank banks②" have become part of our language. The one characteristics that distinguishes commercial banks from all other competitors is this: Commercial banks are full-service institutions.

Large industries and corporations, individual consumers, small businesses, and agencies of federal, state, and local government all rely on commercial banks to meet every type of financial need.

The largest commercial bank today may offer over 200 separate financial services and products, but not all of these are essential to continued profitable operations③. For example, every bank does not have an international department or a trust department④. If some of the 200 services to be eliminated, the large bank still could serve most of the customers.

---

① demand deposit: 活期存款
② nonblank bank: 非银行金融机构
③ continued profitable operations: 持续业务盈利
④ trust department: 信托部门

Three functions stand out as major contributions to the economy. They are the building blocks upon which banking and the economy rest. In addition, they satisfy the legal requirement that defines a bank. The three functions are:

The deposit function

The largest single element in the money supply is the demand deposit—funds that can be withdrawn at any time without advance notice to the bank. The most common type of demand deposit is the checking account①. The total amount on deposit, or any part of it, is payable on demand and can be converted② into coin and currency if the funds are collected and available. If an individual with an available balance of ＄100 in a checking account issues a check for that amount, he or she can present it to a teller③ and immediately receive ＄100 in cash.

At a bank, the deposit may be made either into a checking or savings account④, or used to establish some form of time deposit⑤. The depositor's intent is not the same in each case. Deposits into checking accounts are made because the customer intends to withdraw the funds in the very near future to meet current expenses. In today's economy, customers tend to leave the smallest amount possible in excess checking-account balances, which by law cannot earn interest. Instead, they deposit all funds that are not immediately needed into some form of savings account or time deposit. Such funds are set aside for future goals or emergencies while earning interest.

Savings accounts are different from time deposits. The customer who opens a saving account does not establish a maturity date⑥ when it will be closed; deposits and withdrawals affecting the account may be made over a period of many years. On the other hand, a time deposit has a specific maturity—7 days or more from the date of deposit. Whenever a time deposit is withdrawn before maturity, there is a penalty⑦ for the early withdrawal.

In its simplest form, banking consists of obtaining funds through deposits and putting those funds to profitable use in loans and investments. Thus, it is logical to expect banks to be aware at all times of the actual amounts available as deposits and the types of deposits these amounts represent. The ratio between demand deposits on one hand, and time and savings deposits on the other, is extremely important for two reasons. The bank must pay an interest expense on the latter, and there is an essential difference in the rate of turnover. The turnover rate⑧ for demand deposits is extremely high. They can be used for short-term loans and investments. Time deposits, however, remain for longer periods and are used in longer-term loans and investments.

The payment function

---

① checking account: 活期存款账户
② convert: 转换
③ teller: 出纳员
④ saving account: 储蓄账户
⑤ time deposit: 定期存款
⑥ a maturity date: 到期日
⑦ penalty: 罚金
⑧ turnover rate: 周转率

Checks are safe and convenient vehicles for payment, and are accepted on faith and trust. Before checks gained such wide acceptance, the payments function often involved methods that left a great deal to be desired. Money, for example, is easily lost or stolen. If a payment is made in cash, any receipt that is given also can be lost; and if no receipt is issued, it may be impossible to prove that the payment actually was made.

By contrast, every customer who uses checks as a payment vehicle receives certain forms of protection. The risk of losing cash disappears; the paid check remains the best evidence of payment; and the bank's bookkeeping system is designed to assure that the customer's exact instructions, as contained in the check, are followed in every detail.

By continually improving the payments mechanism and by supplying the personnel, equipment, and technology to handle 100 million checks every day, banks have made a great contribution to the economy. There is a constant search for a better way to serve the interests of customers and banks, and this has led to the development of various Electronic Funds Transfer Systems (EFTS).

Whenever automated, paperless bookkeeping entries can be used to debit one account and credit another, tremendous benefits can be gained. Electronic transfers are far less costly, more accurate, and faster than paper-based payment systems.

Social Security Administration officials have had great success in persuading recipients to accepts direct deposit of their monthly payments, which avoids the use of checks and guarantees payment on the due date. Many employers also use direct deposit for their payroll[①] activity so that an employee's account, wherever it is located, can be credited with his or her net pay[②]. In growing numbers, customers are using ATMs to obtain cash without issuing checks. A depositor can authorize in advance direct payments from his or her bank to cover insurance premiums[③], mortgage[④] and loan payments, and other fixed charges.

The credit function

Today many sources of credit are available to customers. Individual consumers can approach personal finance or auto finance companies for credit and can borrow from insurance companies against the cash surrender value[⑤] of their policies or from brokerage firms against the value of their securities. Individuals also can buy merchandise on credit through a retailer, obtain mortgage or home equity loans[⑥] from thrift institutions[⑦], borrow from a credit union to which they belong, or as savings depositors, use their passbooks as security for loans.

Despite the diversity of available lenders, banks remain the dominant force in the credit

---

① payroll: 薪资
② net pay: 薪酬净额
③ cover insurance premiums: 支付保险费
④ mortgage: 抵押贷款
⑤ cash surrender value: 人寿保险退保解约金值
⑥ home equity loans: 房屋净值贷款
⑦ thrift institutions: 储蓄机构

market. More money is borrowed each year from banks than from any other source. Banks have not become the largest lenders simply because they are required to make commercial loans under the legal definition of banks; they do so because the loans constitute their largest source of income. Typically, two-thirds of a bank's yearly earnings results from interest on loans. Moreover, lending fulfills the bank's traditional role of serving their customers and communities.

In keeping with their full-service philosophy, banks extend credit under virtually every conceivable set of conditions to every segment of the market. No other lender can match them in either the size or diversity of the credit extended. There are bank loans to meet the needs of the small or large business, the government, and the consumer.

Business, governments, and consumers are the three main categories of borrowers. The ability of banks to serve the credit needs of the three groups is vital to the prosperity of the American economy. In addition, by granting loans and crediting the proceeds to customers' accounts, banks are directly responsible for creating money, thereby directly affecting the nation's money supply.

How do banks create money? Essentially, by generating a cycle of funds. Assume that reserve① requirements are 20%, that all loans proceeds are deposited into checking accounts, and that all payments are deposits to a checking account in the same bank. A $1,000 cash deposit is made in the bank by A. After the 20% reserve is deducted, the bank can lend $800 to B. Following the reserve deduction, $640 is available to lend to C. Continuing the same process, the bank theoretically could lend $512 to D and $409 to E. From the original cash deposit of $1,000, a total of $2,361 in new funds has been created through this succession of bank loans.

Banks can build up their deposits by increasing loans, as long as they provide for reserve requirements and depositors' withdrawals.

III. Notes

1. Nonbank bank. An institution that provides most of the services of a bank but is not a member of the federal reserve systems and does not have a charter from a state banking agency. A *nonbank bank* may offer credit cards, consumer and commercial loans, savings accounts, and accounts with services similar to bank checking accounts. By avoiding government regulation, such businesses may be able to be more innovative and profitable than traditional government-regulated banks.

2. Electronic Funds Transfer System (电子金融转账系统). It is the use of automated technology to move funds in institution for use of paper checks. The growing popularity of EFT for online bill payment is paving the way for a paperless universe where checks, stamps, envelopes, and paper bills are obsolete. The benefits of EFT include reduced administrative costs, increased efficiency, simplified bookkeeping, and greater security. However, the number of compa-

---

① reserve: 储备

nies who send and receive bills through the Internet is still relatively small.

3. Social Security Administration（社会保障）. The United States Social Security Administration (SSA) is an independent agency of the United States federal government that administers Social Security, a social insurance program consisting of retirement, disability, and survivors' benefits. To qualify for these benefits, most American workers pay Social Security taxes on their earnings; future benefits are based on the employees' contributions.

4. Thrift institution（储蓄机构）. A thrift institution is a financial institution formed primarily to accept consumer deposits and make home mortgages. The primary types of thrift institutions are mutual banks, savings and loan associations, and credit unions. Thrift institutions often pay out more in dividends (interest) than do traditional financial institutions and have access to lower cost funds from organizations like Federal Home Loan Banks. Thrift institutions are more community-focused than other types of financial institutions and tend to focus more on consumers than businesses. Since financial services have become increasingly deregulated, thrift institutions have been able to offer more services to businesses, however.

Ⅳ. Useful Expressions

1. advance notice: 提前通知
2. rest upon: 依赖，取决于
3. convert into: 转换成
4. meet expenses: 应付开支
5. set aside: 留出，拨出
6. in advance: 提前
7. build up: 增长，扩大

Ⅴ. Reading Comprehension

Questions

1. What is the legal definition of a bank? What are the three basic functions of a commercial bank?
2. What is the legal difference between a savings deposit and a time deposit?
3. How is bank interest generated?
4. In what ways are checks better than cash in payment?
5. How do commercial banks create money?

Decide whether each of the following statements is true or false.

1. Banking is the one industry that is related to every other. Without the services the banks provide, other industries would find it difficult or impossible to continue operating.   (   )
2. Deposit is the largest source of banks' income.   (   )
3. Banks meet the needs of all economic entities except governmental organizations.
    (   )

4. Other types of financial institutions might have offered each customer the necessary services; yet only a commercial bank could have offered all of the services to all of the customers. (   )

5. That people set aside some amount of money for future goals or emergencies is called checking accounts. (   )

6. Savings accounts can not earn interest, while time deposits can earn interest. (   )

7. Banks accept various types of deposits, process both checks and electronic funds transfers as payment vehicles. (   )

8. Bank is the only source for corporation to borrow money. (   )

9. Since new application of an Electronic Funds Transfer System reduces check usage, there will be situations in which checks will not continue to be used. (   )

10. Banks have a strong comparative advantage in making commercial and industrial loans than other financial institutions. (   )

VI. Discussion

Without the services the banks provide, other industries would find it difficult or impossible to continue operating. Do you agree with it?

Text B
BEC Reading Texts

PART ONE
Questions 1—8

· Look at the statements below and the five extracts about money & banking from an article.

· Which extract (A, B, C, D or E) does each statement (1—8) refer to?

· For each statement (1—8), make one letter (A, B, C, D or E) on your Answer Sheet.

· You will need to use some of these letters more than once.

1. The commercial banking systems of the major industry countries have become internationalized.

2. By controlling the money supply, commercial banks can keep themselves grow at an appropriate rate.

3. Relations between the Central Bank and the government are complex.

4. Central Bank acts as the government's bank.

5. One of the function of a central bank is to prevent massive bank failures.

6. One consequence of the internationalization of commercial banking is that there is now

more extensive competition in the major national financial centers due to the presence of foreign banks.

7. One of the Central Bank's roles is a lender of last resort.

8. The Central Bank is not owned and operated completely by the government.

A. Each commercial bank, as it obtains reserves and expands its deposits, could grow at an inappropriate rate. One way of controlling the growth rate of deposits is to require banks to stand ready to redeem their deposits in some valuable commodity. Another is to institute a central bank charged with keeping reserves.

B. Central bank needs to guard against bank failures, particularly if there are many relatively small banks. This is not to say that central banks always did prevent widespread bank failures. But a central bank should act as institution able and willing in a crisis to make loans to banks when other banks cannot, or will not to do so.

C. In addition to its services for commercial banks, a central bank provides many other services. The government keeps an account at the central bank, writes its checks on this account, and, in some countries, sells its securities through central bank. Another group of services to the government arises directly out of the central bank's close relation with commercial banks. Thus the central bank typically administrators certain controls over commercial bank.

D. Although central banks are part of the government, they maintain a certain detachment from the rest of it. They usually have much more independence from the administration than do such government agencies as the Treasury.

E. Banking in Great Britain is dominated by four major banks (National Westminster, Barclays, Midland, and Lloyds), but twenty major non-British banks compete for the British pound deposits and loans of major and modest customers. Similarly, the three big German banks (Deutsche, Dresdner, and Commerz) have encountered increased competition for loan and deposit business from fifty branches of foreign banks in Frankfurt, Düsseldorf, and Hamburg.

PART TWO
Questions 9—14

· Read the text about the pulse of the economy.

· Choose the best sentence to fill each of the gaps.

· For each gap (9—14), mark one letter (A-H) on your Answer Sheet.

· Do not use any letter more than once.

Taking the Pulse of the Economy

Reading the financial news is somewhat complicated when the subject is overall economic activity. In fact, when measuring the performance of the aggregate economy there is no single number that does the job. Instead, a variety of statistics released by the government on a monthly or quarterly basis, and published in major newspapers, (9)... It is useful to divide these statistics into measures of aggregate output and unemployment on the one hand, . (10)...

Aggregate output and employment. The most comprehensive measures of economic activity is real GDP. Estimates are released in April for the first quarter (January-March), (11)... Although real GNP is released as a dollar figure, the most important feature is its rate of growth. Thus, if real GNP grows at an annual rate of 4% during a quarter, that is considered a fast pace of economic activity; if it grows by only 1% that would be slow.

The most important number released on a monthly basis is the unemployment rate. Increases in the unemployment rate of one-half of one percent during a one-or two-month period implies that (12)...

The price level. The GNP deflator is the most comprehensive measure of the price level. (13)... It is released quarterly along with data on GNP. A rate of increase in the deflator of 3% or 4% on an annual basis has been considered acceptable in recent years.

Two somewhat narrower measures of inflation are released monthly: the consumer price index and the producer price index. As suggested by their names, (14)..., while the latter measures price changes at the wholesale level. For obvious reasons, although the consumer price index is a less comprehensive measure of the price level than the GNP deflator, it receives the lion's share of attention because it measures how inflation influences each of us directly in our role as consumers. Once again, a 3% or 4% increase on an annual basis is considered acceptable; 6% or 8% is not.

A. Our knowledge of how best to construct such a model is far from complete

B. in July for the second quarter (April-June), and so on

C. serve as important indicators

D. in terms of the results that formal econometric models of the economy have produced

E. the former measures the rate of change in prices of goods purchased by the typical consumer (as defined by the Department of Commerce)

F. It is a weighted average of prices of all goods and services produced in the economy

G. economic activity is slowing down sufficiently to take its toll on the work force

H. and the price level and inflation on the other

PART THREE
Questions 15—20

· Read the following article Bank of American's new decision.

· For each question (15—20) mark one letter (A, B, C or D) on your Answer Sheet for the answer you choose.

Bank of America struck a nerve this week when it announced it would charge many debit card users a $5 monthly fee when they shop. The company's stock price fell. Customers complained. One cable business anchor sliced up her debit card live on air. Why such a public backlash over a few extra bucks a month? Perhaps the bank's decision simply reminded us all over again that we are living increasingly in a fee-littered world, where companies continually seek out new ways to nibble away at our wallets by charging for the smallest of once-free services, leaving many customers feeling nickel-and-dimed. "The proliferation of a la carte fees has inundated the economy," said Ed Mierzwinski, consumer program director for the U. S. Public Interest Research Group. Companies "are inventing new fees; they are making it harder to avoid fees; they are increasing the fees... It's much more complicated to be a consumer." Bank of America's new debit card fee, which also has been tested or implemented by other banks, joins a long and growing list of similar charges that consumers now encounter in the course of daily life. Among them: airline baggage fees, hotel Internet fees, "convenience charges" for concert and sporting tickets, ATM fees, bank teller fees, paper statement fees, fees hidden in phone and cable bills, taxicab fuel surcharges and exorbitant shipping and handling costs. As many businesses find themselves squeezed by new regulations, rising fuel prices or the generally sluggish economy, they have sought new ways to extract more money from customers, despite the public relations hit that often results, said John Ulzheimer, president of consumer education at SmartCredit. com. "It's absolutely a math equation: How many people am I going to lose?" Ulzheimer said. "I don't know that companies care so much about being loved; they care more that people continue to use them. What's important is the bottom line." That doesn't mean the tactic can't backfire. It's little surprise that consumers feel slighted when something that used to be free — be it airline pretzels or hotel gyms — suddenly costs money. But the businesses behind those fees often argue that they simply are covering their costs. Bank of America's debit card fee marks just one of the ways banks are modifying consumers' accounts in the wake of the financial crisis, which resulted in a regulatory overhaul for the banking system and a fundamental shift in the industry business model. Even so, many customers have shown little sympathy for the bank's woes in the wake of news about the new monthly debit card fee. "It's not fair," Elizabeth Romero of the District said Friday outside a Bank of America branch in Capitol Heights. "I started looking into changing banks."

15. What did Bank of America decide to do?

A. To invent new fees.

B. To make consumers more complicated.

C. To encourage people to deposit more money.

D. To charge debit card users some amount of fee.

16. Why was there a public backlash over Bank of America's new decision?

A. Because many companies' stock price fell down.

B. Because customers feel unimportant when receiving services now

C. Because customers have to pay for once-free service.

D. Because customers can't avoid fees.

17. Which of the statement is not true?

A. There are still many services that do not charge in our living word.

B. Not only Bank of America but also other banks have already implemented new debit card fee.

C. Customers need to pay airline baggage fees.

D. Customers felt angry when Bank of America announced its new policy.

18. How do customers feel when they are charged for something that used to be free?

A. Pleased.

B. Respected.

C. Uneasy.

D. Contemptuous.

19. What can be inferred about Bank of America?

A. It is facing financial crisis. .

B. It needs changing in its regulatory overhaul and industry business model.

C. It has modified customers accounts in the way of debit card fee marks.

D. It will get more profit by charging debit card fee.

20. Why did Elizabeth Romero say: "It's not fair" at the end of the passage?

A. American banks shifted their financial burden to the working people.

B. The fee American banks charge for debit card just covers the cost.

C. American banks are in a critical period.

D. Customers show their sympathy to banks' plight.

PART FOUR
Questions 21—30

· Read the article below about gold investment.

· Choose the correct word to fill each gap from A, B, C or D.

· For each question (21—30), mark one letter (A, B, C or D) on your Answer Sheet.

Is Gold A Good Investment?

Gold is probably the favorite (21)... for hoarding by both governments and individuals around the world, and it has been for centuries. Should you buy some gold, perhaps in the (22)... of a few gold coins? Is gold a good investment?

Because gold earns no interest or dividends, it immediately suffers in comparison with such (23)... as savings accounts, bonds, stocks, and rental property. In this respect it is similar to diamonds, stamps, rare coins, and art objects. Because it yields no current income, the (24)... of buying gold thus depends entirely on the prospect for future price appreciation.

If gold can be expected to rise in price by more than 5 to 10 percent annually, which is (25)... what one can earn in a savings account or over the long run in bonds or stocks, then it is worth considering seriously as an investment.

The price of gold, just like the price of other commodities, is determined in the free market by supply and demand. And in this case, supply and demand factors make the price of gold highly volatile. (26)... respect to supply, new production adds to the existing stockpile at the rate of only about 2% a year. This means that the overwhelming element on the supply side is not the amount of current ore production but uncertainty as to how much holders of the existing stockpile might decide to unload. (27)..., sales by large holders are always a threat to break the price.

When consumer prices threaten to rise rapidly and/or international tensions increase, the private demand for gold (28)... But when inflation subsides and/or international tensions ease, demand often vanishes overnight. This sort of demand typically fluctuates erratically on short notice, and rather small changes in supply or demand can produce (29)... price swings.

Thus gold is a highly (30)... investment. Large gains can occasionally be made, but on the basis of the historical record over the past hundred years large losses are just as likely.

21. A. asset   B. property   C. capital   D. wealth
22. A. form   B. way   C. value   D. means
23. A. alternates   B. options   C. alternatives   D. alternations
24. A. usage   B. benefit   C. profitability D. wisdom
25. A. exactly   B. roughly   C. probably   D. similarly
26. A. For   B. By   C. With   D. In
27. A. As it were   B. In summary
    C. In other words   D. Generally speaking
28. A. decreases   B. shrinks   C. extends   D. expands
29. A. serious   B. wide   C. terrible   D. broad
30. A. speculative   B. profitable   C. lucrative   D. risky

PART FIVE
Questions 31—40

· Read the article below about environment.

· For each question 31—40, write one word in CAPITAL LETTERS on your Answer Sheet.

Helping the Environment While Saving Money

The management of Neckermann, a $2.4 billion German mail-order firm, wanted to help protect the environment, (31)... it formulated a policy directing its employees to work to this end. The (32)... department, responsible for handling imports from European countries and Asia, proposed sending more imports to Rotterdam, (33)... where they would be forwarded in barges via the Rhine waterway to the firm's three warehouses in Frankfurt. Under the old arrangement, imports arriving in Hamburg were sent by rail or road to Frankfurt. The 120,000 tons of merchandise from European suppliers now comes by rail (34)... of truck as it formerly did. These changes have provided two (35)...: less environmental damage and (36)... costs.'

Based on estimates by the prestigious Planco Institute, the company calculates that the new environmentally friendly system of waterways and rail has (37)... total costs to the environment (air, ground, water, and noise pollution) from $1.6 million under the old road-intensive arrangement to ＄722,000. In addition, the firm is saving ＄241,000 annually by shipping containers over Rhine waterway from Rotterdam to Frankfurt instead of using (38)... from Hamburg to Frankfrut. It is now considering supplying its Manngeim warehouse by barge, and it may also use barges on the Rhine (39)... to handle the 500 containers that come each year from Eastern Europe. This has been made (40)... by the new Main-Danube canal that extends the Rhine waterway all the way to the Black Sea.

Other firms, among them Ford and Unilever, had already changed to the more environmentally friendly river system. These companies predict that others will increase their use of waterways when, as expected, the European Union deregulates waterway rates.

PART SIX
Questions 41—52

· Read the text below from a report about central reserve.

· In most lines (41—52), there is one extra word. It either is grammatically incorrect or does not fit in with the sense of the text. Some lines, however, are correct.

· If a line is correct, write CORRECT on your Answer Sheet.

· If there is an extra word in the line, write the extra word in CAPITAL LETTERS on your Answer Sheet.

Central Reserve

41. The US ＄ has been the most used central reserve asset in the world since then the end of

42. World War Ⅱ. Somewhat analogous to a savings account, the dollars were available when

43. needed to finance trade or investments or to intervene with in currency markets. Held in the

44. form of U.S. Treasury Bonds, the US ＄ s earn an interest, and the more held in the savings/central reserve account, the better. But the countries don't want their central reserve

45. asset US ＄ to lose value, and there lies a contradiction: at some point, more greater numbers of US ＄ in supply cause them to lose value-supply and demand. At the same time, the US ＄ is the

46. national currency of the United States of America, that whose government must deal with inflation, recession, interest rates, unemployment, and other national, internal problems. The U.S. government uses fiscal and monetary policies to meet those problems-higher or lower

47. taxes, decisions so as to how to spend available revenue, growth or contraction of the money

48. supply, and rate of its growth or contraction. It would be accidental if only the national

49. interests of the United States in dealing with its internal problems are coincided with the

50. interests of the multitude of countries who holding US＄in their central reserve asset accounts.

51. The United States may be slowing money supply growth and raising taxes to combat against U. S. inflation while the world needs more liquidity, in the form of US＄, to finance growth, trade, or investment. Or the United States may be stimulating its economy through faster money supply growth and lower taxes at a time when so many US＄are already outstanding that their

52. value is dropping-not a happy state of affairs for countries holding US＄.

第15单元　商务礼仪
Unit 15　Business Etiquette

Text A

Ⅰ. 课文导读

　　商务礼仪是基于不同文化、不同习俗,在一系列商务活动中所产生的礼貌、礼节、行为等的约定俗成。在不同国家、不同地域,应采取不同的礼仪方式。商务活动中,商务礼仪的作用是为了使社会关系更为和善,使商务活动得以顺利进行。商务礼仪在针对不同对象时也有所不同。在老板面前应该注意礼貌,对待同事同仁,也应该注意自己的行为是否妥当,是否表现出尊重他人。此外,个人礼仪同样重要,包括个人习惯、卫生等。

Ⅱ. Text

　　Etiquette is dependent on culture; what is excellent etiquette in one society may shock another. Etiquette can vary widely between different cultures and nations. In China, a person who takes the last item of food from a common plate or bowl without first offering it to others at the table may be seen as a glutton① and insulting the generosity of the host. Traditionally, if guests do not have leftover food in front of them at the end of a meal, it is to the dishonor of the host. In America a guest is expected to eat all of the food given to them, as a compliment② to the quality of the cooking. However, it is still considered polite to offer food from a common plate or bowl to others at the table.

　　The etiquette of business is the set of written and unwritten rules of conduct that make social interactions run more smoothly. Office etiquette in particular applies to coworker interaction, excluding interactions with external contacts such as customers and suppliers. Opening the door for a coworker or picking up a ringing telephone at an unattended③ desk are nice things to do, and they are part of business etiquette — but they're just the tip of the iceberg④.

　　Business etiquette, simply put, is how you politely and considerately present yourself at work and work-related social gatherings. Exhibiting proper business etiquette brands you in a

---

① glutton: 贪吃鬼
② compliment: 赞美
③ unattended: 没人照料的
④ tip of the iceberg: 冰山一角

positive way, earning you the respect of your boss and your coworkers and ensuring that you're taken seriously. I believe that corporate culture starts at the top of the organizational chart. If the president/CEO of a company is respectful of his employees and shows them that he is genuinely interested in their professional development, employees will strive to work hard and try to impress him. Show me an organization where the boss is a yeller and screamer, and I'll guarantee you their office has a revolving door①.

Business etiquette shouldn't be limited to how you behave around your boss; coworkers should be given respect too. There are a few things you may (or may not be) doing that affect whether people view you as a polite person who's pleasant to work with or as "that guy/that woman." Here are a few tips I've learned throughout many years.

Etiquette towards your boss:

· If you are in your supervisor's office and their phone rings, politely excuse yourself and step out to give them privacy (unless they tell you to stay).

· If your boss asks you to tally up② travel and expense (T & E) reports, do not mention how much they spent.

· Listen carefully to what is being said to you and then follow through.

· If you need to make an appointment with your supervisor, ask for it verbally or in writing. Do not expect them to drop everything and see you immediately.

· Be early for work. If you are on time, you are late.

· Supervisors may not notice every time you do the right thing, but you can be sure they'll notice if you do the wrong thing.

Etiquette towards your coworkers:

· Greet coworkers by name when you see them.

· If you work in a cubicle③ do not play music, talk loudly, or eat foods with a strong aroma④; this can be bothersome and distracting to your coworkers.

· If you want to speak to someone in another cubicle, knock before you enter.

· Copy machines are for everyone in an office to use. If you need to make several copies and see there is a wait for the machine, let a coworker who just needs one or two copies jump in⑤.

· Be mindful of wearing perfume or cologne in an office. You may think you smell fantastic, but your coworkers may not agree.

· If your office has a refrigerator, keep track of your food and be courteous⑥ enough to

---

① a revolving door: 旋转门
② tally up: 结算
③ cubicle: 小隔间
④ aroma: 浓香
⑤ jump in: 插队，先做
⑥ courteous: 有礼貌的

throw it away before it spoils.

· Do not chime in① on other people's conversations if you aren't part of the conversation.

· Refrain from commenting on the food choices others make.

· Do not use a speakerphone② at work unless you have a private office.

· If you are in an open environment, do not speak loudly into your phone.

· Go to business meetings prepared.

· If you are late for a staff meeting or presentation, do not walk in front of the speaker. Find a way to be as inconspicuous as possible and quietly take your seat.

· Do not try to speak over a colleague during meetings; simply wait your turn.

· Do not walk out of a meeting while someone is speaking. Wait until there is a break.

· Return voicemails, emails and general correspondences in a timely manner③.

· Do not say or imply that a member of the opposite sex is looking sexy.

· Restrict your romantic inclinations and advances to people you don't work with. Office romance is not good for either party, and you may find yourself in hot water.

· Do not drink alcohol at holiday/office parties.

It's important to remember that you must respect your colleagues. You do not have to like them, but you owe it to them (and yourself) to learn to work together.

Personal etiquette:

· Pay attention to your appearance and make sure you're neatly and professionally groomed④ when you go to work.

· Look alert at your desk and do not slouch⑤ in your seat.

· Be sure your desk is not hidden under a heap of clutter⑥.

· Do not share your darkest secrets with your coworkers. Your place of work is a professional environment — not a social club.

· Do not share other people's darkest secrets with your coworkers. The office is no place for gossip.

· Do not use foul⑦ or potentially offensive language at work.

· Do not whine⑧.

· Do not be a clock-watcher.

· Keep confidential correspondences truly confidential.

· Avoid downloading personal information on your work computer.

---

① chime in: 插话
② speakerphone: 免提
③ in a timely manner: 及时地
④ groom: 打扮
⑤ slouch: 懒散地坐着
⑥ clutter: 杂乱
⑦ foul language: 粗言秽语
⑧ whine: 抱怨,发牢骚

· Do not tweet about work or your personal life through Twitter while you're at work. I know I promote social networking through the web, but work is not the place to catch up with people in your network.

· YouTube videos are not appropriate to review at work —even if it is the funniest thing you've ever seen, save it for home viewing.

· If you are running late and have a client waiting, let them know you will be with them shortly and offer them a beverage①.

· Send thank-you notes within one day to express your appreciation when necessary.

When you behave professionally on a personal level, you're showing your supervisor and coworkers that you're serious about your job — and setting yourself up for success.

Ⅲ. Notes

1. Twitter (非官方中文惯称:推特). It is an online social networking and microblogging service that enables its users to send and read text-based posts of up to 140 characters, informally known as "tweets". Twitter was created in March 2006 by Jack Dorsey and launched that July. Twitter rapidly gained worldwide popularity, with over 300 million users as of 2011, generating over 300 million tweets and handling over 1.6 billion search queries per day. It is sometimes described as "the SMS of the Internet." Twitter Inc., the company that operates the service and associated website, is based in San Francisco, with additional servers and offices in San Antonio, Boston, and New York City.

2. YouTube (视频分享网站). YouTube is a video-sharing website, created by three former PayPal employees in February 2005, on which users can upload, view and share videos. Unregistered users may watch videos, and registered users may upload an unlimited number of videos. Videos that are considered to contain potentially offensive content are available only to registered users 18 years old and older. The company is based in San Bruno, California and uses Adobe Flash Video and HTML5 technology to display a wide variety of user-generated video content, including movie clips, TV clips, and music videos, as well as amateur content such as video blogging and short original videos. Most of the content on YouTube has been uploaded by individuals, although media corporations including CBS, BBC, VEVO, Hulu, and other organizations offer some of their material via the site, as part of the YouTube partnership program. In November 2006, YouTube, LLC was bought by Google Inc. for US $1.65 billion, and now operates as a subsidiary of Google.

Ⅳ. Useful Expressions

1. earn sb. respect: 赢得尊重
2. simply put: 简单地说
3. take sb. seriously: 认真对待某人

---

① beverage: 饮料

4. tally up the expenses: 结算费用

5. follow through: 完成

6. keep track of: 记录；了解进展情况

7. chime in: 插话

8. be mindful of: 注意

9. restrict to: 仅限于

V. Reading Comprehension

Questions

1. What is business etiquette?
2. How do you manage the relationship with your boss?
3. What should you avoid doing in communication with your coworkers?
4. What does it mean by saying "I'll guarantee you their office has a revolving door"?
5. What is the etiquette toward the coworkers of the opposite sex?

Decide whether each of the following statements is true or false.

1. Business etiquette is a variety of rules of conduct applied to help social interactions. ( )
2. Business etiquette can be different according to different nations. ( )
3. In China, you should always take the last item of food before the others do. ( )
4. Table etiquette is more important in Western counties. ( )
5. Office etiquette is a set of principles you should follow to please your colleagues. ( )
6. Presenting proper business etiquette can earn the respect of your customers. ( )
7. You should listen carefully to what the boss says to you and raise an objection. ( )
8. You ought to always be punctual at work. ( )
9. If you work in a cubicle, do not listen to music, talk loudly or eat food, because this will bother your coworkers. ( )
10. You should not promote your social circle through network while you are at work. ( )

VI. Discussion

Compare the different etiquettes between China and Western countries.

Text B
BEC Reading Texts

PART ONE
Questions 1—8

- Look at the statements below and the five extracts about business etiquette from an article.
- Which extract (A, B, C, D or E) does each statement (1—8) refer to?
- For each statement (1—8), make one letter (A, B, C, D or E) on your Answer Sheet.
- You will need to use some of these letters more than once.

1. Business etiquette is fundamentally concerned with building relationships founded upon courtesy and politeness between business personnel.

2. There are many written and unwritten rules and guidelines for etiquette, and it certainly behooves a business person to learn them.

3. Etiquette is about being comfortable around people and making them comfortable around you.

4. People are a key factor in your own and your business' success. Many potentially worthwhile and profitable alliances have been lost because of an unintentional breach of manners.

5. Trying to understand the astonishing diversity of an ancient yet vibrant culture and yet finding rules for behaving in an effective manner is a daunting challenge for anyone.

6. The most important thing to remember is to be courteous and thoughtful to the people around you. Consider other people's feelings, stick to your convictions as diplomatically as possible.

7. One area of culture that is important for the international business person is etiquette.

8. There is a lot to consider, in business etiquette but the caveat is that there is no possible way to avoid all of mistakes.

A. Business etiquette is made up of significantly more important things than knowing which fork to use at lunch with a client. Unfortunately, in the perception of others, the devil is in the details. People may feel that if you can't be trusted not to embarrass yourself in business and social situations, you may lack the self-control necessary to be good at what you do. Etiquette is about presenting yourself with the kind of polish that shows you can be taken seriously.

B. These guidelines have some difficult-to-navigate nuances, depending on the company, the local culture, and the requirements of the situation. Possibilities to commit a faux pas are limitless, and chances are, sooner or later, you'll make a mistake. But you can minimize them, recover quickly, and avoid causing a bad impression by being generally considerate and attentive to the concerns of others, and by adhering to the basic rules of etiquette. When in doubt, stick to the basics.

C. When doing business abroad it is important to understand the local culture. Culture includes areas such as a country's norms, values, behaviors, food, architecture, fashion and art. Understanding business etiquette allows you to feel comfortable in your dealings with foreign friends, colleagues, customers or clients. Knowing what to do and say in the right places will help build trust and open lines of communication.

D. Westerners going to India to do business find out pretty soon that India is a culture where it is absolutely impossible to just drop in to conduct business and then fly away unaffected. The pace of life, the vivacity of the teeming masses, the mêlée of sounds, the richness of colors and smells, the tenacity of the unpredictable to surface like an ubiquitous spook amidst all attempts on both sides to make business smooth and manageable-all this is India.

E. Etiquette, and especially business etiquette, is a means of maximizing your potential by presenting yourself positively. Writing a business letter is not simply a matter of expressing your ideas clearly. The way you write a letter and the etiquette you employ may have a significant impact on your success or failure in business. Failure to observe correct business letter etiquette can result in you adopting an inappropriate tone, causing offense or misunderstandings, lack of clarity or purpose and hostility or soured relations.

PART TWO
Questions 9—14

· Read the text about the tips on business phone etiquette.

· Choose the best sentence to fill each of the gaps.

· For each gap (9—14), mark one letter (A-H) on your Answer Sheet.

· Do not use any letter more than once.

Business Phone Etiquette

Etiquette is in essence about proper conduct and presenting yourself favorably. Demonstrating good etiquette is important if one seeks to be successful. An area in which this is essential is the business phone call.

(9)... Business people that interact solely over the phone yet never meet still form strong opinions of one another. Practicing good business phone etiquette helps encourage clear lines of communication, build rapport and avoid misunderstandings. Most of us can recollect a phone call that left us feeling frustrated or irritated. How much of this could have been attributed to poor phone etiquette? (10)...

All successful business interaction needs preparation. The phone call is no exception. It is important to know who you are calling, the most convenient time to do so, the reason for your call and what you can do for them. Be structured, short and sharp. If the caller is not known to the receiver, it is important that the purpose of the call and the caller's credentials are established immediately. (11)...

Particularize your intention behind the call. (12)... Expand upon information and specify the purpose of the call. Pass on information that the receiver will understand, appreciate and find useful. Waffling and speaking generically will lose attention and generally reflect poorly on the caller.

(13)... When speaking to someone you do not know avoid informal speech or personal questions. Once a relationship has been built it is considered polite to enquire about weekends, children or other non-sensitive personal matters. (14)... If it is imperative that sensitive discussions take place over the phone, business etiquette requires that you confirm with the receiver whether this is appropriate.

A. Privacy and security around furtive issues must always be borne in mind on the phone.

B. Do not assume the receiver understands why you are calling them and what you expect of them.

C. Here we explore a few simple examples of areas within business phone etiquette that should be employed when making or receiving calls.

D. You should find they can go a long way in contributing to an improved understanding of how to use the phone effectively in the business world.

E. A simple introduction followed by a sentence or two not only shows good phone etiquette but allows the receiver to set the forthcoming information within a context.

F. If the caller is rambling, chances are you can't tell what the point is.

G. Millions of business phone calls are made every hour and day.

H. Good business phone etiquette demands professionalism at all times.

PART THREE

Questions 15—20

· Read the following article on etiquette in business environment.

· For each question (15—20) mark one letter (A, B, C or D) on your Answer Sheet for the answer you choose.

To say that today's business environment is becoming increasingly more global is to state the obvious. Meetings, phone calls and conferences are held all over the world and attendees can come from any point on the globe. You may never have to leave home to interact on an international level.

While the old adage "When in Rome, do as the Romans do" still holds true. Not to do your homework and put your best international foot forward can cost you relationships and future business. One small misstep such as using first names inappropriately or not observing the rules of timing bouquet can be costly.

Keeping in mind that there are as many ways to do business as there are countries to do business with, here are a few tips for minding your global P's and Q's.

Americans like to dress for fashion and comfort, but people from other parts of the world are generally more conservative. Your choice of business attire is a signal of your respect for the other person. Leave your trendy clothes in the closet on the days that you meet with your foreign guests.

It is not always a simple matter to know who the highest-ranking member is when you are dealing with a group. To avoid embarrassment, err on the side of age and masculine gender, only if you are unable to discover the protocol with research. If you are interacting with the Japanese, it is important to understand that they make decisions by consensus, starting with the younger members of the group.

With a few exceptions, business people around the world use the handshake for greeting. The American style handshake with a firm grip, two quick pumps, eye contact and a smile is not universal. Variations in handshakes are based on cultural differences. The Japanese give a light handshake. Germans offer a firm shake with one pump. Middle Eastern people will continue shaking your hand throughout the greeting. Don't be surprised if you are occasionally met with a kiss, a hug, or a bow somewhere along the way.

Not everyone in the world is as time-conscious as Americans. Don't take it personally if someone from a more relaxed culture keeps you waiting or spends more of that commodity than you normally would in meetings or over meals. Stick to the rules of punctuality, but be understanding when your contact from another country seems unconcerned.

Whether the world comes to you or you go out to it, the greatest compliment you can pay your international clients is to learn about their customs. Understand differences in behavior and honor them with your actions. Don't take offense when visitors behave according to their norms. People from other cultures will appreciate your efforts to accommodate them and you will find yourself building your international clientele.

15. What does the author mean by using the old adage "When in Rome, do as the Romans do" means?

    A. Different countries have different cultures and customs.

    B. You should do what is done by Romans when you in Rome.

    C. Business clients who are visiting this country should be with an awareness of their unique culture.

    D. You can not use the etiquette of your own country to treat your business clients.

16. What do you understand by the slang "P's and Q's"?

    A. It means there are as many ways to do business as there are countries to do business with.

    B. It refers to someone's behaviors.

    C. It represents your attire in a business environment.

    D. It signifies your respect to your business clients.

17. To do business with Japanese, you should not stick to the principle of

    A. learning about their customs before you meet.

B. giving a light handshake.

C. wearing casual clothing to show your honor.

D. starting the negotiation with the younger members of the group.

18. Which is not one of the appropriate behaviors in a business with an American?

A. Stick to the rules of punctuality.

B. Dress your trendy cloths and being fashionable.

C. Offer a firm grip, two quick pumps, eye contact and a smile.

D. Give him a hug or a kiss when meet him for the first time.

19. What do we learn about from the last paragraph?

A. It is the greatest compliment that you can learn about your clients' country and their customs.

B. Don't take offense when visitors behave according to their norms.

C. Understand the difference of your clients and show your respect with actions.

D. Clients from other cultures will appreciate your efforts to accommodate them.

20. Which is the best title of text?

A. Tips on business etiquette

B. Global business, global etiquette

C. Seek common points while reserving difference

D. Different culture, different etiquette

PART FOUR

Questions 21—30

· Read the article below about the need of business golf etiquette.

· Choose the correct word to fill each gap from A, B, C or D.

· For each question (21—30), mark one letter (A, B, C or D) on your Answer Sheet.

The Need of Business Golf Etiquette

Building and maintaining solid business relationships is the key to success, but how can you (21)... escape the tense office environment and spend dedicated time getting to know a customer, client or boss on a personal level?

Business Golf, once the domain of the executive elite is now (22)... for anyone wishing to create and strengthen business relationships in a relaxed atmosphere. In fact, according to a 2002 COMPAS Leader Poll, "business leaders use golf as an important tool in doing business and say that it is extremely (23)...; for each dollar they spend on golf they earn over $1500 in business revenue as a result. (24)..., only restaurants surpass the golf course as an effective place to conduct business outside of the office."

The strong demand for golf has resulted in several new (25)... being opened every year thereby reducing membership costs. Corporate and charity tournaments also represent a tremendous networking opportunity where organizational hierarchy may be temporarily eliminated and a common (26)... created for building (27)...

An important benefit of golf is that it provides a unique window into the personality, values and conduct of others. This could prove to be very useful in future business dealings as one's behavior on the course is a (28)... of their business character and ethics. For example, a golfing partner who cheats on every (29)... might be someone to be careful with when making deals. It must be realized, however that this window is made of two way glass. Take advantage of this opportunity to project a positive image of yourself by (30)... proper Business Golf Etiquette.

21.	A. rightfully	B. legitimately	C. reasonably	D. rationally
22.	A. acceptant	B. accessible	C. recipient	D. susceptive
23.	A. economical	B. valid	C. remunerative	D. efficient
24.	A. However	B. Further	C. Nevertheless	D. Whereas
25.	A. courses	B. ways	C. items	D. means
26.	A. goal	B. interest	C. destination	D. ground
27.	A. relations	B. cooperation	C. rapport	D. affinity
28.	A. presentation	B. response	C. reflection	D. report
29.	A. game	B. business	C. negotiation	D. hole
30.	A. demonstrating	B. proving	C. conveying	D. manifesting

PART FIVE
Questions 31—40

· Read the article below about business meal etiquette.

· For each question 31—40, write one word in CAPITAL LETTERS on your Answer Sheet.

Business Meal Etiquette: the Soup Course

Many (31)... business meal starts with a soup course. (32)... you have already begun by munching on the bread, this is your first opportunity to demonstrate your table manners to impress or unimpress-your dining companions.

Choosing the right spoon is step number one. If the table has been preset, your soup spoon will be the large round or oval one to the far (33)... of your place setting. If the table has not been fully set, the server will bring your spoon with the soup. I recently found myself on a hunt for my soup spoon (34)... the waiter had brought the bowl. There was no soup spoon to the right of the place setting and it didn't seem to be anywhere else close (35)... Just before confessing that I was without a spoon, I spotted a handle sticking out from under the oversized soup bowl. So check the plate first (36)... you give up.

With soup spoon in (37)..., spoon the soup away from you towards the opposite side of the bowl. If a bit of the liquid should fall from the spoon this will ensure that it will drop into the bowl and not on the front of your nice business attire. Sip your soup quietly from the side of the spoon. Slurping is never acceptable.

No matter (38)... hot the soup, at no point should you blow on it to cool it off. You may lift a spoonful slightly level with the bowl and hold it for a (39)... seconds while it cools off. Be patient and grateful that your soup is (40)...

PART SIX
Questions 41—52

· Read the text below from a report about business email etiquette.

· In most lines (41—52), there is one extra word. It either is grammatically incorrect or does not fit in with the sense of the text. Some lines, however, are correct.

· If a line is correct, write CORRECT on your Answer Sheet.

· If there is an extra word in the line, write the extra word in CAPITAL LETTERS on your Answer Sheet.

Business Email Etiquette

Business email etiquette is of utmost importance when it comes to the activity of conveying

41. information or making formal requests. A single email can make a way for your successful future

42. endeavors or rule out of the scope of any business with the recipient. Though emailing can be

43. done even by a 3 year old, being exhibiting proper business email etiquette can be just a tad

44. difficult. Still the whole ballyhoo over email etiquette is uncalled for necessary. The first

45. commandment of business email etiquette is never to make spelling and grammatical mistakes.

46. Include all the details in the email so that you do not have to reply to queries by again and again.

47. Make sure that the tone of the email is proper and is actually what you wanted to. To find out that

48. tone of the email is appropriate, you can read the email aloud. Business letters and likewise,

49. business emails are supposed to be formal and devoid of any other errors. But unlike business

50. letters, business emails have a scope of being written light and crisp and can express pleasant

51. disposition of yours. Write correct names and addresses because the client or customer wouldn't

52. appreciate anything else less than that. If you are sending an attached file of considerable size, then ensure that your email would actually reach the desired destination without bouncing.

第16单元 股票市场
Unit 16　Stock Market

Text A

Ⅰ. 课文导读

股票市场是股民从事股票交易的场所。历史证明,从长期来看,购买股票是实现资产增值的最简单和有效的方式。福布斯财富排行榜前400位富豪,都拥有大量的股票。一般说来,股票的价格由供求关系所决定。对于一支股票来说,购买的人越多,它就变得越稀缺,价格也就会上扬。反之,购买的人越少,抛售的人越多,价格也就会迅速下跌。因此,股价会经常上下波动。如果大股东执意要卖掉大量的股票,即使发行股票的公司并没有出现任何问题,该股股价仍然会应声下挫。

Ⅱ. Text

The stock market is essentially a giant auction—only instead of antiques and heirlooms①. Stocks are traded at places called exchanges. At these exchanges, traders buy and sell shares of companies. Generally, the price of a stock is determined by supply and demand. For example, if there are more people wanting to buy a stock than to sell it, the price will be driven up because those shares are rarer and people will pay a higher price for them. On the other hand, if there are a lot of shares for sale and no one is interested in buying them, the price will quickly fall.

Because of this, the market can appear to fluctuate② widely. Even if there is nothing wrong with a company, a large shareholder who is trying to sell millions of shares at a time can drive the price of the stock down, simply because there are not enough people interested in buying the stock he is trying to sell. Because there is no real demand for the company he is selling, he is forced to accept a lower price.

History has shown that owning stocks is one of the easiest and most profitable ways to grow your wealth over the long-term. Virtually③ every member of the Forbes 400 list got there because they own a large block of shares in a public or private corporation, ranging from manufacturing and oil drilling to cosmetics and money management. Although your beginning may be

---

① heirloom: 传家宝
② fluctuate: 波动
③ virtually: 实际上;几乎

humble, this guide to investing in stocks will explain what stocks are, how you can make money from them, and much more.

Have you ever asked yourself, "What is stock?" or wondered why shares of stock exist? This introduction to the world of investing in stocks will provide answers to those questions and show you just how simple Wall Street really is. It may turn out to be one of the most important articles you've ever read if you don't understand what stocks represent.

Imagine you wanted to start a retail store with members of your family. You decide you need $100,000 to get the business off the ground so you incorporate a new company. You divide the company into 1,000 pieces, or "shares" of stock. (They are called this because each piece of stock is entitled to① a proportional share② of the profit or loss). You price each new share of stock at $100. If you can sell all of the shares to your family members, you should have the $100,000 you need (1,000 shares x $100 contributed capital per share = $100,000 cash raised for the company).

If the store earned $50,000 after taxes during its first year, each share of stock would be entitled to 1/1,000th of the profit. You'd take $50,000 and divide it by 1,000, resulting in $50.00 earnings per share (or EPS as it is often called on Wall Street). You could call a meeting of the company's Board of Directors (these are the people the stockholders elected to watch over their interest since they couldn't run the business) and decide to use the money to pay cash dividends③, repurchase stock, or expand the company by reinvesting in the retail store.

At some point, you may decide you want to sell your shares of the family retailer. If the company is large enough, you could trade on a stock exchange. That's what is happening when you buy or sell shares of a company through a stock broker. You are telling the market you are interested in acquiring or selling shares of a certain company and Wall Street matches you up with④ someone and takes fees and commissions⑤ for doing it. Alternatively, shares of stock could be issued to raise millions, or even billions, of dollars for expansion. When Sam Walton formed Wal-Mart Stores, Inc., the initial public offering that resulted from him selling newly created shares of stock in his company gave him enough cash to pay off most of his debt and fund Wal-Mart's nationwide expansion.

Shares of Stock on Wall Street Are No Different

It doesn't matter if you invest in shares of stock of multi-billion dollar conglomerates⑥ or tiny publicly traded retailers, when you buy share of stock, you are purchasing a tiny piece of a company. For instance, McDonald's Corporation has divided itself into 1,079,186,614 shares of

---

① is entitled to: 享有
② a proportional share: 定额；一定比例的份额
③ dividend: 红利
④ match up with: 匹配
⑤ commissions: 佣金
⑥ conglomerate: 企业集团

common stock. Over the past twelve months, the company earned net income of ＄4,176,452,196.18 so management took that profit and divided it by the shares outstanding, resulting in earnings per share of ＄3.87. Of that, the company's Board of Directors voted to pay ＄2.20 out in the form of a cash dividend, leaving ＄1.67 per share for the company to devote to other causes such as expansion, debt reduction, share repurchases, or whatever else it decides is necessary to produce a good return for its owners, the stockholders.

The current stock price of McDonald's is ＄61.66 per share. The stock market is nothing more than an auction. Individual investors, just like you, are making decisions with their own money in a real-time auction. If someone wants to sell their shares of McDonald's and there are no buyers at ＄61.66, the price would have to continually fall until someone else stepped in and placed a buy order with their broker. If investors thought McDonald's was going to grow its profits faster than other companies, they would be willing to bid up the price① of the stock (which is affected by supply and demand because there are only a fixed amount of shares in existence, in this case 1,079,186,614 shares). Likewise, if a large investor were to dump his or her shares on the market, the supply could temporarily overwhelm the demand and drive the stock price lower.

Keep Perspective on② Stocks and Never Forget What They Represent

What happens if you believe McDonald's will generate far higher earnings per share of stock within five years, you buy 1,000 shares at ＄61.66 (for a total investment of ＄61,660), and the very next day, the stock falls to ＄30 per share? Should you be upset?

In this situation, you need to remember that the stock market is an auction. If you still believe the company will generate the earnings per share you calculated several years from now, to be upset that the stock price got cheaper would be, in the words of the legendary Benjamin Graham, to allow yourself to get upset by "other peoples' mistakes in judgment". The share price may move around wildly as millions of investors throughout the world make decisions about how much they are willing to pay, but the ultimate value of your shares will come from the profit the company generates.

If McDonald's did reach, say, ＄8 in per share earnings within five years, and kept the same dividend policy, your shares would collect ＄4.55 in cash dividends each year. That means you'd be earning 15.17% in cash dividend yield on the stock you purchased when it fell to ＄30 per share. This is why you see many successful investors completely unemotional about stock market crashes; they view the events as nothing more than the opportunity to buy a greater stake③ in businesses they like that generate lots of cash.

---

① bid up the price: 哄抬价格
② keep perspective on: 明察
③ stake: 股份

Stock typically takes the form of shares of either common stock① or preferred stock②. As a unit of ownership, common stock typically carries voting rights that can be exercised in corporate decisions. Preferred stock differs from common stock in that it typically does not carry voting rights but is legally entitled to receive a certain level of dividend payments before any dividends can be issued to other shareholders. Convertible③ preferred stock is preferred stock that includes an option for the holder to convert the preferred shares into a fixed number of common shares, usually anytime after a predetermined date. Shares of such stock are called "convertible preferred shares" (or "convertible preference shares" in the UK)

New equity issues④ may have specific legal clauses attached that differentiate them from previous issues of the issuer. Some shares of common stock may be issued without the typical voting rights, for instance, or some shares may have special rights unique to them and issued only to certain parties. Often, new issues that have not been registered with a securities governing body⑤ may be restricted from resale for certain periods of time.

Preferred stock may be hybrid⑥ by having the qualities of bonds of fixed returns and common stock voting rights. They also have preference in the payment of dividends over common stock and also have been given preference at the time of liquidation⑦ over common stock. They have other features of accumulation⑧ in dividend.

Ⅲ. Notes

1. Forbes(福布斯杂志). Forbes is an American publishing and media company. Its flagship publication, the Forbes magazine, is published biweekly. Its primary competitors in the national business magazine category are Fortune, which is also published biweekly, and Business Week. The magazine is well-known for its lists, including its lists of the richest Americans (the Forbes 400) and its list of billionaires.

2. Wall Street (华尔街). Wall Street refers to the financial district of New York City, named after and centered on the eight-block-long street running from Broadway to South Street on the East River in Lower Manhattan. Anchored by Wall Street, New York City is one of the world's principal financial centers.

3. Common stock (普通股). Common stock is a form of corporate equity ownership, a type of security. It is called "common" to distinguish it from preferred stock. In the event of bankruptcy, common stock investors receive their funds after preferred stock holders, bondholde-

---

① common stock: 普通股
② preferred stock: 优先股
③ convertible: 可转换的
④ new equity issue: 新股票发行
⑤ securities governing body: 证券管理机构
⑥ hybrid: 混合物
⑦ liquidation: 清算
⑧ accumulation: 积累

rs, creditors, etc. On the other hand, common shares on average perform better than preferred shares or bonds over time.

4. Preferred stock（优先股）. Preferred stock, also called preferred shares, preference shares, or simply preferreds, is a special equity security that has properties of both an equity and a debt instrument and is generally considered a hybrid instrument. Preferreds are senior (i.e. higher ranking) to common stock, but are subordinate to bonds. Preferred stock usually carries no voting rights, but may carry a dividend and may have priority over common stock in the payment of dividends and upon liquidation. Preferred stock may have a convertibility feature into common stock. Similar to bonds, preferred stocks are rated by the major credit rating companies. The rating for preferreds is generally lower since preferred dividends do not carry the same guarantees as interest payments from bonds and they are junior to all creditors.

5. Benjamin Graham(本杰明·格雷厄姆). Benjamin Graham (May 8, 1894-September 21, 1976) was an American economist and professional investor. Graham is considered the first proponent of value investing, an investment approach he began teaching at Columbia Business School in 1928 and subsequently refined with David Dodd through various editions of their famous book Security Analysis. Graham had such an overwhelming influence on his students that two of them, Buffett and Kahn, named their sons, Howard Graham Buffett and Thomas Graham Kahn, after him.

IV. Useful Expressions

1. get ... off the ground: 开始,使有进展
2. be entitled to: 享有,应得
3. match up with: 与……匹配
4. pay off one's debt: 还债
5. keep perspective on: 明察事理
6. differentiate sth. from: 与……区别开来
7. differ from in: 在……方面不同
8. take the form of: 以……形式(出现)
9. in existence: 存在
10. in the words of sb.: 以……的话说

V. Reading Comprehension

Questions

1. Why is a stock market a giant auction?
2. How does a stock market operate?
3. What's the difference between preferred stock and common stock?
4. What rules are there for new equity issues?
5. Why are successful investors not upset when the stock market crashes?

Decide whether each of the following statements is true or false.

1. Traders merely buy and sell stocks at places called exchanges.   (   )
2. Supply and demand determines the price of a stock.   (   )
3. Owing a large block of shares makes people listed the rank of Forbes rich.   (   )
4. If the earned $50,000 is entitled to 1/1,000th of the profit, the EPS is $50.00.
   (   )
5. A large investor shares decides the price of a stock.   (   )
6. People are upset since they are influenced by other stock-holders' judgments.   (   )
7. The profit the company ultimately earns decides the value of the shares.   (   )
8. Preferred stock carries voting rights and is entitled to receive a certain level of dividend payments.
9. If a preferred stock that includes an option for the holder to convert the preferred shares into a fixed number of common shares, it could be viewed as "convertible preferred shares"
10. Every share of common stock may be issued without the typical voting rights.   (   )

Ⅵ. Discussion

What kind of stocks would you choose? Why?

Text B
BEC Reading Texts

PART ONE

Questions 1—8

· Look at the statements below and the five extracts about equity and preferred stock from an article.

· Which extract (A, B, C, D or E) does each statement (1—8) refer to?

· For each statement (1—8), make one letter (A, B, C, D or E) on your Answer Sheet.

· You will need to use some of these letters more than once.

1. This definition is helpful in understanding the liquidation process in case of bankruptcy.
2. In accounting and finance, equity is the residual claim or interest of the most junior class of investors in assets, after all liabilities are paid.
3. Public companies usually pay dividends on a fixed schedule, but may declare a dividend at any time, sometimes.
4. The rating for prefer reds is generally lower since preferred dividends do not carry the same guarantees as interest payments from bonds and they are junior to all creditors.
5. For a joint stock company, a dividend is allocated as a fixed amount per share.

6. Thus owners' equity is reduced to zero. Ownership equity is also known as risk capital or liable capital.

7. After liabilities have been accounted for the positive remainder is deemed the owner's interest in the business.

8. Similar to bonds, preferred stocks are rated by the major credit rating companies.

A. If liability exceeds assets, negative equity exists. In an accounting context, shareholders' equity (or stockholders' equity, shareholders' funds, shareholders' capital or similar terms) represents the remaining interest in assets of a company, spread among individual shareholders of common or preferred stock.

B. Therefore, a shareholder receives a dividend in proportion to their shareholding. For the joint stock company, paying dividends is not an expense; rather, it is the division of after tax profits among shareholders. Retained earnings (profits that have not been distributed as dividends) are shown in the shareholder equity section in the company's balance sheet-the same as its issued share capital.

C. At first, all the secured creditors are paid against proceeds from assets. Afterward, a series of creditors, ranked in priority sequence, have the next claim/right on the residual proceeds. Ownership equity is the last or residual claim against assets, paid only after all other creditors are paid. In such cases where even creditors could not get enough money to pay their bills, nothing is left over to reimburse owners' equity.

D. Preferred stock usually carries no voting rights, but may carry a dividend and may have priority over common stock in the payment of dividends and upon liquidation. Preferred stock may have a convertibility feature into common stock. Terms of the preferred stock are stated in a "Certificate of Designation".

E. At the start of a business, owners put some funding into the business to finance operations. This creates a liability on the business in the shape of capital as the business is a separate entity from its owners. Businesses can be considered, for accounting purposes, sums of liabilities and assets; this is the accounting equation.

PART TWO
Questions 9—14

- Read the text about the stoke trading.
- Choose the best sentence to fill each of the gaps.
- For each gap (9—14), mark one letter (A-H) on your Answer Sheet.
- Do not use any letter more than once.

Stock Trading

Participants in the stock market range from small individual stock investors to large hedge fund traders, who can be based anywhere. Their orders usually end up with a professional at a stock exchange, who executes the order of buying or selling.

(9)..., thus providing a marketplace (virtual or real). The exchanges provide real-time trading information on the listed securities, facilitating price discovery.

Some exchanges are physical locations where transactions are carried out on a trading floor, by a method known as open outcry. This type of auction is used in stock exchanges and commodity exchanges where traders may enter "verbal" bids and offers simultaneously. (10)..., composed of a network of computers where trades are made electronically via traders.

Actual trades are based on an auction market model where a potential buyer bids a specific price for a stock and a potential seller asks a specific price for the stock. (11)... When the bid and ask prices match, a sale takes place, on a first-come-first-served basis if there are multiple bidders or askers at a given price.

The New York Stock Exchange is one of the physical exchanges, also referred to as a *listed exchange*-(12)... Orders enter by way of exchange members and flow down to a floor broker, who goes to the floor trading post specialist for that stock to trade the order. (13)... If a spread exists, no trade immediately takes place—in this case the specialist should use his/her own resources (money or stock) to close the difference after his/her judged time. Once a trade has been made the details are reported on the "tape" and sent back to the brokerage firm, which then notifies the investor who placed the order. (14)..., computers play an important role, especially for so-called "program trading".

A. The other type of stock exchange is a virtual kind

B. The purpose of a stock exchange is to facilitate the exchange of securities between buyers and sellers

C. Although there is a significant amount of human contact in this process

D. stocks listed on one exchange can also be traded on other participating exchanges

E. The specialist's job is to match buy and sell orders using open outcry

F. Buying stock on margin means buying stock with money borrowed against the stocks in the same account.

G. Buying or selling at market means you will accept any ask price or bid price for the stock, respectively

H. only stocks listed with the exchange may be traded

PART THREE
Questions 15—20

· Read the following article on the stock market.

· For each question (15—20) mark one letter (A, B, C or D) on your Answer Sheet for the answer you choose.

On Monday, October 19, 1987, a wave of selling triggered widespread price declines in stock markets from New York to Australia. On that day, now infamous as "Black Monday", over

600 million shares were traded on the New York Stock Exchange. The Dow Jones Industrial Average of the prices of 30 stocks of major US companies lost 22.6 percent of its value on that memorable day, plunging 508 points in the panicked rush to sell.

What is the stock market, and how is it affected by the forces of supply and demand? The stock market is the means through which previously issued corporate stocks, shares of ownership in a corporation, are traded. Stock exchanges are organizations whose members act as intermediaries to buy and sell stocks for their clients. About 80 percent of all stock trading in the United States takes place at the New York Stock Exchange. There are other stock exchanges in the United States as well as in Paris, London, Sydney and Tokyo.

How are stock prices determined? The answer, as you might expect, is by supply and demand. However, the forces influencing the prices of corporate stocks are quite different from those influencing the prices of goods and services. People and organizations that buy and hold stock do so for the incomes they hope to earn. The incomes depend on dividends paid to stockholders, changes in the price of stock over time, and the expected return on alternative investments.

On any given day in the stock market, there are orders to buy and orders to sell. The orders to buy constitute the quantity of a stock demanded at the current (or anticipated) price per share, while the orders to sell constitute the quantity supplied at that price. The chief influence on both the supply of and demand for stocks is the income potential of holding the stock compared to the income potential of holding alternative assets such as bonds, other types of securities, or real property like buildings and land.

On the New York Stock Exchange, trading in all stocks is continuous. A specialist is assigned to oversee trading in each stock. This specialist is a "broker's broker" who tries to adjust the price of the stock so that quantity demanded equals quantity supplied. However, the specialist is also allowed to purchase the stock to hold as a personal investment if no buyer can be found. In this way the specialist can exert some influence on the supply of and demand for stocks, and will do so if it's profitable.

On October 19, 1987, there were hardly any buy orders, and the markets were flooded with sell orders. Because of the tremendous surplus of stocks at the prevailing prices, specialists and call clerks lowered prices until quantity demanded equaled quantity supplied. When Black Monday finally reeled to a close, many a portfolio had lost over a fifth of the value it had the day before.

15. By the word "intermediaries" (line 4, paragraph 2), the author means _____.
A. connections
B. messengers
C. go-betweens
D. spokesmen

16. Which of the following does not determine people's incomes in stock market?
A. Changes in the price of stock.

B. Dividends paid to stockholders.

C. The expected return on alternative investments.

D. The supply of the stock.

17. Which of the following can not be considered as "alternative assets" according to the passage?

A. Buildings

B. Stocks

C. Bonds

D. Securities

18. Which of the following stock exchange centers are mentioned in the passage?

A. Stock exchange centers in London, Sydney and Moscow.

B. Stock exchange centers in Paris, London, Sydney.

C. Stock exchange centers in Frankfurt, Paris, New York.

D. Stock exchange centers in London, Tokyo, Hong Kong.

19. Which of the following is NOT the right description of stock market on October 19, 1987?

A. The markets were flooded with sell orders.

B. More than 600 million shares were traded on the New York Stock Exchange

C. The Dow Jones Industrial Average of the prices of 30 stocks of major US companies lost 22.6 percent of its value

D. Many a portfolio had lost a fifth of the value it had the day before.

20. What might be the most appropriate title of the passage?

A. Stock Market

B. Stock Exchange

C. Infamous "Black Monday"

D. The Caprice Stock Market

PART FOUR

Questions 21—30

· Read the article below about the function and purpose of stoke markets.

· Choose the correct word to fill each gap from A, B, C or D.

· For each question (21—30), mark one letter (A, B, C or D) on your Answer Sheet.

Function and Purpose of Stock Markets

The stock market is one of the most important (21)... for companies to raise money. This allows businesses to be publicly (22)..., or raise additional financial capital for expansion by selling shares of ownership of the company in a public market. The (23)... that an exchange provides affords investors the ability to quickly and easily sell securities. This is an attractive feature of (24)... in stocks.

Exchanges also act as the (25)... for each transaction, meaning that they collect and deliver the shares, and guarantee payment to the seller of a security. This eliminates the risk to an individual buyer or seller that the counterparty could (26)... on the transaction. The smooth functioning of all these activities facilitates economic growth in that lower costs. In this way the financial system is assumed to contribute to increased prosperity.

History has shown that the price of shares and other (27)... is an important part of the dynamics of economic activity, and can influence or be an indicator of social mood. An economy where the stock market is on the rise is considered to be an up-and-coming economy. In fact, the stock market is often considered the primary indicator of a country's economic strength and development.

(28)... share prices, for instance, tend to be associated with increased business investment and vice versa. Share prices also affect the wealth of households and their consumption. (29)..., central banks tend to keep an eye on the control and behavior of the stock market and, in (30)..., on the smooth operation of financial system functions.

21. A. sources   B. assistants   C. reasons   D. ways
22. A. bought   B. traded   C. conducted   D. done
23. A. convenience   B. liquidity   C. superiority   D. celerity
24. A. indulging   B. engaging   C. investing   D. funding
25. A. clearinghouse   B. greenhouse   C. whitehouse   D. workhouse
26. A. counter   B. breach   C. default   D. fail
27. A. exchanges   B. transactions   C. assets   D. investments
28. A. Decreasing   B. Steadying   C. Learning   D. Rising
29. A. However   B. Besides   C. Moreover   D. Therefore
30. A. return   B. general   C. short   D. fact

PART FIVE
Questions 31—40

· Read the article below about stock market crashes.

· For each question 31—40, write one word in CAPITAL LETTERS on your Answer Sheet.

Stock Market Crashes

A stock market crash is often defined as a sharp dip in (31)... prices of equities listed on the stock exchanges. In parallel (32)... various economic factors, a reason for stock market crashes is also (33)... to panic and investing public's loss of confidence. Often, stock market crashes end speculative economic bubbles.

There have been famous stock market crashes that have ended in the (34)... of billions of dollars and wealth destruction on a massive scale. An increasing (35)... of people are involved in the stock market, especially since the social security and retirement plans are (36)... increasingly privatized and linked to stocks and bonds and other elements of the market. There have been a number of famous stock market crashes like the (37)... Street Crash of 1929, the stock market crash of 1973-4, the Black Monday of 1987, the Dot-com bubble of 2000, and the Stock Market Crash of 2008.

One of the most famous stock market crashes started October 24, 1929 on Black Thursday. The Dow Jones Industrial lost 50 % during this stock market crash. It was the beginning of the Great Depression. (38)... famous crash took place on October 19, 1987-Black Monday. The crash began in Hong Kong and quickly (39)... around the world. By the (40)... of October, stock markets in Hong Kong had fallen 45.5 %%, Australia 41.8 %%, Spain 31 %%, the United Kingdom 26.4 %%, the United States 22.68 %%, and Canada 22.5 %%.

PART SIX
Questions 41—52

· Read the text below about disintermediation.

· In most lines (41—52), there is one extra word. It either is grammatically incorrect or does not fit in with the sense of the text. Some lines, however, are correct.

· If a line is correct, write CORRECT on your Answer Sheet.

· If there is an extra word in the line, write the extra word in CAPITAL LETTERS on your Answer Sheet.

Disintermediation—A Remarkable Transformation

41. The financial system in most western countries has been undergone a remarkable transformation. One feature of this development is disintermediation. A portion of the funds

42. involved in saving and financing, it flows directly to the financial markets instead of being routed

43. via the traditional bank lending and deposit to operations. The general public interest in investing

44. in the stock market, either directly or through mutual funds, has been an important component of

45. this process. Statistics show that in recent decades selling shares have made up an increasingly

46. large proportion of households' financial assets in many countries abroad. In the 1970s, in

47. Sweden, deposit accounts and any other very liquid assets with little risk made up almost 60

48. percent of households' financial wealth, compared to less than 20 percent in the 2000s. The

49. major part of this adjustment is that financial portfolios have gone directly to shares but not a good deal now takes the form of various kinds of institutional investment for groups of individuals,

50. e. g. , pension funds, mutual funds, hedge funds, insurance investment of premiums, etc. The

51. trend towards forms of saving with a higher risk which has been accentuated by new rules for

52. most funds and insurance. Similar tendencies are to be difficult found in all developed economic systems, such as the European Union, the United States, Japan and other developed nations: saving has moved away from traditional bank deposits to more risky securities of one sort or another.

附录一　剑桥商务英语证书考试真题(一)

PART ONE
Questions 1-8
- Look at the statements below and the five news items on various companies on the opposite page from an article .
- Which extract **(A, B, C,D or E)** does each statement**(1-8)** refer to ?
- For each statement **(1-8)**, make one letter **(A, B, C,D or E)** on your Answer Sheet .
- You will need to use some of these letters more than once .

1 This company reports not being able to pass on higher costs to its customers.

2 The sale of part of a company has had an adverse affect on profits.

3 This company's response to fluctuations in sales has not had the desired effect.

4 Jobs have been lost because a company has ended one of its activities.

5 There are fears about the impact of internal competition within the company.

6 This company has reported contrasting results from different parts of its operations.

7 This company has spent money on moving part of its operation.

8 Efforts are to be made to turn around sales at a store.

A. New Store

Parkin's search for a site for its next store has been ended by Marsden's misfortunes, with Parkin agreeing to buy half of the latter's Birmingham store for £40m. Parkin's main store is in London, but it opened its second, in Birmingham, three years ago, and has been seeking sites in other large cities. There was surprise that the new store, likely to open next year, is so close to the existing one, where profits have so far beaten Parkin's sales targets, in case it draws customers away from the existing outlet.

B. Capacity Cut

The packaging industry has typically suffered from a vicious cycle, with rising prices leading to excess capacity, which in turn leads to a collapse in prices, and Johnson Keithley is no exception. The company has been attempting to smooth the boom/bust cycle by better capacity management, but it admitted yesterday that it has been forced to make significant cuts to capacity because of a surprisingly sharp downturn in demand. The group now expects its second-half results to fall below expectations, and warned of further problems on the horizon.

C. Hit by Higher Costs

Higher raw-material costs have reduced full-year profits at Bonner's, the plastics manufacturer, with prices of polyethylene, the main component of its business, rising 8% since last year. Profits were also held back by the disposal of its packaging division, which accounted for over half of turnover the previous year. Additional costs were incurred by relocating the head office from Wrexham to Cardiff, and I from reorganization and redundancy in its plastics business. Bonner's said that trading in the current year has started slowly, particularly in its European markets.

D. Surprise Fall

Shares in regional supermarket chain Couldson fell steeply yesterday after the retailer warned of losses at its biggest outlet, in Bristol. The warning was in stark contrast to its trading statement three months ago, which reported a rise in like-for-like sales of 5% in the preceding month. However, trading across the rest of the chain, including seven outlets bought last year from Luxona, showed a healthy improvement. The company has promised to do all it can to stem the decline of the last four weeks at the Bristol outlet.

E. Modest Improvement

Dorcas Foods has posted a modest rise in interim profits. However, the company says it has had to absorb increased costs at its Quality Sugar subsidiary and the impact of a margin squeeze at its Australian baking operations. In sugar, the continued strength of sterling has capped profits, and with Dorcas's move out of sugar-beet refining, expenditure on redundancy is having a serious impact. At the same time, floods in Australia have led to higher wheat prices, which in turn have reduced margins in the company's baking operations.

PART TWO

Questions 9–14

- Read this article from the business pages of a newspaper.
- Choose the best sentence from the opposite page to fill each of the gaps.
- For each gap **(9-14)**, mark one letter **(A-H)** on your Answer Sheet.
- Do not use any letter more than once.

High fliers of the future head for specialist fairs

Despite the recent development of online recruiting, graduate job fairs are still proving hugely popular in Britain with both employers and job hunters. **(0)** …H….. Any graduate with big ambitions could be forgiven for thinking that the north-west of England is the centre of the north-west of England is the centre of the universe next week. **(9)** …….. As usual, they will all be looking for the brightest, best and most suitable graduates to employ.

November 2 sees Expo Management (the finance, business and management fair), and on November 3, Technology for the Future (the IT, science and engineering fair), will be held. **(10)** …….. Expo Management has also expanded, to incorporate a broad range of careers in business and management, as well as the finance sector. There are excellent transport links from all parts of the country to where the fairs are being held. An accommodation booking service is available, and there is plenty of entertainment on offer.

Employers are keener than ever to take part. **(11)** ……,. Having said that, employers use the fairs in order to make contact with the specific kinds of graduates they are looking to recruit. **(12)**…….. However, all graduates visiting the fairs with the right skills and motivation are likely to get a very positive response from employers.

Preparation is the key to getting the most from these fairs and visitors should have done their homework. **(13)** …….. It is sensible to exploit this opportunity by coming armed with a good CV and a list of relevant questions to ask. Also, this year the fairs' organizers have introduced a new support facility. **(14)**……. By visiting http://www.networld.co/gradfairs, they will get instant access to the full list of exhibitors and their vacancies, as well as links to their company websites. With the world of business changing and expanding so rapidly, ambitious graduates will find that time spent at the fairs makes an excellent investment in their future.

A They are keen for graduates to make use of this innovation before they attend the fairs.	**E** After all, they may not have another chance to see such a huge range of prestigious employers under one roof.
B Graduates can take advantage of these to ensure that they know how to make the best applications possible in the weeks following the fairs.	**F** The reason is that is where a 170-strong list of employers will be setting up their stands at the start of November's round of graduate fairs.
C The latter, only a few years old, has proved so successful that this year it has doubled in size: it now plays host to more than 40 employers.	**G** This enthusiasm means that the prospects for graduate job-hunters are excellent at the moment.
D In particular, it is those with technical qualifications who are most sought after.	**H** As a result, they are getting bigger and bigger each time they hit the road again.

PART THREE

Questions 15-20

- Read the article below about management styles and the questions on the opposite page.
- For each question **(15-20)** mark one letter **(A, B, C or D)** on your Answer Sheet for the answer you choose.

Generally, the culture of any firm can be described as principally action-orientated, people-orientated or system-orientated. That is to say, the behavior that the managers exhibit tends to emphasize one of these three approaches to leadership and management.

In successful firms where leadership is action-orientated, the culture is generally driven by one or a handful of managers who present a strong vision for the firm and lead by example. The emphasis is on getting things done, on driving for change. Such leaders constantly infuse energy throughout the firm and reinforce it through training that emphasizes individual action, showing initiative, taking considered risks and stressing individual output and results. It is a dynamic culture that rests on individuals being motivated to rise to the challenges of the business and being willing to take on responsibilities, often beyond what is considered their normal role.

The downside is that the approach can be somewhat 'one-sided', overlooking the need for systems to handle routine matters, and taking for granted that people are all driven by a sense of challenge. It can result in the strong and quick riding roughshod over the more considered and thoughtful. When overdone, action-orientation becomes 'flare' behavior, insensitive to differences in situations and people.

Successful people-orientated cultures derive from leadership that trains people to be ready to take responsibility and then invests them with it. Such firms delegate responsibility down as far as possible. They are not the 'do it, check it, recheck it, double-check it and then check it again to be sure' types of cultures. They empower trained people and trust them to build quality in. They ask people to make decisions and expect them to do so. If the decisions prove wrong, the experience is used as the basis for learning rather than for criticism or punishment. They emphasize commitment and mutual support, reinforced through training that focuses on how and when to delegate responsibility, on understanding and recognizing that people are not all the same, learning how to get the best out of everyone.

However, people-orientated cultures are not warm and cuddly. They respect people, support them and develop them – but they expect them to perform. If people fail to live up to expectations after proper training investment, appropriate steps are taken. The downside of people-orientated cultures occurs when responsibility is not appropriately delegated. Insufficient challenge for bright, trained people leads to poor performance. Equally, giving people more than they can handle without properly preparing them, and without providing adequate support if they initially falter, leads to the same result.

Successful system-orientated cultures focus on trying to deal systematically with recurring problems and situations. Basically, they have their feet on the ground; in most organizations, 80o7o of what is done is routine, and the system-orientated firm knows this. So its procedures handle the routine, leaving managers to use their energy on that 20% of the work that needs their expertise.

The essence of a successful system-orientated culture is its ability and willingness to constantly question its systems. Such organizations tend to have strong corporate cultures, and people have to buy into them before being given the right to question and criticize. But given that, every process is up for evaluation and improvement. The rule book really matters, but it is not cast in stone. Away from the rule book, initiative is a key characteristic, but it is initiative in a strong team environment. People consult where possible and take individual decisions only when it is not.

15 According to the text, a company that has an action-orientated approach to management is likely to
    A accept that some initiatives will be more successful than others.
    B view staff in terms of their personal achievements.
    C emphasize the importance of staff input into strategy.
    D expect staff to work extra hours without remuneration.

16 Which of the following does the writer consider a disadvantage of action-orientated management?
    A It attracts people who are unreliable.
    B It focuses too heavily on controversial issues.
    C It gives out the wrong kind of message to new recruits.
    D It makes a questionable assumption about human behavior.

17 Unlike action-orientated companies, those who favor people-orientated
    A keep a watchful eye on what their employees do.
    B are unwilling to tolerate errors of judgment.
    C are sensitive to individual differences.
    D see indecision as a positive feature.

18 According to the text, which type of person may under-perform in a people-orientated company?
    A an intelligent person who lacks stimulation
    B a new member of staff who is keen to learn new skills
    C a new employee who is given a challenging role
    D an individual who learns less quickly than others

19 In the writer's view, the system-orientated approach is
    A visionary.
    B realistic.
    C uninspiring.
    D outdated.

20 In a system-orientated culture, employees are
    A encouraged to share ideas.
    B not expected to criticize colleagues.
    C trained to focus on self-improvement.
    D not allowed to challenge company policy.

PART FOUR

Questions 21-30

- Read the article below about customer relationship management.
- Choose the correct word to fill each gap from **A, B, C** or **D** on the opposite page.
- For each question (**21-30**), mark one letter (**A, B, C** or **D**) on your Answer Sheet.

Customer Relationship Management

In today's fast-moving market, it is a simple fact that products are constantly being replaced by something new. For companies large and small, the most important real **(21)**…….. with measurable, long-term value is loyal, one-to-one customer relationships. However, despite their importance, they do not **(22)** ………. On any company's balance sheet. If a company lost 10% of its inventory to theft, it would react swiftly, but if the company loses 10% of its customers, this may not be **(23)** ……… .

In this age of product **(24)** ……….. , in which the market fails to perceive any profound difference between products or companies, effective management of customer relationships is critical in achieving a competitive **(25)** ………. . Delivering quality service and achieving high customer satisfaction have been closely **(26)** ………. to profits, and consequently the **(27)**…….. all companies are trying to make is to provide more internal and external customer relationship focus. By **(28)**……..available information technology, leading companies have already shortened process and response times, increasing customer satisfaction.

But companies must make a profit to survive, so telling a chief executive to focus more on customers, through the use of expensive information technology, may fall on deaf ears unless it can be demonstrated that such investments will be **(29)** ……… In terms of revenue, market share and profits. Certain companies are responding to this new customer focus by completely **(30)**………their traditional financial-only measurements of corporate performance, and seeking new ways of measuring customers' perceptions and expectations.

21	A	worth	B	value	C	asset	D	property
22	A	turn out	B	make up	C	write out	D	show up
23	A	detected	B	regarded	C	conceived	D	distinguished
24	A	coincidence	B	similarity	C	agreement	D	connection
25	A	authority	B	command	C	advantage	D	preference
26	A	joined	B	linked	C	associated	D	combined
27	A	shift	B	fluctuation	C	motion	D	displacement
28	A	profiting	B	capitalizing	C	exploiting	D	benefiting
29	A	reinstated	B	restored	C	replaced	D	recouped
30	A	modifying	B	mending	C	refurbishing	D	overhauling

PART FIVE

Questions 31-40

- Read the article below about working abroad for your company.
- For each question 31-40, write one word in CAPITAL LETTERS on your Answer Sheet.

JUST HOW FAR WILL YOU GO FOR YOUR JOB?

These days, a great many companies require more staff to spend more time working abroad on business assignments, as a result of the trend towards economic globalization.

Nearly **(31)**...... senior managers believe that it is going to be more important than ever **(32)**.........executives to be globally mobile over the next five years. Ambitious young managers are also increasingly realizing that international experience is essential if they want to get anywhere near the boardroom of a modern, successful company.

But **(33)**...... is a downside to this. A majority of top managers say they are now unwilling to make the personal sacrifices involved in meeting this demand. Severe shortages **(34)** .... the supply of globally mobile executives are therefore on the cards.

The solution that has now **(35)**......., commonplace is a significant increase in the use of short-term assignments. International 'commuting' – living **(36)** .... home but traveling regularly around the world – is now the norm for many managers. A **(37)** .... companies are even known to pay for key staff to travel home once a week from workplaces in another continent Airlines have recognized the trend and are adapting their services to accommodate the demands of steadily increasing numbers of business people traveling on short-term assignments, for **(38)**.........by reducing check-in times and scheduling late flights.

However, it remains to be seen **(39)** .... or not even this can make international commuting attractive to those employees **(40)**...... are already struggling to balance the competing demands of work and family life.

PART SIX

Questions 41-52

- Read the text below from a report about sales figures.
- In most lines **(41-52)**, there is one extra word. It either is grammatically incorrect or does not fit in with the sense of the text. Some lines, however, are correct.
- If a line is correct, write **CORRECT** on your Answer Sheet.
- If there is an extra word in the line, write the extra word in **CAPITAL LETTERS** on your Answer Sheet.

REPORT TO MANAGING DIRECTOR ON SALES FIGURES

After six successful quarters of sales in the Seattle area, results for the last quarter were disappointing. General sales were down

41 16 per cent, on average, across our nine area stores. While as I noted
42 in my last report, it is my view that some of this downturn can then be attributed
43 to layoffs at IMP plc, which, as you know, it is the area's largest employer.
44 During the quarter, IMP plc gave layoff notices to something in the region of
45 5 per cent part of its workforce. But it would be dangerous, I believe,
46 to assume that our sales slump is due simply to such layoffs. In the same
47 period of time, two powerful competitors – as SaveMarts and Bargain
48 Buys – opened a total sum of eight stores within our main catchments'
49 area. However, the grand openings of these stores were accompanied
50 by their heavy advertising of sales items. I recommend that a thorough
51 assessment of how the impact of such competition upon our sales
52 Equipped with this detailed knowledge, we would scarcely be in a position to review our current strategy.

附录二 剑桥商务英语证书考试真题(二)

PART ONE

Questions 1-8

- Look at the statements below and the reports about five different companies on the opposite page from an article.
- Which extract **(A, B, C,D or E)** does each statement(**1-8**) refer to ?
- For each statement (**1-8**), make one letter **(A, B, C,D or E)** on your Answer Sheet .
- You will need to use some of these letters more than once .

1   This company has expanded at a time of high demand.

2   Good results in one part of this company made up for disappointing results in another part.

3   It is difficult to predict future prospects for the kind of products this company sells.

4   Profits for this company are likely to be different from those that were earlier predicted.

5   This company produced more goods than were needed for certain markets.

6   This company has denied rumors about its future plans.

7   A recovery in this company's financial position is expected.

8   This company is likely to benefit from charging more for its products.

A. Following the company's poor annual results in November, the share price plunged and has since remained around 200p. Analysts now believe that the company is seriously undervalued by the stock market. The company's biggest problems were in Germany and France last year where supply outstripped demand, leading to a 20 million loss for the year. However, the company has recently appointed a new chairman who has a first-rate track record of reviving failing companies. It is believed that he will be successful in turning round the company's fortunes.

B. Analysts are impressed with the company's recent performance. In the last six months, it has managed to increase prices by 3 per cent without adversely affecting sales. In such a low-margin, high-sales sector, this ought to translate directly into increased profits. The company's recent sale of its packaging division has eliminated all its debts. Shares have risen in the past month from 80p to 100p. Despite these promising. Signs, it must be remembered that the company is trading in an extremely volatile market.

C. For some weeks, there has been widespread expectation that the company will announce the sale of its troubled newspaper-and-magazine distribution arm. Speculation came to an end when this was firmly ruled out as a possibility at the annual general meeting last week. Profits from this division were down from 13 million to 8 million. However, this drop was more than offset by an improvement in the company's retail division, which has taken the innovative step of opening stores in places such as hospitals and colleges. Profits in this division rose from

D. The company has had steady growth prospects since it opened four more upmarket hotels and several health and fitness clubs. This move has come at a time when the market is particularly buoyant. There were rumors that the company might become the subject of a takeover bid by one of the large American corporations. However, this has not materialized, and it now seems unlikely that any such bids will be made in the immediate future. This is expected to lead to

E. The company has always been popular with shareholders as, for the past ten years, it has consistently provided them with above average returns. Profits for the first half of the year were up by 15 per cent. Development profits from some 30 projects around the country will provide a balanced stream of earnings in the second half of the year. Given this, and the sale of a loss-making division in Bradford, pre-tax profit forecasts have been increased to 21 million and

PART TWO

Questions 9–14

- Read this text taken from the results of a survey on employees' priorities at work in the UK.
- Choose the best sentence from the opposite page to fill each of the gaps.
- For each gap **(9-14)**, mark one letter **(A-H)** on your Answer Sheet.
- Do not use any letter more than once.

WHAT EMPLOYEES SAY THEY WANT

Employees say one thing and do another, a recent UK-based report claims. **(0)** ...H.... Addressing these problems is especially important when there are skills shortages, and companies are trying hard to retain the workers they have. According to the report, there is a consistent discrepancy between what really attracts staff and keeps them, and what they say are priorities.

The report found that, although there are differences in preferences, depending on age, home country and gender, all age groups say they rate the work/life balance as an extremely important consideration for staying with their particular company. **(9)** …… This is followed by job security and financial rewards.

However, despite their proclamations about wanting a work/life balance, it was established that this does not have a positive effect on retention for any subgroup. Similarly, people profess to identify more closely with a company which has a clear strategy for success, but in fact that does not result in improved retention either. **(10)** ……

Another finding was that it is the high-flyers in a company who are most likely to be ungrateful and leave. This is despite the fact that they are more likely to attract fast-track promotion, career development, training and financial rewards, which should be the glue to keep them loyal. **(11)** ……

All this makes life difficult for managers. **(12)** …… This is because they have to spend as much time creating an employment brand that attracts the best talent as they do in creating a consumer brand that builds customer loyalty.

That is all the more important for major companies, who, increasingly these days, are no longer viewed as the employer of choice by top graduates. **(13)** …… This involves both corporate attitudes and individual encouragement. At corporate level, there is a need for a clear and convincing strategy for the business, and an innovative environment low in bureaucracy. One level down from that, there should be tasks that interest and challenge employees, and sharpen their skills. At individual level, profit-related bonuses go down well. **(14)** ……

Above all, companies should remember that since the requirements are different for the young, middle-aged and elderly, as well as for men and women, the package has to be enticing to the right target age and gender.

A Top executives find that they can no longer delegate personnel matters.	**E** Moreover, when it comes to choosing a job, women rate it even more highly than men.
B That is possibly because they are most likely to find other jobs.	**F** As a result, the report concludes that focusing on the top performers can be counterproductive because it can cause underdevelopment, underutilization and demotivation of the rest of the workforce.
C What the report did conclude though, was that money, especially performance-related pay, does increase commitment, as do share options and profit-sharing.	
	G The report reckons that in order to change this situation, a two-stage policy is required.
D In addition, companies need to motivate key people with appropriate recognition and by giving them what they actually want, rather than just relying on an attractive basic salary, which can easily be matched by any other employer.	**H** This will come as no surprise to anyone involved with market research, but it is causing problems for employers trying to recruit staff.

PART THREE

Questions 15-20

- Read the following article about James Linton, CEO of RoCom, and the questions on the opposite page.
- For each question **(15-20)** mark one letter **(A, B, C or D)** on your Answer Sheet for the answer you choose.

In the world of big business, James Linton is precocious in the extreme. Just two years into the job of reviving one of the most illustrious names in retail finance, RoCom, he has found himself a key player in one of the richest and certainly most audacious deals in the industry: PTL's takeover of RoCom.

PI'L is paying 25 a share for RoCom – approximately 40 per cent more than the market value of the shares – and its offer document boasted that 'PTL attaches great importance to key employees having appropriate, performance-related remuneration'. Initially wary about the takeover, Linton has now negotiated a hands-off agreement with PTL, which confirms its intention to leave him very much to his own devices to continue building the business. All this and he will not turn 38 for another fortnight!

Although Linton is credited with turning RoCom around, this is more a matter of work in progress than actual achievement. Yet he does seem to have instituted the biggest top-level shake-up in its near 70-year history, promoted some big-hitters amongst key staff and transformed RoCom's way of doing business.

Linton has, however, warned that the takeover is by no means a guarantee of future success; indeed, deteriorating market conditions suggest that the way forward will be anything but smooth. Linton recently ventured the hypothesis that being shareholder-owned had, in recent years, helped the business focus and argued that the sector's experience of rival takeovers was not encouraging. Indeed, the recently reported performance of rival organizations such as Maften Limited has not promoted the notion that big corporations are happy homes for experienced staff and managers such as Linton

It may have been his ideas about independence that made Linton address RoCom's 900 staff on the day the takeover was announced, rather than doing high-profile media interviews on what was immediately seen as a fantastic deal for share-holders. He is acutely aware of the business is to succeed, something which is not lost on them. This is not a management-school dictum. It is a genuine belief that every member of staff has contributed to the firm and enabled it to net 1.9 billion from PTL. Other CEOs say he is arrogant, but this probably reflects the fact that Linton may find talking to them difficult. He is also ferociously intelligent, and, while in others this could appear intimidating, in Linton it awakes further admiration amongst loyal employees. They clearly do not feel they have to grovel in front of this mastermind, and claim that although he's incredibly dedicated to his work, he has an affable manner.

Linton boasts that staff turnover rates at RoCom have remained low for the industry, at about 12 per cent since he took over as CEO two years ago. 'People have a real affection for RoCom, and that runs right through the office here. They all want us to be number one,' he says. He is aware of the possibility that the collegiate ethos he has worked so hard to create, the meritocracy on which he thinks much of RoCom's success depends, could be destroyed if PTL is too heavy-handed. He will need all his skills to keep RoCom on course, particularly when attention has immediately focused on the possibility that Susan Marshall, its respected investment chief, might be the first casualty of the takeover. Whatever the future holds for RoCom, we are certain to go on hearing a lot more of James Linton.

15 What is PTL doing, according to the second paragraph?
   A allowing Linton to run RoCom in the way he wishes to
   B purchasing almost half of the RoCom shares on offer
   C giving all RoCom staff regular bonuses to promote motivation
   D drawing up new employment contracts for RoCom employees

16 What do we learn about Linton's work at RoCom in the third paragraph?
   A He has achieved more than anyone in RoCom's history.
   B He has widened the range of RoCom's business activities.
   C He has taken on a number of new employees.
   D He has made changes to senior management.

17 What does Linton say about RoCom in the fourth paragraph?
   A The company is likely to face difficult times.
   B The company has lost a number of experienced staff.
   C The company is expecting to report encouraging results shortly.
   D The company needs to change its focus to remain competitive.

18 Which of the following is said about Linton's management style?
   A He involves others in the decision-making process.
   B His staff find him approachable.
   C He expects his staff to work as hard as he does.
   D His style differs from that of other CEOs.

19 How does Linton feel about the takeover, according to the sixth paragraph?
   A pleased that staff turnover finally started to fall two years ago
   B afraid that he will lose his job to Susan Marshall
   C worried that the company culture might change
   D happy that employees have been so supportive of his work

20 Which of the following would be the best title for the article?
   A The Linton way of getting the best from staff
   B A thin line between success and failure for James Linton
   C James Linton – a man who will go far
   D How a good idea went wrong for James Linton

PART FOUR

Questions 21-30

- Read the extract below from a book about corporate planning.
- Choose the correct word to fill each gap from **A, B, C** or **D** on the opposite page.
- For each question (**21-30**), mark one letter (**A, B, C** or **D**) on your Answer Sheet.

WHAT IS CORPORATE PLANNING?

Corporate planning may be described as the careful and systematic taking of strategic decisions. In contrast to a short-term plan like a budget, a corporate plan is concerned with taking a long-term **(21)** …… of future developments and with designing a strategy so that the organization can achieve its chosen objectives. Many large companies now recognize the importance of **(22)** …….. a formal approach to developing a corporate plan. They prepare 'scenarios' or forecasts of future developments in the **(23)** ………… in which they wish to operate, in order to examine whether decisions taken in the present will result in success in the future. In recent years, companies have been developing more sophisticated **(24)** ……- with which to analyze the risks involved in such decisions.

(25)……… for example, an oil company deciding if it should invest in a new refinery. Faced with this decision, involving the **(26)** ………..of millions of pounds on something which might have a life of 15 years or more, the company must have a sound basis for its decision. In this case, it needs to know whether it can be **(27)** ………. of a market for the extra volume of its refined products, and it needs to know whether they can be produced profitably. In addition, it is necessary to study the **(28)** ………… Of crude oil and other supplies needed in the process.

Corporate planning, therefore, involves three main areas: **(29)** ………… the long-term objectives of an organization, deciding what market **(30)**…….. there may be and formulating a product policy to satisfy them.

21	A	sight	B	picture	C	scene	D	view
22	A	carrying	B	practicing	C	placing	D	adopting
23	A	element	B	condition	C	environment	D	atmosphere
24	A	techniques	B	ideas	C	styles	D	ways
25	A	Refer	B	Consider	C	Think	D	Suppose
26	A	outlay	B	output	C	outset	D	outcome
27	A	assured	B	insured	C	confirmed	D	ascertained
28	A	utility	B	availability	C	attainability	D	usability
29	A	guiding	B	leading	C	determining	D	concluding
30	A	chance	B	potential	C	room	D	scope

PART FIVE

Questions 31-40

- Read the newspaper article below about entrepreneurs.
- For each question 31-40, write one word in CAPITAL LETTERS on your Answer Sheet.

Can anyone be an entrepreneur?

Who wants to be an entrepreneur? Just about everybody — or **(31)** .... it seems these days. The values of entrepreneurship are hailed everywhere, **(32)** .... the more enterprising small shop owner to the boardrooms of multinationals. Entrepreneurs are seen as the true 'wealth creators' and as the initiators of change. They are often creative and always self-driven, and **(33)** .... a result, they and the companies they head possess a sense of vision which larger, more amorphous organizations often aim for but hardly ever achieve. So how do you become one? The received wisdom is that entrepreneurs with talents **(34)** .... As these are a breed apart. They are born, not formed through education.

If that's **(35)** .... case, then is there any point in going to business school to learn how to become an entrepreneur, as many do? There are trainers who think it's perfectly feasible. They compare it to training an opera singer **(36)** .... the sense that for singers, natural talent is essential, but then trainers instruct and develop it. The **(37)** .... goes for would-be entrepreneurs. Trainers develop their skills and impart knowledge. In **(38)** .... words, so the argument goes, to be trained, you must be the right kind of person to start with. What is such a person's essential characteristic: It is the ability to distinguish between acceptable and unacceptable levels of risk and act accordingly. That more than **(39)** .... else marks entrepreneurs out from others **(40)** .... preference is for the safer option of a salaried and structured career.

PART SIX

Questions 41-52

- Read the advertisement below about a service for small businesses.
- In most lines **(41-52)**, there is one extra word. It either is grammatically incorrect or does not fit in with the sense of the text. Some lines, however, are correct.
- If a line is correct, write **CORRECT** on your Answer Sheet.
- If there is an extra word in the line, write the extra word in **CAPITAL LETTERS** on your Answer Sheet.

HELP FOR SMALL BUSINESS

It is never going to be easy running a business, so it is good to know that sound financial help and advice are close at hand with Maxton Bank. With a customer

41 base of half a million, our reputation has been built on years of experience of

42 dealing with small businesses like yours. We have a commitment to helping you can

43 achieve your goals by offering a special service for either old and new customers.

44 This service provides with expert guidance and support, as our business

45 managers have extensive experience in working with companies and too have

46 valuable local knowledge and connections. All them have undergone specialist

47 training, and many have successfully completed an externally accredited training

48 course. Their aim is to understand you and your business as fully as possible, so

49 that they can supply you the best possible assistance. This is all supported by a

50 pack of free material which covering all aspects of running a business, such as

51 understanding cashflow and identify break-even point. In addition, if you have

52 any special requirements. Our business managers will put you in touch with the most

right people.

附录三 剑桥商务英语证书考试真题(三)

PART ONE

Questions 1-8

- Look at the statements below and the five extracts from company reports on the opposite page from an article .
- Which extract **(A, B, C,D or E)** dose each statement**(1-8)** refer to ?
- For each statement (**1-8**), make one letter **(A, B, C,D or E)** on your Answer Sheet .
- You will need to use some of these letters more than once .

1 Some of this company's outlets were affected by competition from its own new outlets.

2 This company expects the number of companies in its sector to be reduced.

3 Not all of this company's competitors are increasing their turnover.

4 This company has had to allow for covering a loss made on a particular contract.

5 This company has paid off the money it owed.

6 It is likely that this company will make more money on reduced sales revenue.

7 Some of this company's outlets will be required to change their name.

8 This company has decided against going ahead with a plan.

A. COLEMAN'S As was widely reported, we closely examined the possibility of merging with a food-distribution business during the year. However, whilst the strategic rationale for combination was sound, it became clear that it would not be in our shareholders' best interests to proceed with the deal, with its risk of increasing debt. Instead, we intend to concentrate on our core activity. Nevertheless, the market within which we operate is fiercely competitive, and the advent of new entrants is creating market conditions in which continued earnings growth will become increasingly challenging.

B. SHERIFF This is a momentous period for the pharmaceutical industry. Against the background of scientific and economic change, we are seeing inevitable further consolidation of what remains one of the most fragmented of the great global industries. Sheriff will not shrink from participating in this process if circumstances necessitate such action in the interests of future success. However, today, the overwhelming preoccupation of your Board, executive management and staff is with the job at hand, which is to grow the business and deliver the promises we have made in terms of turning around our losses of recent years.

C. BVL Profit before taxation was 20m, in comparison with the 32m achieved in the previous year. This disappointing result includes a provision of 26m on one project, due to costs exceeding the guaranteed maximum price quoted to the client. One result is that the Construction Division has been set targets to increase the level of partnering and fee work. Turnover, already stagnant, may decline, but profits are expected to recover. In addition, improvements will be made to the control processes relating to tendering, and to the quality of project management.

D. MARTIN'S Martin's has developed a distinctive retail format based on convenient locations for the shopper. Last year's merger of Martin's and Hoyle has provided us with the opportunity to build on our leadership in this neighborhood retail market. Building awareness of the Martin's brand continues, and its visibility and familiarity will grow as we convert Hoyle stores into Martin's operations. In line with our vision, we aim to set the pace in developing new shopping services and channels such as home and office shopping.

E. TAYLOR'S Despite a downturn in consumer confidence during the period, we continued to experience positive like-for-like sales growth for the financial year, unlike many others in our peer group. Encroachment by our new openings on 38 of our established restaurants had a 3c7o negative effect on like-for-like sales, but this percentage is certain to be reduced. Since the year-end, our like-for-like sales trend continues to be positive. We have changed a net debt position of £11.2m this time last year to net cash of £1.7m this year.

PART TWO

Questions 9–14

- Read this text about business schools.
- Choose the best sentence from the opposite page to fill each of the gaps.
- For each gap **(9-14)**, mark one letter **(A-H)** on your Answer Sheet.
- Do not use any letter more than once.

BUSINESS SCHOOLS HAVE THE EDGE

Business schools are facing increasing competition from other providers of management training such as consultancies. The key to their future success as manager-trainers lies in the quality both of their research and of their partnership with the business world.

In the most general sense, being a good manager is a matter of being marginally better than and different from your competitors. **(0)** ….H…. These are the elements which make the difference between a successful and a less successful manager. This marginal edge may be based on talent, flair or natural leadership. **(9)** …….. And this is where business schools come into their own.

The education of managers should include on-the-job training, workshops, conferences and training courses. **(10)** ……….. Traditionally, business schools have three major differentiating characteristics. First, they offer a complete package ranging from basic to very sophisticated training. Next, they enable managers to benefit from the research they carry out. **(11)** ………

In contrast to other providers of management education, business schools often offer a complete portfolio of educational programmes. MBA programmes exist alongside general management programmes, as well as specialized programmes for experienced managers. For the business school, this has the advantage that teachers can use the information they get from one programme to cross-fertilize with their teaching on another. **(12)** …….. This in turn offers substantial advantages to the companies concerned. It means that managers and executives at different levels of the organization can be confronted with the same concepts, expressed in the same language. In this way, a close partnership with a business school enables a company to create some coherence between the education and the development of its different management levels. People in the company will communicate more effectively because they use the same terminology. **(13)** …….. In short, thanks to contact with the business school, more people within the same company will be embracing similar ideas.

Obviously, the value of these concepts to the company increases if they are state-of-the-art concepts. **(14)** ………. Only then can the company genuinely improve its management practice and competitive performance. Working with a business school is for many companies a privileged method of accessing the latest management thinking, before it is published in trade journals or popular books.

A Different departments will be able to discuss internal issues with a considerable amount of mutual understanding.	**E** For them in fact to be so, a business school's teaching must be supported by first-class research.
B Yet good management is also essential to the competitive performance of companies.	**F** Thus insights gained from top executives might impact positively on what they cover in a graduate programme.
C And no less important, they are able to preserve an independent outlook towards the world of business.	**G** Business schools have a special role to fulfill in the delivery of this portfolio.
D However, acquired knowledge of management can also provide this decisive advantage.	**H** He or she needs to be a little faster, able to spot opportunities earlier and react more quickly.

PART THREE

Questions 15-20

- Read the following extract from an article about brand stretching (using an existing brand name on new types of products) and the questions on the opposite page.
- For each question **(15-20)** mark one letter **(A, B, C or D)** on your Answer Sheet for the answer you choose.

A manufacturer of sports shoes starts selling consumer electronics. A soft drink lends its name to a range of urban clothing. What's going on? In simpler times, you knew where you were with brands. One brand name meant good-quality sports shoes, another a soft drink. No confusion. Today, however, big companies try to redefine brands as not so much a product, more a way of life, and stretch them into new areas. In the early years of the consumer society, a brand name on a box simply identified what was inside. People were looking for products that would improve their quality of life, and chose brands most likely to achieve that purpose. But as people in industrialized nations became more affluent and fulfilled their basic needs, brands acquired other attributes. The functionality of the product was still important, but people also started using brands to say something about themselves, for example, choosing a brand of cosmetics which would suggest that they were sophisticated jet-setters.

Now, we have entered a third age of branding, in which so many companies are making roughly the same product at roughly the same price that functionality rarely succeeds as a point of differentiation. Instead, companies are trying to make their brands stand out by emphasizing their emotional aspects, hoping consumers will identify with the set of values the brand represents.

One disadvantage of a product-based brand is that if the product goes out of fashion, the brand goes with it. This is a serious concern for manufacturers of breakfast cereals, who are struggling to counter weak demand for the products that bear their names. So far, their marketing efforts seem to be having little effect. The advantage for emotional brands is that companies can transfer their brand strength into other areas, increasing revenues and reducing their exposure to the lifespan of a single product.

The elasticity of brands seems to be related to their position on a spectrum ranging from those rooted in solid, tangible assets to those with highly intangible, emotional qualities. At the one end, you have train companies that tend to associate themselves with infrastructure. And their ability to get you from A to B, and at the other end would be a leisure brand that positions itself on dreams and making people have fun. It is the latter which has the maximum potential for stretch.

But even emotional brands have a limit to their elasticity. The merchandise has to be consistent with the brand promise. Just to sell merchandise with your logo on it is a short-term, mistaken idea. From this viewpoint, the decision to move from sports shoes into consumer electronics makes sense. Most items in the range, such as the two-way radio for hikers, are sports-focused, even though the products may be adopted as fashion accessories, and the sports shoe customers will probably snap them up.

When the move was made from soft drinks into clothing, however, it left the branding consultants cold. It was a difficult mental leap into clothing from the drink so closely associated with that particular brand name. On the other hand, the emotional attributes that youngsters seem to find appealing in the drink, like its heritage and global appeal, are fashionable at the moment, and in fact response to the clothes with the same name has been overwhelming. Maybe this just shows that an inspired move – and by all accounts a snap decision –sometimes pays off against the odds, leaving the manufacturer laughing all the way to the bank.

15 What led to a change in attitudes to brands?
    A the influence of consumers on each other
    B the personal circumstances of consumers
    C more sophisticated marketing
    D greater choice of products

16 According to the writer, an attribute of the third age of branding is that
    A competing products may serve their purpose equally well.
    B the range of products available is too large for all to survive.
    C consumers are becoming confused about the products available.
    D price has become a key factor in consumers' choice of products.

17 The writer mentions manufacturers of breakfast cereals to illustrate how
    A competition can have an impact on a product.
    B a brand can lose its popularity despite a strong market for the product.
    C advertising can affect sales of a product.
    D changes in the popularity of products can cause difficulties.

18 The writer refers to railways to show that brands like this
    A do not recognize the value of stretching.
    B suffer from having an unattractive image.
    C are unlikely to lend themselves to stretching.
    D are notoriously difficult to advertise.

19 The writer argues that the stretch from sports shoes into consumer electronics is likely to be successful because
    A existing customers have demanded the new products.
    B they will be sold in the same outlets.
    C the new lines will expand the manufacturer's market.
    D there is a connection in the way that the goods can be used.

20 The writer argues that the stretch from soft drinks into clothing
    A was a gamble which succeeded.
    B built on the popularity of certain types of clothing.
    C showed the value of careful planning.
    D created production problems for the manufacturer.

PART FOUR

Questions 21-30

- Read the article below about teamwork and stress.
- Choose the correct word to fill each gap from **A,B,C** or **D** on the opposite page.
- For each question (**21-30**), mark one letter (**A,B,C** or **D**) on your Answer Sheet.

TEAMWORK AND STRESS

Stressful working conditions lead to a breakdown in group co-operation which can damage effectiveness and productivity, a study has found. Psychologists have discovered that when employees work in crisis **(21)**.......... they are less willing to work together. The study showed that when workers are under stress, they have a strong **(22)** .... to concentrate on their own personal **(23)**........ to the detriment of their colleagues.

In the study, 100 naval personnel worked in groups of three, and each group was given a computer **(24)** .... of a naval decision-making task. Under a high **(25)** .... of stress, they had to monitor a radar screen with their own ship at the centre and numerous unidentified contacts around the ship.

As **(26)**....... participants operating in this highly stressful situation performed worse than those operating under normal circumstances. But the results also showed that under stress, the workers' **(27)** .... of attention shifted from group involvement to a more narrow individual perspective, which led to a severe breakdown in team performance.

The author of the study concludes that it is possible that, for many team tasks, the importance of teamwork behavior such as co-ordination and communication may be **(28)** .... as secondary to basic individual demands. In his opinion, the **(29)** ....to achieve efficiency under stress is by delegation. Simplifying tasks by delegating parts of them, making them less demanding, is one of the best ways of **(30)** .... the effectiveness of the group.

21	A	moments	B	states	C	conditions	D	positions
22	A	likelihood	B probability		C	liking	D	tendency
23	A	intentions	B	goals	C	purposes	D	objects
24	A impression		B conception		C imitation		D simulation	
25	A	measure	B	degree	C	standard	D	rate
26	A	supposed	B wondered		C	expected	D questioned	
27	A	focus	B	area	C	direction	D	point
28	A	perceived	B	estimated	C	determined	D calculated	
29	A	manner	B	way	C	procedure	D	route
30	A	persisting	B	holding	C maintaining		D confirming	

PART FIVE

Questions 31-40

- Read the article below about the problem of ageism.
- For each question 31-40, write one word in CAPITAL LETTERS on your Answer Sheet.

Younger Does Not Always Mean Better

Recruitment policies in Britain's businesses favor the young. Mature men and women are being marginalized and their considerable skills lost to the economy. Cost-cutting policies such as delayering and downsizing, now widely criticized **(31)** .... causing loss of valuable knowledge and experience, are hardest on more mature staff.

All around us can **(32)** .... seen the effects of ageism. Highly qualified, middle-aged people with excellent CVs apply for jobs, but do not get them because younger applicants are preferred **(33)** .... the basis of age alone. Similarly, when it comes **(34)** .... promotion, younger employees are often more successful than their older colleagues, because **(35)** .... former are seen as more dynamic and ambitious.

Our research, however, suggests otherwise: it is the mature manager who is considerably **(36)** .... capable of handling the complex dynamics of office life and creating an effective team. The challenge of working in today's flatter organizations is best handled **(37)**.........experienced, older managers, provided they have positive personalities.

Our research demonstrates that it **(38)** .... older senior managers, not younger executives, who take the more balanced view **(39)** ....required to take decisions, and are more likely than younger colleagues to evolve positive relationships with people from other departments and from outside the organization. Similarly, the effectiveness of strategic decision-making and the implementation of company policy benefit **(40)** ....the presence of older senior managers in the top team.

PART SIX

Questions 41-52

- Read the text below about an advertisement for information systems trainees.
- In most lines (41-52), there is one extra word. It either is grammatically incorrect or does not fit in with the sense of the text. Some lines, however, are correct.
- If a line is correct, write **CORRECT** on your Answer Sheet.
- If there is an extra word in the line, write the extra word in **CAPITAL LETTERS** on your Answer Sheet.

Advertisement for Information Systems Trainees

You are a graduate with a good degree which proves you have the capacity for to learn. Your degree course probably included plenty of Information Technology,

41 which you really enjoyed yourself, or you have a real interest in this exciting area.
42 It is a career you would like to follow, but how do you go about getting into it?
43 Median Life is currently recruiting graduates for entry up to the Information
44 Systems division. After eight weeks' intensive training, you will be all equipped
45 with the skills to start making such a real contribution to the running of Europe's
46 largest life-assurance company. You will join a small team and work on the projects
47 of varying size and complexity, or using some of the most up-to-date technology in
48 existence. If you show the necessary enthusiasm and determination, that we will give
49 you every opportunity to work your way up to the very top. While trainees will
50 be based at our head offices, which are in the centre of the lively and beautiful
51 city of Edinburgh. If you are interested in applying us for one of these exciting
52 positions, should email us at the address below to request an information pack.

参 考 答 案

第1单元 经济全球化

Text A

V. Decide whether each of the following statements is true or false.

1. F 2. T 3. F 4. T 5. F 6. T 7. T 8. T 9. T 10. F

Text B

PART ONE

(1) C (2) A (3) E (4) B (5) E (6) C (7) B (8) D

PART TWO

(9) B (10) D (11) G (12) H (13) A (14) E

PART THREE

(15) C (16) A (17) D (18) B (19) A (20) D

PART FOUR

(21) C (22) B (23) B (24) A (25) D (26) D (27) A (28) C (29) B (30) D

PART FIVE

(31) FOR (32) APPLIED (33) FROM (34) ROUTINES (35) RATHER

(36) BECAUSE (37) WHICH (38) WHERE (39) EMPLOYEE'S (40) WITHOUT

PART SIX

(41) WHICH (42) THEM (43) NOT (44) AT

(45) IN (46) OUT (47) ALTHOUGH (48) HAD

(49) THEY (50) HAD (51) OVER (52) TO

第2单元 市场机制

Text A

V. Decide whether each of the following statements is true or false.

1. T 2. F 3. T 4. F 5. T 6. T 7. F 8. F 9. F 10. T

Text B

PART ONE

(1) A (2) C (3) B (4) D (5) A (6) A (7) E (8) E

PART TWO

(9) G (10) A (11) B (12) H (13) D (14) F

· 235 ·

PART THREE

(15)D (16)B (17)D (18)D (19)D (20)C

PART FOUR

(21)D (22)C (23)D (24)B (25)A (26)B (27)B (28)C (29)C (30)A

PART FIVE

(31)NO (32)NEITHER (33)THEREFORE (34)CHEAPER (35)ON

(36)WERE (37)TO (38)FAIL (39)ACCORDING (40)WHAT

PART SIX

(41)CORRECT (42)TO (43)OFF (44)WHO

(45)POOR (46)CORRECT (47)FROM (48)CORRECT

(49)NOT (50)AN (51)ACCORDING (52)WHERE

第3单元 国际贸易

Text A

V. Decide whether each of the following statements is true or false.

1.T 2.T 3.T 4.T 5.T 6.F 7.F 8.F 9.F 10.F

Text B

PART ONE

(1)C (2)E (3)D (4)B (5)C (6)A (7)E (8)A

PART TWO

(9)C (10)D (11)A (12)H (13)E (14)G

PART THREE

(15)C (16)D (17)C (18)D (19)A (20)D

PART FOUR

(21)C (22)B (23)C (24)A (25)C (26)D (27)D (28)A (29)A (30)B

PART FIVE

(31)COUNTRIES (32)THAN (33)LONG (34)IF (35)AT

(36)EITHER (37)DIFFERENT (38)FINDS (39)COST (40)EFFICIENT

PART SIX

(41)AS (42)SHIPPING (43)IF (44)SHOULD

(45)CORRECT (46)BE (47)CORRECT (48)NOT

(49)IS (50)AND (51)CORRECT (52)ABOVE

第4单元 营销策略

Text A

V. Decide whether each of the following statements is true or false.

1.T 2.T 3.T 4.T 5.F 6.F 7.T 8.F 9.T 10.F

Text B

PART ONE

(1) D (2) C (3) C (4) A (5) E 6) B (7) A (8) B

PART TWO

(9) D (10) A (11) G (12) E (13) C (14) B

PART THREE

(15) C (16) C (17) D (18) A (19) D (20) D

PART FOUR

(21) B (22) C (23) A (24) C (25) A (26) D (27) A (28) C (29) B (30) D

PART FIVE

(31) MORE (32) RATHER (33) WITH (34) CHANGE (35) ABOUT

(36) WHAT (37) EITHER (38) TIME (39) ENOUGH (40) DIFFERENT

PART SIX

(41) BEING (42) DO (43) ALL (44) CORRECT

(45) UP (46) CORRECT (47) ELSE (48) GOING

(49) THEY (50) CORRECT (51) ON (52) MEANS

第5单元　广告和促销

Text A

V. Decide whether each of the following statements is true or false.

1. T 2. T 3. F 4. T 5. T 6. F 7. T 8. T 9. F 10. F

Text B

PART ONE

(1) D (2) D (3) B (4) C (5) E (6) C (7) B (8) A

PART TWO

(9) D (10) F (11) A (12) C (13) G (14) B

PART THREE

(15) C (16) B (17) C (18) D (19) B (20) C

PART FOUR

(21) D (22) D (23) C (24) D (25) B (26) C (27) B (28) A (29) A (30) B

PART FIVE

(31) PROMOTE (32) ADVERTISING (33) OF (34) TOO (35) SERVICE

(36) BEHALF (37) MEET (38) DURING (39) ITS (40) WHICH

PART SIX

(41) CORRECT (42) WELL (43) TOUR (44) WATCHING

(45) HOW (46) CORRECT (47) WHETHER (48) IN

(49) OUT (50) CORRECT (51) TO (52) BY

· 237 ·

第6单元 商业合同

Text A

V. Decide whether each of the following statements is true or false.

1. T 2. F 3. T 4. F 5. F 6. T 7. F 8. F 9. F 10. T

Text B

PART ONE

(1) D (2) C (3) B (4) E (5) A (6) D (7) C (8) B

PART TWO

(9) G (10) B (11) F (12) E (13) C (14) A

PART THREE

(15) C (16) B (17) D (18) A (19) D (20) C

PART FOUR

(21) B (22) C (23) A (24) D (25) B (26) A (27) C (28) B (29) D (30) C

PART FIVE

(31) OF (32) LARGE (33) WITH (34) ALTHOUGH (35) BETWEEN

(36) ACCEPTS (37) FORWARD (38) INVITED (39) LIKE (40) BUT

PART SIX

(41) CORRECT (42) ANY (43) MOSTLY (44) CORRECT

(45) ONE (46) THAT (47) CORRECT (48) IS

(49) TO (50) FOR (51) WITH (52) CERTAIN

第7单元 企业管理

Text A

V. Decide whether each of the following statements is true or false.

1. F 2. T 3. F 4. F 5. T 6. T 7. T 8. F 9. T 10. F

Text B

PART ONE

(1) A (2) C (3) D (4) A (5) D (6) E (7) B (8) C

PART TWO

(9) C (10) A (11) E (12) H (13) F (14) D

PART THREE

(15) D (16) A (17) B (18) C (19) B (20) A

PART FOUR

(21) A (22) C (23) A (24) B (25) B (26) D (27) A (28) C (29) D (30) B

PART FIVE

(31) TOP (32) HOW (33) WORTH (34) SENSE (35) ISN'T

(36) AVERAGE (37) EMPLOYEES (38) LOWEST (39) WORST (40) GLOBAL

PART SIX

(41)MORE (42)IT (43)CORRECT (44)OUT

(45)YEAR (46)NUMBER (47)HAD (48)IN

(49)WITH (50)CORRECT (51)THEN (52)SOMETHING

第8单元 物 流

Text A

V. Decide whether each of the following statements is true or false.

1．F 2．F 3．T 4．T 5．T 6．F 7．T 8．F 9．F 10．T

Text B

PART ONE

(1)D (2)D (3)A (4)C (5)C (6)B (7)D (8)E

PART TWO

(9)F (10)G (11)H (12)C (13)A (14)D

PART THREE

(15)A (16)D (17)B (18)D (19)B (20)B

PART FOUR

(21)A (22)B (23)A (24)D (25)C (26)B (27)D (28)A (29)B (30)C

PART FIVE

(31)BETWEEN (32)REQUIREMENTS (33)DUE (34)TIME (35)EITHER

(36)FROM (37)MAIN (38)TO (39)OTHER (40)CARRY

PART SIX

(41)WITH (42)WHILE (43)EITHER (44)CORRECT

(45)BY (46)MORE (47)IS (48)CORRECT

(49)DUE (50)CORRECT (51)TO (52)AGAINST

第9单元 商业道德和社会责任

Text A

V. Decide whether each of the following statements is true or false.

1．F 2．T 3．T 4．F 5．F 6．F 7．T 8．T 9．F 10．T

Text B

PART ONE

(1)C (2)A (3)D (4)B (5)A (6)A (7)E (8)D

PART TWO

(9)C (10)F (11)E (12)A (13)D (14)H

PART THREE

(15)C (16)A (17)C (18)C (19)D (20)B

PART FOUR

(21)C (22)B (23)B (24)B (25)D (26)C (27)B (28)C (29)D (30)A

PART FIVE

(31) WHICH   (32) USE   (33) HOWEVER   (34) WITH   (35) THAN
(36) AN   (37) IN   (38) BECAUSE   (39) WHETHER   (40) STAKE

PART SIX

(41) OF   (42) CORRECT   (43) WRONG   (44) OUT
(45) THEY   (46) AT   (47) ONLY   (48) CORRECT
(49) MAKING   (50) CORRECT   (51) SUCH   (52) IN

第10单元　电子商务

Text A

V. Decide whether each of the following statements is true or false.

1. T   2. F   3. T   4. F   5. T   6. F   7. T   8. F   9. T   10. F

Text B

PART ONE

(1) D   (2) E   (3) A   (4) D   (5) B   (6) A   (7) D   (8) C

PART TWO

(9) F   (10) C   (11) H   (12) A   (13) E   (14) B

PART THREE

(15) B   (16) B   (17) C   (18) C   (19) D   (20) A

PART FOUR

(21) B   (22) D   (23) A   (24) A   (25) D   (26) C   (27) C   (28) C   (29) B   (30) B

PART FIVE

(31) ALREADY   (32) WAY   (33) ENTER   (34) WITH   (35) WHICH
(36) GOOD   (37) RESULT   (38) TRADITIONAL   (39) SUCCESS   (40) TO

PART SIX

(41) OVER   (42) A   (43) BE   (44) CORRECT
(45) AT   (46) IN   (47) WITH   (48) CORRECT
(49) THAN   (50) BUYING   (51) CORRECT   (52) REASON

第11单元　信息时代的会计

Text A

V. Decide whether each of the following statements is true or false.

1. T   2. F   3. F   4. F   5. T   6. F   7. F   8. F   9. T   10. T

Text B

PART ONE

(1) E   (2) D   (3) A   (4) B   (5) A   (6) C   (7) E   (8) C

PART TWO

(9) H   (10) G   (11) B   (12) D   (13) F   (14) C

PART THREE

(15)D　(16)A　(17)B　(18)C　(19)B　(20)D

PART FOUR

(21)B　(22)A　(23)C　(24)B　(25)D　(26)C　(27)A　(28)C　(29)B　(30)C

PART FIVE

(31)ABOUT　(32)FINANCIAL　(33)WHO　(34)DIFFERENCE　(35)IN
(36)FOR　(37)BEING　(38)CONCERNED　(39)MUCH　(40)THAN

PART SIX

(41)AGO　(42)CORRECT　(43)IS　(44)HAS
(45)AS　(46)NOT　(47)IN　(48)CORRECT
(49)SOMETHING　(50)WITH　(51)CORRECT　(52)EVEN

第12单元　知识产权

Text A

V. Decide whether each of the following statements is true or false.

1. F　2. F　3. T　4. F　5. T　6. F　7. T　8. T　9. F　10. T

Text B

PART ONE

(1)E　(2)B　(3)D　(4)E　(5)C　(6)B　(7)A　(8)C

PART TWO

(9)C　(10)G　(11)B　(12)D　(13)H　(14)E

PART THREE

(15)C　(16)B　(17)D　(18)A　(19)C　(20)B

PART FOUR

(21)B　(22)A　(23)C　(24)D　(25)B　(26)D　(27)A　(28)C　(29)D　(30)B

PART FIVE

(31)PROPERTY　(32)WHY　(33)DESCRIBED　(34)SIMPLE　(35)THAT
(36)SPEAKING　(37)FALLS　(38)EXAMPLES　(39)VERY　(40)RIGHT

PART SIX

(41)CORRECT　(42)ALL　(43)CORRECT　(44)UP
(45)CALLED　(46)IN　(47)THING　(48)MIGHT
(49)THAT　(50)TIME　(51)CORRECT　(52)NOT

第13单元　人力资源管理

Text A

V. Decide whether each of the following statements is true or false.

1. F　2. F　3. T　4. T　5. F　6. T　7. T　8. F　9. T　10. F

Text B

PART ONE

(1) B (2) A (3) A (4) E (5) E (6) C (7) D (8) E

PART TWO

(9) E (10) G (11) B (12) D (13) H (14) C

PART THREE

(15) B (16) D (17) C (18) C (19) D (20) C

PART FOUR

(21) B (22) A (23) D (24) C (25) B (26) B (27) C (28) C (29) D (30) A

PART FIVE

(31) WHICH (32) LEVELS (33) EXTERNALLY (34) EITHER (35) RESOURCE
(36) SOURCE (37) FOR (38) RAPIDLY (39) WITHOUT (40) THIRD

PART SIX

(41) BE (42) THOSE (43) RELATING (44) CORRECT
(45) AND (46) OUR (47) DEVELOPMENT (48) CORRECT
(49) THEM (50) NOT (51) CORRECT (52) ON

第14单元　货币和银行

Text A

V. Decide whether each of the following statements is true or false.

1. T 2. F 3. F 4. T 5. F 6. F 7. T 8. F 9. F 10. T

Text B

PART ONE

(1) E (2) A (3) D (4) C (5) B (6) E (7) B (8) D

PART TWO

(9) C (10) H (11) B (12) G (13) F (14) E

PART THREE

(15) D (16) C (17) A (18) D (19) B (20) A

PART FOUR

(21) A (22) A (23) C (24) D (25) B (26) C (27) C (28) D (29) B (30) A

PART FIVE

(31) SO (32) LOGISTICS (33) FROM (34) INSTEAD (35) BENEFITS
(36) LOWER (37) REDUCED (38) RAIL (39) WATERWAY (40) POSSIBLE

PART SIX

(41) THEN (42) CORRECT (43) WITH (44) AN
(45) MORE (46) THAT (47) SO (48) ONLY
(49) ARE (50) WHO (51) AGAINST (52) CORRECT

第15单元 商务礼仪

Text A

V. Decide whether each of the following statements is true or false.

1. T 2. T 3. F 4. F 5. F 6. T 7. F 8. F 9. F 10. T

Text B

PART ONE

(1) E (2) B (3) A (4) A (5) D (6) B (7) C (8) B

PART TWO

(9) G (10) C (11) E (12) B (13) H (14) A

PART THREE

(15) C (16) B (17) C (18) D (19) C (20) A

PART FOUR

(21) B (22) B (23) C (24) B (25) A (26) D (27) C (28) C (29) D (30) A

PART FIVE

(31) A (32) UNLESS (33) RIGHT (34) AFTER (35) BY

(36) BEFORE (37) HAND (38) HOW (39) FEW (40) HOT

PART SIX

(41) A (42) OF (43) BEING (44) NECESSARY

(45) CORRECT (46) BY (47) TO (48) CORRECT

(49) OTHER (50) WRITTEN (51) CORRECT (52) ELSE

第16单元 股票市场

Text A

V. Decide whether each of the following statements is true or false.

1. F 2. T 3. T 4. T 5. F 6. T 7. F 8. F 9. T 10. F

Text B

PART ONE

(1) C (2) A (3) B (4) D (5) B (6) C (7) E (8) D

PART TWO

(9) B (10) A (11) G (12) H (13) E (14) C

PART THREE

(15) C (16) D (17) B (18) B (19) D (20) C

PART FOUR

(21) A (22) B (23) B (24) C (25) A (26) C (27) C (28) D (29) D (30) B

PART FIVE

(31) SHARE (32) WITH (33) DUE (34) LOSS (35) NUMBER

(36) BEING (37) WALL (38) ANOTHER (39) SPREAD (40) END

PART SIX

(41)BEEN (42)IT (43)TO (44)CORRECT
(45)SELLIGN (46)ABRAOD (47)ANY (48)CORRECT
(49)NOT (50)CORRECT (51)WHICH (52)DIFFICULT

附录一 剑桥商务英语证书考试真题(一)

PART ONE

(1)E (2)C (3)B (4)E (5)A (6)D (7)C (8)D

PART TWO

(9)F (10)C (11)G (12)D (13)E (14)A

PART THREE

(15)B (16)D (17)C (18)A (19)B (20)A

PART FOUR

(21)C (22)D (23)A (24)B (25)C
(26)B (27)A (28)C (29)D (30)D

PART FIVE

(31)ALL (32)FOR (33)THERE (34)IN (35)BECOME
(36)AT (37)FEW (38)INSTANCE/EXAMPLE (39)WHETHER (40)WHO

PART SIX

(41)WHILE (42)THEN (43)IT (44)CORRECT
(45)PART (46)CORRECT (47)AS (48)SUM
(49)HOWEVER (50)THAT (51)HOW (52)SCARCELY

附录二 剑桥商务英语证书考试真题(二)

PART ONE

(1)D (2)C (3)B (4)E (5)A (6)C (7)A (8)B

PART TWO

(9)E (10)C (11)F (12)A (13)G (14)D

PART THREE

(15)A (16)D (17)A (18)B (19)C (20)C

PART FOUR

(21)D (22)D (23)C (24)A (25)B
(26)A (27)A (28)B (29)C (30)B

PART FIVE

(31)SO (32)FROM (33)AS (34)SUCH (35)THE
(36)IN (37)SAME (38)OTHER (39)ANYTHING/EVERYTHING
(40)WHOSE

PART SIX

(41)CORRECT (42)CAN (43)EITHER (44)WITH

(45) TOO   (46) THEM   (47) CORRECT   (48) CORRECT
(49) YOU   (50) WHICH   (51) IDENTIFY   (52) MOST

附录三 剑桥商务英语证书考试真题(三)

PART ONE
(1) E   (2) B   (3) E   (4) C   (5) E   (6) C   (7) D   (8) A

PART TWO
(9) D   (10) G   (11) C   (12) F   (13) A   (14) E

PART THREE
(15) B   (16) A   (17) D   (18) C   (19) D   (20) A

PART FOUR
(21) C   (22) D   (23) B   (24) D   (25) B
(26) C   (27) A   (28) A   (29) B   (30) C

PART FIVE
(31) FOR/AS   (32) BE   (33) ON   (34) TO   (35) THE
(36) MORE   (37) BY   (38) IS   (39) WHEN/IF   (40) FROM

PART SIX
(41) YOURSELF   (42) CORRECT   (43) UP   (44) ALL
(45) SUCH   (46) THE   (47) OR   (48) THAT
(49) WHILE   (50) CORRECT   (51) US   (52) SHOULD